CHURCH COUP

A CAUTIONARY TALE OF
CONGREGATIONAL CONFLICT

Jim Meyer

CONTENTS

DEDICATION

To my family and everyone who believed in us

"You are those who have stood by me in my trials." Luke 22:28

*W*arning: This book may break your heart. As you read about what Jim and Kim endured at the hands of those who were supposed to be supporting them, and you magnify that times the thousands of pastors who go through similar events, there is something wrong with your heart if it doesn't break. But interwoven throughout their story is an abundance of hope, and a lot of practical and biblical advice concerning church conflict. The hopeful part of the story involves a combination of healing and prevention. This book should be read by every pastor and church board member and every lay leader. The story is compelling, and the lessons are critical.

Dave Rolph, senior pastor of Calvary Chapel Pacific Hills, Aliso Viejo, California, and teacher on the nationally-syndicated radio program *The Balanced Word*

Rick Warren says: "God intentionally allows you to go through painful experiences to equip you for ministry to others." And that is exactly what Jim is doing in his book: equipping pastors, church leaders and lay people to handle the conflicts that inevitably arise in congregations. With candor and balance, Jim outlines a godly approach to handling the heartbreak of a ministry divided. A must read for anyone who is in the midst of considering letting a pastor go.

Kathi Lipp, author and speaker

If you are a pastor or active lay person in the church and have picked up this book expecting a quick and easy read, I suggest you read no further. You may find yourself experiencing the all-too-real pain Jim shares about an unexpected turn in his ministry as a pastor when he becomes the target of those in the church that want him to leave. If you start reading and stop too soon, you might assume that this is merely a cathartic journal of this very tough time but there is more. Jim has been willing to be transparent about his experience so that others in the work of the church will read this, learn from it, and act differently. After counseling pastors for over thirty-five years, Jim's story is not a new one to me. This book offers churches helpful insight as they search for more constructive outcomes in their dealings with ministers.

Dale Frimodt, founder and director of Barnabas Ministries, Omaha, Nebraska

ACKNOWLEDGEMENTS

I am grateful to God for the many Christian leaders who have publicly and privately shared with me their wisdom about managing conflict in churches.

Thanks to Homer Benton, Dr. Archibald Hart, Dr. David Augsburger, and Dr. Leith Anderson for their teaching about conflict in a classroom setting.

Thanks to Speed Leas for his many writings, especially his manual *Moving Your Church through Conflict* – the single greatest resource on managing church conflict that I know.

Thanks to Dr. G. Lloyd Rediger for his pioneering work in exposing "clergy killers."

Thanks to Dr. Charles Wickman for sharing meals and insights with me concerning pastor-centered conflict.

Thanks to Dr. Charles Chandler from the Ministering to Ministers Foundation – both a mentor and a friend – who knows more about forced termination than anyone on the planet.

Thanks to Dr. Earl Grant, my first and best ministry mentor, who has provided counsel for me concerning conflict situations for forty years.

Thanks to every person who reviewed the manuscript and offered suggestions, including Suzy Arena, David Ekstrand, Karen Harrington, Michael Hawbecker, Russ Jones, Ryan Meyer, Sarah Meyer and Cecile Pecoraro.

For my children and family members – who have suffered along with me – thanks for your ongoing love and support. It means more than you'll ever know.

And for my beloved wife Kim – who has dedicated her life to advancing Christ's kingdom – thanks for working with me to tell our story. May God use it to benefit other pastors and congregations.

While I sincerely appreciate the contributions that each of the above individuals has made to my thinking in the area of conflict, I am solely responsible for the contents of this work.

FOREWORD

*C*hurch Coup: A Cautionary Tale of Congregational Conflict is a
must read for ministers, key lay leaders, as well as denominational leaders (judicatories). Jim shares openly about his pilgrimage
through the deep and traumatic valley of a pastor-centered church conflict that ended in an involuntary resignation. The layers of feelings of
betrayal, shock, disbelief, disillusionment, grief, eroding self-esteem,
loss of self-confidence, sense of failure, guilt and shame, isolation,
inability to trust and an enormous amount of anger – though usually
suppressed – are given a face through Jim's story.

Those who have experienced a severe church conflict and/or forced
termination will identify with much of Jim's journey and find his processing and search for answers to be therapeutic. Unlike many who tell
their story, Jim accepts responsibility for his choices and responses,
recognizing that all choices – good and bad – have consequences. He
also recognizes that healing comes through honesty in looking back.

Those who have not experienced severe church conflict and/or
forced termination can learn from Jim's experience also. A part of his
willingness to share his painful story is to expose the problems that
ministers face while doing ministry in today's world. His desire is that
ministers, lay church leaders, and denominational leaders will be able
to put in place procedures as pastoral tenures begin that will help prevent such painful and destructive experiences for both ministers and
their families as well as for congregations.

Sadly, Jim's experience is not an isolated event. And forced termination among clergy has reached epidemic proportions. The dynamics
are so similar – the minister is blindsided at a time when he is vulner-

able. It often happens after the minister has been away, has been ill, is dealing with a family trauma, is on the brink of burnout, or has been beaten down by adversaries.

At the Ministering to Ministers Foundation, we have worked with approximately 10,000 ministers and spouses during the past eighteen years. We have observed similar dynamics over and over, regardless of church polity or theological perspectives. And the ripple effect reaches far beyond the minister and his or her family and congregation. It affects the entire community. The joy of the gospel message is dampened. Some congregations never recover.

The Apostle Paul, writing to the Christians at Corinth – a conflicted church – concludes chapter 12 with these words, "And yet I will show you the most excellent way" – then follows with his great exposition on love (1 Corinthians 13). I wonder what church life would look like if Paul's admonition was taken seriously?

I admire Jim's transparency, honesty, and desire to redeem his pain by shedding light on a dark area of too many church-minister experiences. I encourage you to read the book carefully and to recommend it to other ministers as well as key church leaders who can make a difference.

Charles H. Chandler, D.Min.
Executive Director
Ministering to Ministers Foundation, Inc.
Richmond, Virginia
www.mtmfoundation.org

INTRODUCTION

*D*id you know that hundreds of pastors are forced to leave their churches every month?

Christians rightly lament the persecution of believers worldwide, but they are being terrorized by *secular authorities* or *religious extremists*. But in far too many cases, pastors and their families are being mistreated in local assemblies by their *spiritual brothers and sisters* – and the toll keeps escalating.

If a group in a church attacks their pastor and he is forced to resign, the consequences are tragic for everyone involved. The pastor may leave church ministry for good. That church's reputation will be sullied. Some believers will flee their church. Friendships will end. Outreach will stop cold. And the evil one will dance. I've seen it all my life.

When I was a boy, my father felt pressured to resign as pastor from a church he founded, even though he was innocent of any major offense. He died twenty months later at age thirty-eight, leaving behind a homemaker wife who didn't drive, two sons (ages thirteen and ten), and a five-year-old daughter who has only vague recollections of the father she lost.

During the ensuing years, the pastors of the churches I attended were subjected to similar pressures. In my early teens, one pastor abruptly resigned in the middle of a church meeting. My next pastor was forced to resign after five years of ministry. In my second staff position, the pastor was voted out of office in another contentious public meeting. And in my next staff position, the pastor was verbally threatened until he lost the will to serve.

When I became a rookie pastor, I learned that my predecessor had been forced from office after just one year of ministry. When our church merged with a sister church two years later, the *other* church's pastor was forced to leave. Five years after the merger, a disgruntled churchgoer formed an alliance with a faction inside that church and pressured *me* to resign – but the board stood by me and that group left to form their own church nearby.

The next decade went so well that I hoped that I'd finally out-lasted any ecclesiastical opponents. And after becoming the pastor of an impactful church entering the millennium, I entered the Doctor of Ministry program at Fuller Seminary and wrote my dissertation on dealing with church antagonists using a biblical model informed by family systems theory. After studying how powerbrokers operate in a church, I thought I had finally come to a place where peace and under-standing reigned. But sadly, I was mistaken.

In the autumn of 2009, after my wife and I returned from a mis-sion trip to Eastern Europe, our church's governing leaders stunned us by making drastic decisions. Seven weeks later, I resigned as pastor because too many people believed a litany of false allegations. We were not guilty of heresies, immoralities, illegalities, or any major offenses. While we both had made minor mistakes in our ministries, we were treated like we *had* committed ecclesiastical felonies.

As I have related our story to family, friends, and colleagues, I have learned how frequently this kind of situation is replicated in local churches. While there are unique features to our story, the template for forcing pastors from their positions has remained the same for decades, if not centuries. Forced exits have become so common in American churches that Rediger writes:

> Abuse of pastors by congregations and the breakdown of pas-tors due to inadequate support are now tragic realities. This worst-case scenario for the church, one that is increasing in epidemic proportions, is not a misinterpretation by a few dis-contented clergy. Rather, it is a phenomenon that is verified by both research and experience.[1]

Guy Greenfield, who was forced out of his position as pastor in his early sixties, comments:

This problem is a growing phenomenon. Numerous publications of observations and research indicate that it is in fact a major problem approaching crisis proportions. Talk to any group of ministers, and you will hear stories of tragedy and heartache. In recent years I have interviewed a considerable number of former ministers, now in secular work, and nearly everyone I talked with told me a similar story that resulted in forced termination. Many of them are now cynical, bitter, angry, and discouraged. Most tell me they will never return to a full-time paid church position. Their wounds continue to be painful.[2]

While pastors have always faced the possibility of forced termination, the problem has been growing steadily worse, which is why wounded pastors are flocking to specialized ministries that offer professional assessments, intensive counseling, and peaceful retreats.

For the past three years, my wife and I have been living hundreds of miles from the church we once joyfully served. We've asked ourselves, "How did we get here? Why did we lose so many friends so quickly? What did *we* do to contribute to our exile?" What's ironic is that I possess a good-sized library on managing and resolving church conflict, and I think I understand the field fairly well. Yet part of me continues to engage in self-reproach because *I didn't see the conflict coming* – and neither did our church family. The whole experience still seems surreal.

While there are fascinating *studies* on the forced termination of pastors, Christians need to hear more *stories* about this tragedy that happens behind closed doors. Yet pastors are afraid that if they tell their stories publicly, they will look foolish, rehearse their pain, sully their reputations, and damage their chances for future employment. So except for rare forays into the light, the involuntary dismissal of hundreds of pastors every month has escaped the notice of most Christians. Because most books on conflict are aimed at pastors and church leaders, my hope is to enlighten and empower lay people as well to ensure that conflicts involving pastors or staffers are handled in a just, deliberate, and *biblical* manner.

I may be violating some unwritten rule that says, "What happens in church stays in church." Wouldn't it be better for our careers and mental health if my wife and I refused to look back, learned from our mistakes, kept our mouths shut, and advanced full-speed ahead? But I believe it's a greater evil to remain silent. What kind of a New Testament would we have if Paul had been mute about the problems in Rome, Corinth, Galatia, Ephesus, Philippi, Colossae, Thessalonica, and Crete? We have learned so much from *those* churches and *their* blunders.

Part of me wants to travel back in time and prevent my father's forced exit. If I could help him with that situation, would he still be alive today? Although that notion may be unrealistic, I have sensed God calling me for years to do something to limit (and even eliminate) the unchristian practices that are inherent in forcing an innocent pastor to leave a church. Wouldn't it advance the kingdom to prevent this tragedy from happening to other pastors and churches?

Let's acknowledge that troubled pastors *do* exist. Some have character disorders or a narcissistic bent. Others are control freaks. A few are lazy. Some can even be tyrants. There are pastors who should be terminated – and even leave pastoral ministry altogether. But Alan Klaas, who investigated the causes of pastoral ousters in different Christian denominations, concluded that in 45 percent of the cases, a minority faction caused the pastor to leave, while "only seven percent of the time was the cause the personal misconduct of the minister."[3]

I have written this book with three purposes in mind. First, *I want to share my side of a conflict as forthrightly as I can.* Several weeks after the conflict surfaced, I sat in two public meetings and did not respond to any of the charges leveled against me. Three years later, I am able to articulate my responses with greater perspective. Others have differing views as to what happened, and that's fine. This is not the *final* version of what happened in 2009, but *my* version as I experienced it. While the conflict occurred, I took careful notes, generated and received scores of emails, interacted with key players, and interviewed congregational experts.

Next, *I want to seek redemption for what we've experienced.* Rick Warren says that our greatest ministries emerge from our greatest sufferings:

> God intentionally allows you to go through painful experiences to equip you for ministry to others . . . . The very expe-

riences that you have resented or regretted most in life – the ones you've wanted to hide and forget – are the experiences God wants to use to help others. They *are* your ministry! For God to use your painful experiences, you must be willing to share them. You have to stop covering them up, and you must honestly admit your faults, failures, and fears. Doing this will probably be your most effective ministry.[4]

While my wife and I are unimportant in the larger Christian community, maybe our willingness to share honestly about a painful experience will turn out to be our "most effective ministry."

Finally, *I want to prevent these kinds of conflicts from happening altogether.* At present, the Christian community permits and even enables destructive behavior against pastors, and the pastor is expected to take it without recourse. If this is just one pastor's story, it may not be worthwhile – but tens of thousands of pastors could relate similar stories if they had the right forum and could just push past their pain. My prayer is that by reducing the fifty-day conflict to slow motion, God's people will be able to identify key junctures and learn from both the wise – and foolish – decisions that were made. I also pray that believers will institute safeguards so that a similar conflict won't invade their churches.

It is not my intent to seek revenge on those who hurt us. Although it took time, my wife and I have forgiven them and wish them God's best in the days ahead. But for this story to help others, it must be reported with authenticity and emotion. My goal is to let believers know how quickly a conflict can spiral out of control and to recommend ways to handle matters that go against our feelings but are consistent with Scripture.

Because I come from a tradition where mostly men are considered for ordination, I will use terms that reflect that reality, although I greatly value the contributions women make in ministry.

Except for members of my immediate family, I have used aliases throughout this book to protect the identity of the individuals involved. I have also avoided naming my former community or church – but the events related in this story are real.

May God use this book to help his people treat pastors and staff members with greater dignity and respect so they can serve him passionately and productively until Christ returns.

CHAPTER 1

PUSHED

The events of October 24, 2009 are lodged in my memory forever. It was a beautiful Saturday morning in our community. Still jet-lagged after a flight from London three days earlier, I awoke and quickly dressed for that morning's scheduled meeting of our church's board of directors. The board planned to finalize the general fund budget for the following year, and as senior pastor, I had volunteered to bring ideas for raising more donations. After putting the finishing touches on my presentation, I made the five-minute drive to the campus, stopped into my office, and then entered the adjacent room where the board was gathered. That's strange, I thought, for all the board members to arrive early for a meeting.

When I entered the room, I was excited. Along with four other participants – including my wife Kim – I had just returned from a mission trip to the Eastern European country of Moldova, our fourth trip there within three years. The ministry overseas exceeded our expectations, and I couldn't wait to share with the board what God had done, though some weren't thrilled about such trips for financial reasons. Upon entering the room, the group seemed unusually quiet, solemn even. I don't remember anyone greeting me or asking me how the trip went. Feeling uncomfortable, I hurriedly sat down.

Taylor, the chairman, began the meeting by saying that the board had made a difficult decision and had lost sleep over it. He had a stack of documents before him, and although he didn't read from them, they seemed to serve as reminders in case he went off track. As the chairman prefaced his remarks, my immediate reaction was that the board was going to fire me, and I could feel my heart rate increasing. But then Taylor looked squarely at me and told me that my wife, the church's outreach director for the past eight-and-a-half years, was being terminated "effective immediately" for the way she had managed her ministry budgets. The board had dismissed the pastor's wife!

Then the chairman told me that I was being reprimanded as well. He specified two complaints against me, based on incidents that had happened two-and-a-half months previously, even though I assumed one incident was in the past because I had already apologized for it and changed my behavior. While the complaints meant that the board was serious, they concerned offenses they claimed I had committed against *them* rather than the way I served the *church*. All I could think was, "What is going to happen to us?"

I was completely off balance and responded, "So *this* is what you've been doing while we've been overseas!" The board and I had been out of sync for several months, so before leaving for Moldova, one of my mentors asked me, "Are you sure you want to leave for three weeks with the problems you've been having with the board?" While overseas, Kim asked me one day, "Do you think we'll have jobs when we get back?"

As I sat at the table with the six board members, I felt betrayed.

The church's governing body was called a board of directors – a title inherited from my predecessor – rather than elders or deacons. We began 2009 with only four board members (three men and one woman), but our governing documents stated we needed a minimum of five. Since I didn't see anyone among the four who could be chairman, I received board consent to ask Taylor (whose term had just ended) to return as chairman for one year, and for a newcomer to fill the role of treasurer. Both men accepted my invitations.

For the first time in my ministry career, every board member was younger than me, even though I had veto power as senior pastor over prospective leaders. But now it felt like my wife and I were being stabbed in the back. On the Sunday before going overseas, these same leaders laid hands on us and prayed for us in front of the congregation, but now those identical hands were wrapped around our throats. What had my wife done to justify her dismissal?

When I asked that very question, the treasurer claimed that she had overspent her outreach budget for an event (which occurred before we went overseas) and her Moldova missions' budget by a wide margin. When the treasurer mentioned a total, I should have asked to see his accounting in writing, but I was too numb to think straight. But since no one gave me written evidence of her spending, I couldn't challenge their figures.

I tried to explain how our Moldova team had to pay unexpected fees to transport five large suitcases to Chisinau, the capital of Moldova. The suitcases were full of aid packets for the vulnerable children, education supplies for church workers, and personal items for the pastor's family with whom we would be staying. (Since Moldova is the poorest country in Europe, and the authorities regularly confiscate things sent from outside the country, our gifts were greatly needed and appreciated.) Kim had called the airlines the day before our departure to confirm that the suitcases would be transported to Chisinau without additional charges (as they had been the previous year), but the domestic airline claimed that the suitcases were too heavy at the airport and charged us accordingly. After our team arrived in London, we discovered just before our flight to Romania that the suitcases were left in Heathrow's baggage area rather than sent through as promised. After quickly negotiating with the Romanian airline – which charged us double the fee of the domestic airline to transport the suitcases – I charged the payments to the church credit card with the intent of explaining the situation when we returned home. I even called the domestic airline's United States' headquarters from London (it was the middle of the night back home) to try and get the charges reversed, but to no avail. Kim later wrote the airline as well, requesting a refund. (They never responded.) As the missions' leader, Kim always made a full financial accounting whenever she returned from an overseas excursion. Why couldn't the board wait to see *her* accounting? What was the hurry besides group anxiety?

Inside that meeting, it dawned on me that someone must have looked at charges put on the church card while we were overseas and assumed that Kim was spending money without authorization, when I had approved those expenditures myself. (In fact, I explicitly told our

23

team when we were in London that *I* was making the decision.) However, without waiting to check with us, the charges were undoubtedly counted against her budget. As pastor, I had also authorized several other necessary trip expenditures which were probably assigned to the missions' budget as well. I offered a few other explanations, but the board seemed uninterested. Then Taylor told me that the board felt so strongly about their decision that they were all willing to resign over this issue. I had never heard of such a power tactic being used by a board before.

During the meeting, the board told me that I was a gifted teacher, I could stay as pastor, and Kim could serve as a volunteer. I asked the six leaders if Kim could still lead Fall Fun Fest, our Halloween outreach event which was only seven days away. (Kim had spent months planning for the event.) The board was clear: Kim could not lead the event. She was finished as a staff member. I didn't ask, but I assumed this meant that she couldn't tell the church about the Moldova trip, either.

I reminded the board that Kim was our most effective staff member, the most beloved person in the church, and the face of the church to the community (she was an ambassador with the Chamber of Commerce), but they didn't budge. I quickly realized that the group wasn't going to change their mind, so for my family's sake, I needed to negotiate the best terms possible. I asked about severance pay, and they told me that she would be given one month's pay as a "love offering." That seemed highly unjust, especially since a different board had been much more generous when they had terminated another staff member years before. I told the board about the hardship Kim's loss of income would have on our family, but they merely listened. (Pastors and staff members are rarely eligible for unemployment benefits.)

Sitting there that morning, I no longer felt I knew the six people around the table. I told the board that they did not know what they were doing and that there were many other ways this could have been handled. In addition, I told them something they had undoubtedly discussed already: there was no way my wife would want to attend services or volunteer for a church that had dismissed her. "If you worked for a grocery store," I told the half-dozen leaders, "and you were released, you wouldn't want to shop at that store ever again. Kim won't want to attend church here anymore and I can't be pastor if she won't attend services." Nobody seemed sympathetic to my argument. They had the luxury of deliberating for at least three weeks without us around, and they knew that by dismissing my wife, they were in effect terminating me as well, even if that was not their stated intention. It was two for the price of one. This led me to mention that if I resigned immediately, it could take at least a year for me to find a new church position, and at my age, it could be the end of my pastoral career altogether. (While I *felt* like resigning, I had trained myself over the years never to quit in haste.)

It was amazing that I remained calm during the meeting. At both the July and August meetings, I had become visibly angry inside a board meeting for the first time in thirty-five years of ministry, and yet the Lord helped me control my emotions during *this* meeting. But while I talked with the board, I kept wondering how I was going to tell Kim about their decision. Her ministry was in many ways her identity. She absolutely *loved* her job.

Even though I was not being terminated, it *felt* like I was being dismissed as well. Kim reported to me as her supervisor, and at times I had to veto one of her entrepreneurial ideas. But there were also times when she persuaded me to let her do something that I wasn't convinced would work – but it usually did. In some respects, Kim was being punished simply for doing the job I expected her to do. However, I had discussed her budgets with her all year long, and to this day, I feel confident about the way I supervised her, but my protests fell on deaf ears.

When you're in a meeting like that, you quickly transition into survival mode. You feel permanently rejected. Whenever I had a major problem with someone in the church, I could consult with the chairman or the board itself – but who could I consult with when the conflict concerned the board? While I couldn't wait to bolt out of that upstairs room, I had to stay and negotiate terms. Our careers, reputations, and legacies were hanging in the balance, as was the health and unity of our beloved church.

While our missionaries received the same amount of support each month, outreach spending was more sporadic depending upon the season. For instance, whenever we had an outreach event – and they were essential in our community – we'd aim to reach a certain number of people but we could never control how many attended. We planned optimistically (so we had enough food, for example) but sometimes the weather wouldn't cooperate or people had scheduling conflicts. Events were intended for our people to invite their friends or to meet newcomers. If we made money, that was great. While we didn't want to lose money, if we did, I considered that an investment in people's lives – and good advertising for the church – but not everyone thought like me. Kim thought she had received approval from the board chairman to spend ahead on her outreach budget, but evidently that no longer mattered.

Sometime during the meeting, the chairman told me that everything said in the meeting should remain confidential. While that was normal procedure for a board meeting, I did not respond to his statement. If I had been *asked* to keep the contents of that meeting private, I would have refused. Had I been able to *participate* in their decision, of course I would have kept matters confidential. But I didn't know how the board arrived at their decision, and if it turned out that they had misrepresented facts or conspired to remove us from our positions, I needed to reserve the right to tell my story or appeal to the congregation. Maybe I should have shared my thinking in the meeting, but with their "gotcha" attitudes, they might have found a way to use my refusal against me. While in the meeting, I remembered this statement from Christian conflict expert Speed Leas:

> Confidentiality just increases the amount of fear in the system. If we believe that we cannot share what is going on in a meeting or in a conflict, the secretive aura enhances rather than diminishes assessments of just how dangerous this situation is. *The more that is shared, the more that is talked about, the less threatening the experience* . . . . I can't say enough about the problems of confidentiality in organizational settings. In my experience the norms of confidentiality are serious barriers to managing conflict. Secrets inhibit rather than open up communication, secrets raise fear, secrets keep out people who might be able to help, secrets presume that truth will enslave rather than set one free, secrets are often lies that keep the accused from confronting them because he or she supposedly doesn't know the 'charges.'[1]

During the meeting, I asked the board if Roger, the associate pastor, had been involved in their decision. Roger had told me many times that he never wanted to be a senior pastor, primarily because he didn't want to receive all the flak the lead pastor receives. When I told the board this, they seemed surprised. Aha, I thought, they assume that if I leave, Roger will assume pastoral leadership for a while. Boy, are they in for a shock!

Ironically, while we were in Moldova, the chairman had sent a letter to the entire church soliciting monetary gifts for Clergy Appreciation Month, which our church celebrated every October. Since our trip overseas encompassed the first three Sundays in October, the last Sunday of the month – the following day – was the final opportunity for the board to present our three pastors with a gift in front of our church family. Since the board planned to announce their decision to the church the next day, they asked that neither of us attend services. I then asked, "Who do you have to preach tomorrow?" Someone answered, "No one." Their plan was to show a DVD featuring a Christian speaker, but I told the board, "I finished a message on giving before leaving for Moldova. I would be happy to give it, and I promise I won't go off the reservation on you." Since they hadn't asked anyone else to speak – and since they hadn't fired *me* – they reluctantly agreed, which meant they would announce Kim's dismissal on the following Sunday, November 1. Without any of us knowing it, their failure to schedule a speaker affected their ability to control subsequent events.

The entire meeting lasted nearly two hours. The board told me that as staff supervisor, they wanted *me* to tell my *wife* that she was terminated. They also wanted me to ask Kim if she wanted to resign or be fired. In retrospect, I should have vehemently protested – especially since I was not shown any evidence against her – because according to church bylaws, the staff worked for the senior pastor, not the board, and it was *their* decision, not mine. In reality, I was caught in an emotional triangle between Kim and the board:

One of the most common types of triangles occurs in a board meeting when the board discusses a problem between two persons or groups – and then suggests that you should go to one of the parties and tell them thus-and-such. It all seems so innocent. The board is concerned and wants the pastor to use his influence to settle the matter. But as soon as you go to one of the parties, you are caught in a triangle between the two opposing groups.[2]

I told the board that although I didn't agree with their decision, I wouldn't accuse or defend Kim in the meeting. But I did ask that two board members meet with her and explain to her their reasoning for letting her go. She needed to hear directly from her accusers rather than hope I was accurately conveying the board's thinking. They agreed, although the timing was left open.

Finally, I mentioned that I thought the severity of any conflict we were having was at a "2" or a "3" level (a skirmish) rather than an "8" or a "9" level (a perpetual war). While the board may have assumed they had spoken forthrightly about certain issues in the past, to me they stopped well short of declaring their true feelings. The board reminded me of the wife who hints to her husband that she wants to see changes in their marriage until one day she demands that he move out of the house. While she assumed she had been speaking assertively, her husband failed to discern her clues. In a similar way, I felt blindsided.

Before leaving the meeting, I told the board that a pastor's authority and responsibility should match. If you are responsible for the ministry, you need to have a corresponding amount of authority to accomplish your goals. But while the board wanted me to be entirely *responsible* for the ministry, it seemed like they increasingly wanted to seize *authority* for themselves. Looking into the faces of now-former colleagues, I could sense the message they were sending: no matter how it's been in the past, you no longer lead this church. We do.

I was in the midst of a church coup.

I tried to put myself in their place. To be fair, with one exception, board members demonstrated sensitivity during the meeting. From their perspective, it took courage to terminate the pastor's wife, especially since the pastor might choose to resign over their verdict. They knew that once their resolution became public, they would have to account to the church for the dismissal. It sounded like they were trying to be just, letting Kim go and letting me stay. But after what they did, and how they did it, I could never work with them again. While there was a remote possibility that we might someday enjoy *personal* relationships, our *working* relationship had been destroyed.

It's sad that the board required three weeks of secret deliberations to muster up the courage to speak with me authentically. Because of cultural and mindset differences, I never felt I could entirely be myself with that particular group.

Before the meeting ended, someone commended me for my professionalism. Based on my recent track record, he may have feared I would become upset again, but God's Spirit assisted me in supernatural ways. After someone prayed – it may have been me, I don't remember – I walked slowly to my car while the board remained behind.

It was my last official meeting with them.

Let me briefly introduce my wife and I to you. Kim was born on the East Coast but her family moved to San Diego shortly after she was born. When she was nine, her parents sensed God calling them to serve as medical missionaries in Saudi Arabia. From ages ten through fifteen, Kim lived in boarding schools in India and Pakistan and only saw her parents in Arabia during vacations. Three years after returning to America, her dad became the pastor of my home church.

Kim is a gifted leader who can mentor leaders, organize groups for projects, and attract crowds with large events. She is a *catalyst* who thinks *big*! For example, due to Kim's boldness, our church once held the closing rally of Vacation Bible School in the headquarters of a National Football League team. Several times a year, so many people came out for outreach events that our property could barely contain the crowds. She also attracted and followed up guests, recruited volunteers for everyone's ministries, and led various ministries superbly. People flocked to her seminars at the regional church convention, and she even began her own consulting practice, later helping a pastor turn around a dying church. She also spearheaded various ministries to hurting people in the area, looking for ways to build bridges between our church and the community. She wasn't a control freak or a one-woman show, but did all she could to empower others. While Kim has loads of vision and creativity, she is also a sweetheart who makes people feel special, especially wounded people. (Every Valentine's Day, she made sure that every person in the church who was single received a gift basket on their doorstep.) On the Myers-Briggs test, Kim and I are exact opposites, but we complement each other and have always worked well together as a team, both at home and at church.

Like Tom Sawyer on the day he whitewashed the fence for Aunt Polly, most people are willing to give *her* things because they enjoy serving with her so much.

In contrast to Kim, I was born on the West Coast in Southern California. My father was one of the initial seven graduates of Talbot Seminary (now School of Theology) and my mother was the first president of the seminary wives. Our family moved to Anaheim, California, when I was four years old. My dad became a pastor and eventually founded a church in nearby Garden Grove. I had a happy childhood until age eleven when my father involuntarily left the pastorate. Twenty months later, he was dead. My mother went back to school and began working to support our family and asked me – her thirteen-year-old son – to look after my younger brother and sister.

When I was fourteen, my best friend invited me to his church for special youth meetings, and our family eventually made that church our home. Five years later, the elders hired me as a youth pastor for the summer, and soon afterward, I met Kim, our new pastor's oldest daughter. I graduated from Biola College (now University) two years later, and we were married several months after that. While working full-time at two different churches, I completed my Master of Divinity degree and nearly three decades later, earned a Doctor of Ministry degree. God has graciously permitted us to serve him in various churches for thirty-six years. During that time, I have served as a youth pastor and an associate pastor, and for twenty-six of those years, a solo or senior pastor. Kim and I have also enjoyed thirty-seven years of wedded bliss.

I love preaching more than anything in ministry and worked tirelessly on my messages. While my top two spiritual gifts are teaching and prophecy, I have always exercised them in love. For some reason, I've also been involved in a variety of ministry transitions, including a church merger and a rebirthed church. I gradually became more of a risk taker than my personality might suggest, using culturally relevant approaches to reach spiritually lost people for Christ. While church ministry can be fulfilling and exciting, even when it's done right, it can result in much pain and heartache, and I have not been immune from those conditions.

The ride home was only five minutes long, but heaviness descended upon me as I drove along the tree-lined streets of our section of the city. How could I tell Kim that her ministry was over? This is her account of what happened next:

I'll always remember that you came home early. I knew there was trouble because you were always at those meetings late. I was sitting in the living room on the couch and your whole posture told me something, and I said, 'They fired you, didn't they?' And then you sat down with me and said, 'No, they fired you, they're letting you go.'

And I will never forget that feeling. I had the biggest pit in my stomach because I had always sworn to myself from the day that you went into ministry that I would never embarrass you or do anything that would affect your ministry. I had made it clear to other people that I would always step down first. And I had caused this and humiliated you to the extent that you had to go to a meeting and they had to tell you that.

I cried uncontrollably for thirty minutes because I just couldn't believe it. I just wanted to throw up. I said I wasn't going to go to church the next day. I didn't know how to explain myself. I felt I had caused it 100 percent. I just couldn't believe it.

Before I could say anything about confidentiality – and it wasn't on my frontal lobes at the time – Kim emailed her good friend Laura:

Please keep this information between you and me. I am very heart broken right now because Jim went to the board meeting today and the board has let me go effective immediately. I can't come to church tomorrow because I am so hurt and not quite sure how to act. I just need to tell a friend because this has never happened to me before. I plan to resign because I don't want to be known as fired. I guess this has been a bad year. I will have no more contact with Moldova or Kenya.

Kim then finished with these words:

> Please keep this quiet because it would hurt even more if the
> church was split over this or hurt in any way. Sometimes I
> don't understand what God is doing.

Laura came over right away. Her friendship would be important in
the days ahead.

I debated what to do for a few minutes and decided I needed expert
guidance. Because of the unexpected decisions that had just been
relayed to me, I was more reactive than rational and needed advice
from objective parties. Proverbs 15:22 says, "Plans fail for lack of
counsel, but with many advisers they succeed." I called my best ministry mentor, Kim's father, and then called a board chairman from a
previous church who told me that the board targeted Kim as a way
of removing me, something that hadn't yet crossed my mind. I then
called Jane, a professional conflict manager from our church with
whom I had consulted about board issues several months before. Her
concern was that Kim's dismissal would split the church.

I also contacted a close friend and former seminary classmate
who served as pastor of a Calvary Chapel. My friend believed that the
board should resign instead of me. In the Calvary system, the pastor
works directly for the Lord, not the board. While his words injected
some fight in me, I wasn't about to lead a rebellion against the board.
Whether or not their actions were justified, they had been duly elected
by the church, and I needed to respect their decision.

The board may have felt that their injunction to keep matters confidential was violated when Kim contacted Laura and I consulted with
Jane, but how could we not ask for the listening ears and prayers of a
few trusted friends at this tragic time? Besides, we didn't share with
friends so they would fight back on our behalf. We just wanted emotional and prayer support. (Not one of my many advisors faulted me
for discussing this situation with experts or friends.) Since the board
met with me but not with Kim directly – and since she had not pledged
confidentiality to them – how free was *she* to tell others about their
decision? Did they expect that we would huddle at home for an entire
week and avoid all contact with church friends? What if someone con-

tacted Kim and wanted to know details about Fall Fun Fest, which normally involved scores of volunteers? If we referred people to board members, wouldn't that raise suspicions even more? And how would the board handle all the people who wanted to know why Kim wasn't leading the event? Regardless of what we said, the news was bound to leak out anyway. The board had placed us in an impossible position.

The board later claimed that they told me to tell Kim that they wanted to meet with her right away, but I don't recall them saying that at all. In fact, over the next few days, I had four contacts with Taylor – one in person and three via email – and he never mentioned any deadline. In the Saturday meeting, the board told me that they wanted to announce to the church the next day that "Kim is no longer the outreach director." They wanted her to decide: would she choose to be fired or resign? While Kim's initial reaction was to resign, she later told me, "I didn't do anything wrong, so I am not going to resign. They are going to have to fire me."

I was thankful that I had already prepared my message for that Sunday. It was based on Mark 12:41-44, the story where Jesus and his disciples watched worshippers deposit their offerings into the temple treasury, prompting Jesus to commend the widow who gave a single mite. The story was replete with timely spiritual and financial lessons for our church, and I had spent a lot of time studying the passage and searching for the right combination of words so I could encourage the congregation in the joys of giving to God.

Since our church shared parking with various businesses and restaurants, I lacked an assigned parking space. Because I wanted to leave the campus quickly after the second service that Sunday, I parked in an alternate lot and had to walk a few hundred feet past some businesses before arriving on campus. Since I am not good at disguising strong feelings, I avoided as many people as possible that morning. After testing my microphone before the first service, I sat in my usual seat in the front row on the center aisle. I could barely sing the worship songs because I was conserving energy for my two messages. At the end of the first service, Taylor presented the associate pastor, youth pastor, and me with individual cards for Clergy Appreciation Month which presumably included monetary gifts from the congregation. Everyone applauded, but I thought to myself, "If you only knew what's really going on around here . . ." When I sat down before the second service, the worship band drummer sat next to me and asked, "Are you okay? I can tell something's wrong." He was right. Something was. But I couldn't tell him. All I said was, "You'll find out soon enough."

God somehow gave me the courage to get through the second service and the whole Clergy Appreciation charade again. After the service, I felt dazed and disconnected from everybody. I wandered over to see Jerry and Angela, two good friends, and briefly told them about the board's decision. As people of grace, they invited Kim and me to their house for dinner that night.

As I slipped off the campus and walked toward my car, I ran into Steve, an Armenian Christian who ran a popular deli. Steve was hosing down the walkway, and as I approached, he asked, "How is Kim?" Because I didn't want to involve Steve in our mess, I responded, "She's not doing well today, which is why she didn't come to church." Because Steve attended a church in another community, he knew nothing about the events of the previous twenty-eight hours, yet his response sounded like a prophecy: "She is an awesome woman of God! That is why she is being attacked!" Steve was far more insightful than he knew.

I slowly opened the door of my Honda and pried open the appreciation card. Each of the board members penned a brief note. While the congregation probably assumed there was a gift inside the card, it was empty. Either the board didn't have their act together or they were sending me a message. Maybe, I thought, it was a little bit of both.

When I got home, Kim was sitting with her best friend Jenny, who stayed with Kim all morning to encourage her. (I had suggested to Kim that she invite someone over because I didn't want her to be alone that morning.) I told Jenny that Kim's dismissal meant that we had to leave the church. If Kim couldn't attend services anymore, how could I stay as pastor? Jenny wanted us to fight the board's decision and felt that the vast majority of the congregation would be with us. But that wasn't something I wanted to do. I knew that any fight would be divisive, and I lacked the drive to mount a counterattack. It was better for us both to leave and keep the church unified than to watch all we'd worked for unravel.

Without our knowledge, the board was meeting that very hour with three staff members on the church campus. The board explained that Kim had been relieved of her duties. When asked why Kim had been dismissed, the staff was told there were three charges, including the fact that Kim was "ungodly," which prompted laughter from the staffer who asked the question. In my meeting with the board the previous day, I was told that Kim was being released because of financial issues, but the board now added more charges. They made the same threat to resign together that they had made to me. A similar meeting had taken place the previous evening with the remaining two staff members. The Kim the board described to the staff was not the Kim they knew and loved. Unbelievably, the board told Kim's co-workers she had been dismissed before ever meeting with Kim herself. I guess confidentiality is a one-way street.

Roger, the associate pastor, had approached me at church earlier that day to say that he was praying for us. Later that afternoon, he sent me an email saying that he was shocked by the news of the weekend and that he and his wife were praying for us and for the unity of our church. He also promised to support me "as best I can" and to continue to build the church. Since he sent the note without prompting on my part, I was reasonably confident that he lacked advance knowledge of the board's decision. Although he invited me to call him, I chose to email him two hours later and carefully wrote:

Thank you for writing. It means a lot to me. I don't really know what this is all about. I spent two hours with the board on Saturday trying to get my head around what they were saying. They haven't talked with Kim yet at all and she hasn't been allowed to tell her side of any story. If she did something wrong, then they need to talk to her about it first, but they've talked to me and the whole staff and haven't talked to her.

This is hard on us right now. I think I know what's going on, but I'm not positive. We have received a lot of great counsel and support. We would appreciate your prayers as we weigh our options.

Later that afternoon, I spoke on the phone with a church leader who already knew about the board's decision and offered to pay for us to consult with a labor attorney for one hour. Several Christian leaders outside the church encouraged us to take legal action against the board, but this was not something that I wanted to do, knowing the biblical injunction against believers taking each other to court in 1 Corinthians 6:1-8. Because of the separation of church and state issue, I didn't think our case had a chance in a secular court of law, but I kept the suggestion in mind.

That Sunday night, Kim and I drove over to the home of Jerry and Angela. Laura was there as well. As honestly as I could, I told our friends about the events that led up to the board's decision. I did not try and cover up any mistakes that Kim or I may have made. Whenever there is a conflict, I try and examine myself first so I can discover how I contributed to the situation. (Pastors tend to blame themselves *completely* for such conflicts.) Yes, Kim and I had made minor mistakes at times, and we both took full responsibility for our actions, although we weren't aware of any major offenses we had committed. (It's better to share everything up front so that your supporters aren't surprised when they hear accusations from others.) Our friends listened, asked questions, encouraged us, and prayed for us. I did not ask them to do anything on our behalf. We just needed to feel safe that night. We left uncertain of our futures but grateful for good friends at such a time. While those friends would become even more valuable in the days ahead, within two weeks, we would have no idea who most of our friends were anymore.

After returning home, I received an email from Taylor. He assured us of his prayers for us and encouraged me to take the next week off. He also stated that he and other board members were available to meet with Kim when she felt ready. He promised not to call her but to let him know via email when she felt comfortable to speak about the situation. At this juncture, Taylor was trying his best to display a sensitive tone. Unlike some boards that demand that a staff member vacate his or her office and leave the campus immediately, the board was allowing Kim to initiate contact with them when she was ready. (However, Taylor was addressing *me* and not *her*.) So far, both sides were acting civilly toward each other.

That was about to change.

36

TAKEAWAYS FROM CHAPTER 1

For pastors and staff members:

- If you are ever blindsided by a board concerning your job status, ask God to help you remain calm. You will interact with the board more clearly, negotiate more wisely, and recount conversations more accurately. If you overreact, the board may use your anger against you at a later date. (However, a pastor should be able to *disagree* with a board and stand up for himself without recrimination.) If necessary, ask for a recess to regain your composure.
- Stay in the meeting as long as possible and discuss every issue that comes to mind. Since you are just learning about matters, ask for issues to be clarified so you understand them fully – and write down all you can for accuracy's sake. You might need to request a second meeting (maybe just with the chairman) so that all your questions and concerns can be addressed.
- If board members claim that you have done something wrong, ask them to explain or show you any evidence they have against you. Do not simply take their word for it. You are entitled to know what you have done wrong so you can defend yourself – or repent.
- Never promise confidentiality needlessly during a time of conflict. Your pledge of silence may hurt you or your church if you need to be forthcoming later. When asked if you will keep matters confidential, the best reply is, "It all depends . . ."

For board members:

- Go "by the book" *before* making any final decisions about a pastor or staff member's job status, making sure to consult your governing documents, insurance company, and a labor attorney.
- If you are unhappy with the performance of your pastor or a staffer, patiently create a progressive improvement plan. Spell out specific behaviors you want him or her to demonstrate and give that person time (such as ninety days) to show progress.

If you display patience, and the person in question does not show improvement, he or she may resign anyway. But if your board fails to use a plan, *you* may later be accused of making decisions out of haste or malice.

- While firing a pastor or a staff member may seem like a quick solution to an ongoing problem, make sure that every process you use is *fair* rather than *fast*. The faster you proceed, the more mistakes you'll make and the more potential harm you will bring to everyone involved.

- If you're thinking about making a personnel decision on the basis of evidence, present the evidence first to the accused for their response. (You could be seeing things inaccurately.) And if you're making a decision based on witness testimony, let the accused face his or her accusers in most cases.

For the congregation:

- Pray for your pastor, staff, and board members on a continual basis. Not only do they have great responsibilities, but Satan is continually trying to deceive, destroy, and divide them as a way of harming your church and its influence. Ask others to pray with you for their protection.

- If you hear rumors about unrest between the top leaders, discreetly try and discover what's happening. Even though you may never know everything, commit the situation to the Lord and trust that he will work out matters for his glory. Do not exacerbate any problems through speculation or gossip.

CHAPTER 2

REINFORCEMENTS

*T*he next day was Monday, and Jane called me that morning to express her concern that the board might send a letter to the congregation announcing that Kim was no longer employed. If they did that, it would become a *fait accompli* and matters might quickly escalate out of control. After she hung up, I called Rebecca, the church's office manager, and asked to meet with her off campus. (She already knew about the board's decision because she had met with the board and staff the previous day.) Because the board wanted to make their announcement as soon as possible, I was concerned they would ask Rebecca to send out a mass mailing to the entire congregation, so I asked her – she still worked for me, not the board – to tip me off if that happened.

As I drove home, Jane called to tell me that Jerry had drafted an email asking if their group of six – Jerry and Angela, Darrell and Jenny, and Laura and Jane – could meet with the board before any announcement about Kim's status became public. As an experienced conflict manager, Jane wanted my approval on letting Jerry send his email. Since the board expected confidentiality from me, if Jerry sent the note, the board would know that I had spoken to others, possibly assuming that I was leading a counterattack. But for me, this was about preserving church cohesiveness. Which virtue was greater: confidentiality or unity? Since I had not explicitly promised confidentiality, I opted for unity and gave the green light for Jerry to send the email.

Jane told me that their group would handle matters from now on, that I needed to trust them to run with things, and that I needed to stay out of sight. While I could strategize, I lacked the stomach for fighting. Although I was not orchestrating matters, I could hear the hoof beats of reinforcements behind me.

After Taylor sent me his email the previous Sunday evening, I delayed answering him until early Tuesday morning, and even then remained noncommittal. I gently tried to reassert my leadership prerogatives when I wrote:

> You have been kind in the way you have handled this, and I appreciate that. It may be that you would prefer I take the week off, including Sunday, but I would prefer to preach this Sunday. Otherwise, we will lay low.

The chairman wrote back within the hour but still insisted that I take the following Sunday off. He offered to arrange for a speaker or use a DVD to fill some time. And he reiterated that he wanted to meet with Kim when she felt up to it. The chairman ended his note by saying he was praying for us.

As it turned out, the longer Kim waited to set up an appointment with board members, the more in control of the situation we inadvertently became. While she wasn't emotionally ready for *any* meeting, I wanted to weigh our options with my advisors. But I sensed the board was becoming increasingly anxious. Maybe they didn't want the information about Kim's dismissal to circulate throughout the church without their interpretation because *they* might be blamed for her departure. People might then contact us to find out our version of events before hearing from the board directly. As events unfolded, we were only able to wait so long.

The church we served was founded in the late 1980s by a pastor friend (I'll call him Norman) who was eighteen years my senior. I had followed the church's progress from its inception. Norman gave me tours of its first two meeting places: a real estate office and a building in the local business park. The church eventually secured land and constructed a building housing a small worship center, ministry rooms, and staff offices. As another pastor once told me, the campus location was both great and terrible. It was great because the property rested on a beautiful lagoon filled with ducks and unique birds, but it was terrible because the property was invisible from the street and located at the back of a long parking area. (The church shared parking with several dozen neighboring businesses.) On Sundays, churchgoers could park anywhere within several lots, but it was often a nightmare to find a space during the week.

The great majority of attendees came from the immediate area, making it a neighborhood church rather than a regional one. In fact, we attracted few people from beyond the local interstate, a ten-minute drive away. The church was also situated in an extreme corner of the city, resulting in poor visibility, but we still became the largest Protestant church in the city for years. In fact, a well-known church growth expert used the word "phenomenal" to describe our ministry. The church had a reputation for being gracious and generous and exceeded ministry expectations for the area. During my tenure, the attendance and giving nearly doubled (the majority of newcomers being unchurched people), and we constructed a new worship center in a field on our single acre of land. But once we maximized the space on our property, we were trapped. To grow more, we either had to buy an adjacent building or sell our property and relocate, and the city had already declared the most logical areas off-limits to churches.

Because of the restrictions involving land, the church was not an ideal setting for an ambitious pastor who needed to see steady growth to feel fulfilled, so it was natural to feel frustrated by the lack of available space. But congregational expectations seemed quite reasonable. People seemed content as long as I loved them, led them, and taught them well. It was a great situation for someone at my stage of life, and I planned to stay until retirement.

Right before I became senior pastor, the board decided to hire a full-time outreach director so we could attract and keep guests. (We had a large reserve fund and the board had designated those funds for ministry.) The board solicited resumes from a wide range of sources and began prioritizing them. During this process, my wife applied for the job even though nearly all her work experience had been in secular positions. While I stayed out of the first round of interviews completely, Kim alone made it to the second round. When it came time for me to interview her along with the board chairman, I grilled her more than I would have done with anyone else. (On our way home, she asked me, "What was *that* about?") Right from the beginning, I wanted her to know that if she was offered the position, she had to earn her way.

The church enjoyed its best-ever year in 2008. We crammed nearly 800 people onto our small campus for Easter, and we seemed ready to make the transition from a medium-sized church to a large one. We were staffed for growth with five full-time people and two part-timers. Our services were creative and uplifting, our outreach ministries were meaningful and thriving, and the spirit of the congregation was positive and contagious. It was a joy and a privilege to lead such an exciting congregation – so what in the world went wrong?

For years, I focused my energies on the church I served and spent a minimal amount of time in professional networking, so after the events of October 24 broke, I contacted Christian leaders that I hadn't spoken with in more than a decade. To my amazement, every person who heard my story gave me invaluable counsel. I contacted nearly twenty leaders within a one-week span, including a seminary professor, several conflict experts, a Christian counselor, three consultants, two former board chairmen, two attorneys, and several pastors. Of particular help was Dr. Charles Chandler from the Ministering to Ministers Foundation in Richmond, Virginia, a group that specializes in assisting pastors and staff members who are in the midst of conflict or have experienced forced termination. Charles warned me not to resign without having a separation package in writing.

Most of my advisors believed that the board's ultimate aim was to remove me as pastor, but since they lacked a strong case, they targeted my wife instead. While I want to believe the best about church leaders, subsequent events demonstrated the wisdom of their analysis. This tactic is sometimes used by boards that find themselves in an adversarial position with their pastor, who is perceived to be too powerful for the board to challenge directly. Since the board doesn't have a slam dunk case against him once matters go public, they make charges against the pastor's family, figuring this will weaken the pastor's resolve as he shields his loved ones from attacks. I know how this feels firsthand.

More than twenty years before, I served as the pastor of a small church. Some members didn't like changes the board and I were making and began meeting in secret to pool complaints. Two of them eventually complained to the board about me – and they targeted my wife, our nine-year-old son, and our six-year-old daughter as well. (When their plan failed, they all left the church together.) When antagonists fire guns at a pastor, his family members are often hit by stray bullets. According to Rediger, this is not uncommon:

> The wakeup call for a pastor under attack by a clergy killer comes when he sees injury to loved ones and the congregation. The thinking of clergy killers resembles military officers who are willing to destroy a village in order to save it from the enemy. Clergy killers pay little attention to collateral damage when pursuing their destructive goals.[1]

Seeing my wife and children become "collateral damage" at that church was difficult to bear. Because of the trauma I experienced when my father left the pastorate, several Christian leaders have told me they are amazed that I am following the Lord, much less that I am in ministry. It's equally amazing that both of our children attend vibrant churches and have served as leaders. I praise God for his faithfulness in our family's life.

Some pastors refuse to hire family as staff members, and I can understand why. Even if the lead pastor is tough on his wife or children in private, the perception may be that the pastor treats hired family members with kid gloves, regardless of their competency. Yet in Christian circles, many pastors place family members on their staffs because they demonstrate loyalty, are known quantities, and possess the giftedness and experience to do a great job. If a pastor's family member is the most qualified person for a position, should he or she automatically be excluded?

I know many situations where a pastor and a family member serve on the same staff together. For example, a pastoral colleague served as the executive pastor of one of America's best-known churches while his wife served as children's director. At a megachurch we attended, the pastor's son was a staff member for more than a decade, and married couples serve on their staff. My daughter attends a church where the wives of the senior pastor, another pastor, and a top staff member are *all* paid staffers. Pastor Norman and his wife served together long before I arrived at the church, so we were following that precedent. While there may be disadvantages to serving with family from a corporate or relational standpoint, it's certainly not an unbiblical concept. Didn't Jesus choose brothers James and John as well as siblings Peter and Andrew for his inner circle? And didn't the married couple Aquila and Priscilla travel with Paul and instruct Apollos together? As long as family members are not given preferential treatment in their hiring, are biblically qualified, and are held to the same standards as other staffers, the practice works great in some situations and not as well in others. (And the same thing can be said about hiring friends.)

Kim was hired as an assistant children's director soon after we came to the church. She did such a great job in that part-time role that when she was hired as a full-time staff member, the announcement of her hiring was met with great enthusiasm. She grew both as a person and as a leader, and was granted more responsibility over time because she got things done. As she demonstrated progress, she was granted more authority, although I made sure never to portray her as a co-pastor. But what does a pastor do when one of the most gifted and productive individuals in a church happens to be his wife?

I wouldn't recommend having a family member serve with the pastor on a board (where the two can form a power block), but I don't see a problem with ministry or support positions. Speaking of pastor's wives, most people don't resent that she is *paid* but that she's *influential*. If the pastor's wife is an assistant small group director and nearly invisible, most people won't care, but if she starts ordering people around as an unpaid *volunteer*, she will draw fire.

Even though the associate pastor knew that Kim had been on the staff for six years prior to his hiring – and we discussed this issue with him and his wife in advance – he later stated emphatically that such an arrangement was inadvisable and that he didn't like having a husband-wife team on staff because of what might happen if we both lost our jobs. (The bigger problem is the hole left in leadership if they leave together.) While he may have felt discomfort with Kim on the staff – and she was a director, not a pastor – he took the job knowing her status. In my mind, if her presence bothered him, he could either accept her role or resign from his position.

While some pastors might allow a family member on their staff to coast with their responsibilities, I could be tough on Kim at times (as the staff knew firsthand), but she also outworked everybody in the church. All in all, I believe we worked well as ministry teammates, although some people referred to us as the "Jim and Kim Show" behind our backs. But without Kim, the church would not have grown as it did, and I suppose a few people resented that fact.

My wife and I sensed the presence of evil in our home during the week after the October 24 meeting, a presence unlike any we had ever felt before. Although we asked God to remove it repeatedly, it remained and might best be characterized as a spirit of fear. We tried to leave home for a few hours every day just to escape it. One day, after collecting the mail, we almost became ill when we received a letter from a local law firm. My first reaction was that we were being sued, but it was just an advertisement for legal services!

My entire week was consumed with making phone calls. One day, I spent fourteen hours on the telephone speaking to advisors. I had never exceeded the allotted minutes on my cell phone plan before, but when I finally checked, I had gone over my limit by hundreds of minutes. During the first two weeks of the conflict, I ate so little I lost ten pounds. Kim felt so wounded she could barely function. It felt like Judgment Day had come to earth, our lives had been divinely scrutinized, and we had been sentenced to hell instead of ushered into heaven.

As our heads cleared, Kim and I tried to discern what we had done to merit the harsh treatment the board had meted out, but we honestly didn't know. I wondered, "Is this payback for something I said in a meeting one night? Have I offended someone personally that I don't know about? Or could this be about the upcoming budget proposal to the congregation?" Although the board had given me a single reason why they had dismissed my wife, it still didn't make sense to me. And if my advisors were correct that I was their real target, why hadn't the board ever spoken with me directly about their concerns? That's the primary reason why I called so many experts. Since I was too close to the situation, I figured they might provide insight that I lacked.

The two of us read Scripture every night, and I must confess, the imprecatory psalms suddenly became appealing. Once I discovered Psalm 35, we began reading it right before bedtime, and for a few weeks, it became our only Bible. David writes in verse 1: "Contend, O Lord, with those who contend with me; fight against those who fight against me." In verses 7-8, the psalmist cries out, "Since they hid their net for me without cause and without cause dug a pit for me, may ruin overtake them by surprise – may the net they hid entangle them, may they fall into the pit, to their ruin." Verse 15 mirrored exactly how we felt: "But when I stumbled, they gathered in glee; attackers gathered against me when I was unaware. They slandered me without ceasing." And then David asks for the Lord's intervention: "O Lord, you have seen this; be not silent. Do not be far from me, O Lord. Awake, and rise to my defense! Contend for me, my God and Lord. Vindicate me in your righteousness, O Lord my God; do not let them gloat over me" (Psalm 35:22-24). Although I'm confident that David's enemies weren't church leaders, his feelings about being falsely accused and ambushed were identical to ours. The genius of Scripture is that it puts our feelings into words in a masterful fashion.

On Wednesday afternoon, Kim finally scheduled an appointment with two board members for the following night on the church campus. She then went online to research the proper way to fire an employee in our state. As a former executive director in a private school, Kim had fired many employees and knew the procedures involved, none of which was used in her case. She wanted to be well prepared for the meeting – but I wondered if it would even occur.

Our six supporters formed an unofficial group that I termed "the pastoral advocacy group." They had scheduled a meeting with the board that very night on the church campus. If the group made their case, they hoped the board might consider alternatives to their decision. Soliciting prayer, Kim sent this note to a good friend in Texas using Facebook's email feature:

Please pray for Jim and me. The board fired me Saturday through Jim and they still have not told me. They are after Jim. The word has gotten out because they told the staff and are announcing [it] this Sunday. It has been a very painful last few days. The people who know now are very angry about the decision and they are having a VERY BIG meeting Wednesday with the board. Pray peace may come.

Shortly after Kim sent this note, she received a phone call from a friend who had just received the same email Kim had sent her Texas friend. When Kim told me that her email had gone to the wrong person, we both screamed out loud in unison and assumed that her note went to *all* of her Facebook friends – which included board members! As it turned out, her note went to seventeen friends whose first names began with "K." It wasn't long before one of those individuals forwarded the email to Taylor who became upset at what he perceived as a breach of confidentiality. Maybe he thought a counterattack was imminent.

As that night's meeting between the advocacy group and board approached, I became increasingly anxious and consequently prayerful. Shortly before the meeting was scheduled to begin, I received a phone call from Jane, who had offered to facilitate a meeting between the two parties without taking sides. Jane had spent much of her day preparing for the meeting and had driven a great distance to the church during rush hour. When she finally arrived in the parking lot, Taylor called to tell her that the meeting was cancelled and that the board needed to meet with Kim before meeting with the advocacy group. (This decision may have been prompted by Kim's email which was now bouncing around cyberspace.) Taylor also reiterated that the board was willing to resign over this issue.

That night, I spent time on the phone with a Christian leader I'll call Harry. This man has the ability to hear a few facts about a situation, size them up quickly, and get right to the heart of the matter. Harry had served as a church consultant many times, and when I candidly told him what had happened, he was concerned that the board might have a vendetta against Kim. He said that if she resigned, it would be a lie. He also said that Kim had the right to meet with the board and clarify matters and that she needed to see documentation of her offenses. He then told me in strong terms to "make it a battle," including taking it before the entire church, if necessary. I asked Harry if he knew of any situations where an entire board had resigned, and he told me about two incidents that he knew about, including one where *he* had recommended mass resignation. Harry's certainty emboldened us and infused us with fresh courage. Up to this time, we assumed that we were totally at fault, although we still didn't know what we had done to provoke such a drastic verdict.

The next day, Thursday, October 29, was a pivotal one in the now five-day-old conflict. To discern our legal status, I spent ninety minutes on the phone that morning consulting with a secular labor attorney. (I couldn't locate a local Christian labor lawyer.) After I explained the situation to him, he asked rhetorically about the board, "What are they thinking? Are they nuts?" Although not a believer, he couldn't believe that the board had fired the pastor's wife. He also told me that the simplest solution to this mess was for the board to resign. (I was starting to hear this theme more often.) He speculated on the real motives for the termination and wondered if the board was jealous, especially if Kim was known throughout the community while far fewer people knew the identity of the board members. But although some Christian leaders urged us to consider a lawsuit, the attorney didn't think we had a chance in court. He said that a judge would notice the case on his docket and remove it based on the separation of church and state. And since employees in that state are hired on an "at will" basis, he believed the board had the *legal* right to do what they did.

The attorney did not understand why Kim was going to meet with two board members that night. He said that if the board would rescind the termination, then it would make sense to meet. He also told me, "If I was the board's attorney, they would be better off to give her a chance to explain." Finally, the attorney said to tell Kim that when she met with the board members that night, she could *think* anything she wanted but she should be as professional and civil as possible. She should go to the meeting, listen, ask for explanations, and secure reasons. Above all, she shouldn't say anything about consulting with an attorney or taking legal action. Before Kim went to the meeting, I made sure she understood the attorney's counsel. I also told her that she would have to endure a crucifixion but that a resurrection would soon be coming. After meeting with Kim that Thursday night, the board had agreed to meet with the pastoral advocacy group on Friday evening. After that meeting, I hoped that the board might be more flexible.

Kim and I prayed before she went to the meeting that Thursday evening. She had wisely invited Darrell, a former board member, to serve as a witness. Kim and Darrell met with two members of the board. My hope was that the board members would be gracious but honest, and that Kim would just listen, tell them she wasn't resigning, and then return home. But when she came home, she was in tears. The meeting had not gone well. Here is Kim's description:

> Going back to Saturday, I remember clearly thinking, 'How could you fire me? Why didn't they have me come?' To me that was humiliating that my own husband would announce my firing. So two friends on the staff took me out to lunch and prepared me for the meeting and said they would pray for me. They said, 'You need to really hold it together. Don't lose it. You're going to be fine.'

> And I was literally shaking when I left for the meeting that night. Jim said, 'Remember, you are going to be the sacrificial lamb.'

> I was shocked because the charges were what I had *heard*. But they added more, so they had a list. And they accused me of being 'ungodly.' That hurt me the most. (Voice trembling.) I was the very person who loved the Lord, went on a Moldova trip. They prayed for me on the stage and blessed me and while I was gone, they did this. So I didn't go there.

One charge against Kim stemmed from the budgetary planning meeting on September 22, which occurred five weeks earlier. After eight-and-a-half years of service, Kim had never received a merit raise and felt she deserved some monetary reward for her hard work. But she also knew the financial constraints the church was undergoing and wanted to reduce her ministry expenses, even proposing that the church not take any mission trips the following year.

To Kim, full-time meant at least fifty hours per week, and although we needed her income, I wanted a healthy wife even more. So I proposed that she reduce her hours to thirty per week but, with a small hourly raise, be paid like she was working thirty-five. By cutting both her hours and overall pay, Kim could keep her job, care for herself better, reduce the church budget, and remain eligible for medical insurance. We both thought it was a great idea and consulted with a ministry professional beforehand. (And it was a request, not a demand, and was entirely negotiable.) But when she tried to talk to the board about it at the September meeting, she was told the board didn't have time to hear her proposal. Five weeks later, at the meeting with two board members, Kim was accused of making the board lie to the insurance company (claiming she was working more hours than she really was), something neither of us envisioned or would ever condone. The board had completely misunderstood her proposal.

Because Kim did not contact the board immediately after the October 24 meeting, they hit her with an *additional* charge, even though I was told through emails that Kim could take her time in responding to them. But now she was indicted for doing just that. Kim comments:

> No matter what I asked for at the budget meeting the previous month, they just brushed me aside and said, 'We don't have time to talk about it,' which told me that I was not valuable. Then they said in the letter that I didn't get back to them in a timely fashion . . . that I was supposed to meet with them right after they met with Jim. And I said, 'Jim never told me that.' And they said, 'Well, it's true.' I said, 'If it was true then why didn't you call me?' 'Well, we tried contacting you.' Then I said, 'If you cared that much you would have come to my front door to see what was going on.'

Kim was also charged with overspending on her budgets. She asked, "Do you have the numbers?" Kim was told that they'd have to go back and look at their notes. Kim told them, "I've done the work for you and I'll be in the black by the end of the year."

> Then I said, 'You know, it really bothers me that you closed down my office. You closed down my email and you closed down my section on the website. You took my name off the bulletin. And you went to the staff and told them why I was fired. That's illegal.'

I then said, 'While I've been sitting here this week I studied wrongful termination. I've never had a verbal or written warning. You did not follow the constitution. You did not use the Bible per Matthew 18.' Then one of them asked, 'But what about when you did this and broke confidence?' And I said, 'I don't know what you're talking about.' One of the board members responded, 'Facebook!' And then I said, 'Okay, that was not supposed to happen. But I have every right to write my friend to pray for me.'

And at that point, one of them said, 'I think we need to take a break.' And I said, 'No, I am finished with this meeting. I could sue you because of what you've done.' When I said that, I was asked to sign a paper. I knew what the paper was because I used to hire and fire staff, and you sign that you had this meeting. I said, 'I'm not signing this.' And that's when Darrell said, 'She did not come to sign. This was not the point of the meeting.' And I said, 'My lawyer said I have 24-48 hours.' Darrell said, 'We will get back with you.'

I was pretty upset. When I stood up, I told the board members, 'You have violated my personal rights.' And when I went outside, I fell apart. Darrell didn't think I could go home. I couldn't stop crying. It was like a sob of someone dying. And I was mad at myself again that I did not hold my tongue. But I felt I was being attacked. I had to stand up for myself. I said, 'Just give me a minute,' and I cried and cried and cried. Got in the car and went home. And I felt I had embarrassed Jim again and all my friends and didn't hold myself together.

The board now had five charges against Kim, up from the single charge they leveled against her on Saturday and the three charges they had shared with the staff. The charges were listed on a single sheet of paper, and evidently they had more because the phrase "among other things" was used. The charges were worded in such a way that those who knew Kim would have had a hard time believing them. In my view, the charges said far more about the board's mindset than about

51

Kim's behavior. She had positively impacted more lives for Christ than anyone at the church.

The charge that wounded Kim the most was that of being "ungodly." If she was so *ungodly*, why did she ignore the advice of her doctor to lead still another mission trip to Moldova? Why did she have more success at sharing her faith than anyone at the church? Was her alleged ungodliness the result of a long-term pattern, or was the charge based on a one-time offense? If a pattern, why hadn't the board addressed the issue with Kim before? If a one-time offense, why didn't anyone bring it to her attention at the time? And if she was so ungodly that she should be dismissed, why didn't anyone discuss their concerns with me as her supervisor? Since I wasn't present during Kim's appearance at the September 22 budget meeting, I have no firsthand knowledge of what took place. However, no board member expressed any concern to me about it afterwards.

I cannot even imagine charging another believer with being "ungodly." Isn't that a word normally used for unbelievers? In my view, it's what Satan would say to halt someone's ministry rather than anything a Christian would say as a corrective. Besides, it didn't come off as a description of her conduct but as a final indictment of her character. (Since the board said she could serve as a volunteer, would they want an *ungodly* one? And was I as a pastor married to an ungodly woman?) Instead of adopting a tone which might lead to repentance and restoration, the board opted for language that made Kim feel demeaned and worthless, resulting in a sense of shame.

When Kim said, "I could sue you because of what you've done," she doesn't believe she said it as a threat. Since she had experience in firing employees, she felt the board had broken protocol and was violating her personal rights. What she meant was, "You [the individual board members] have managed this situation so poorly that you have left yourself wide open for legal action." While I *had* sought legal advice that morning, Kim had not. But that single phrase was later used as ammunition against us.

When I read the board's list of charges against Kim that night – which I as staff supervisor had never seen until that moment – I sensed that the board was throwing all kinds of charges at Kim both to justify their decision and to pressure her to resign, but they were making accusations that few outside their group would believe. While a charge of overspending can be measured objectively, the other charges were all highly subjective.

Although we weren't aware of it at the time, it's possible that the board had been looking to build a case against one or both of us at the September budget meeting five weeks earlier. They may have already decided to dismiss Kim and hoped to catch her saying something they could later use against her. Because I wanted Kim to interact with the board directly that night, I left the room before her budget presentation, a move that I now regret making. (While I was her husband, I was also the pastor and a board member.) Three of the five charges they later made against her stemmed from the thirty minutes she spent with them. Had I been present, I could easily have challenged those charges later on. In fact, the board never mentioned any additional charges to me as her supervisor – only to the staff and to Kim.

But why didn't the board just stick with the overspending charge? Wasn't that enough? And why did they interpret Kim's actions in the worst possible light? Ken Sande, president of Peacemaker Ministries, encourages Christians to make "charitable judgments" about each other:

> Making a charitable judgment means that out of love for God you strive to believe the best about others until you have facts to prove otherwise. In other words, if you can reasonably interpret what someone has said or done in two possible ways, God calls you to embrace the positive interpretation over the negative, or at least to postpone making any judgment at all until you can acquire conclusive facts.[2]

Based on decades of ministry experience, I sensed there was a degree of hatred buried underneath the multitude of charges. How do I know that? In 1 Corinthians 13:5, Paul says that love "keeps no record of wrongs." Christian love does not keep lists of offenses. Mature believers deal with offenses as they arise, before the sun goes down (Ephesians 4:25-26). For example, as staff supervisor, I normally addressed any concerns I had about staff behavior at the first opportunity – and if I waited too long, I viewed that as *my* error and would sometimes let an issue go. (If you don't address issues as they arise, staffers may forget an incident altogether and keep repeating their mistakes.) It's unfair to hoard charges so you can use them against someone in the future.

Revelation 12:10 teaches us that Satan is "the accuser of the brethren" before God. He constantly attacks believers and tells the Lord that his people are sinful and unworthy of his great love. Whenever a believer piles up accusations against another believer, I suspect Satan is at work through the accuser's bitterness (Ephesians 4:26-27). We might call this tactic simply The List. While God usually deals with us one offense at a time – so we can confess our sin and receive his forgiveness – the devil delights in "gunnysacking" us with violations to overwhelm us and render us useless. The Spirit convicts us to bring us back to God while Satan accuses us to drive us away from God. In my experience, whenever a group compiles a *list* of a leader's offenses, they are confessing that they (a) lack a single impeachable offense; (b) have been building a case against him or her; (c) want to end their relationship; and (d) are using that list to justify their decision. When this tactic is used in church settings, it's an implicit confession that the supervisory agent lacks the charity and the courage to address offenses as they arise.

The board did not meet with Kim directly *before* dismissing her. They did not present her with any evidence or seek any explanations from her. They chose to terminate her while she was thousands of miles away serving the Lord. If another staffer had been accused of wrongdoing, and I had been presented with evidence, I would have insisted that we meet with that person before rushing to judgment. Fairness demands that. And yet neither of us ever saw any evidence the board claimed they possessed. And when Kim asked to see documentation of her offenses on October 29, a board member claimed the evidence was somewhere in their files. The board wanted Kim to resign based on their *verbal* charges against her. Should we have believed them? Dr. Marlene Caroselli, a professional development specialist and consultant, provides counsel for supervisors who are considering taking action against an employee: "Stick to the facts, as you perceive them. Ask the employee whether the facts you cite are correct. Give the employee an opportunity to present his or her side. If the employee needs more time to gather other facts, agree to postpone the meeting to a later time."[3] In Kim's case, this time-honored process was completely ignored.

I believe that Kim was victimized both by the process and by the verdict. If you're upset with someone, and you use a predetermined process, the outcome might not come out in your favor. But if you ignore a process, you'll get the result you want – guaranteed. The board's attitude seemed to be, "Since this is an exceptional case, we don't have to use a normal process." But what if the courts adopted that attitude? Isn't working the process *especially* important in major cases? Otherwise, a defendant can claim a miscarriage of justice. You can't skip steps. Proverbs 17:15 declares, "Acquitting the guilty and condemning the innocent – the Lord detests them both."

Speed Leas is one of the premier experts in church conflict over the past half century. Years ago, I had the privilege of meeting him and purchased several of his books directly from him, including his manual *Moving Your Church through Conflict.* Leas states that when pastors (and, by extension, staff members) are charged with offenses, they need to know their accusers, their exact allegations, and be given the opportunity to respond or "the charge is malicious."[4] But the board did not follow Jesus' directions for confronting wrongdoers in Matthew 18:15-17:

> "If your brother sins against you, go and show him his fault, just between the two of you. If he listens to you, you have won your brother over. But if he will not listen, take one or two others along, so that every matter may be established by the testimony of two or three witnesses. If he refuses to listen to them, tell it to the church; and if he refuses to listen even to the church, treat him as you would a pagan or a tax collector."

No board member ever spoke with Kim directly about any alleged violations until the October 29 meeting. The board also did not follow the passage in 1 Timothy 5:19-21 which applies the passage in Matthew 18 to church leaders:

> Do not entertain an accusation against an elder unless it is brought by two or three witnesses. Those who sin are to be

rebuked publicly, so that the others may take warning. I charge you, in the sight of God and Christ Jesus, and the elect angels, to keep these instructions without partiality, and to do nothing out of favoritism.

The board also did not follow church bylaws which stated that the senior pastor must recommend a staff member for dismissal before the board can take action. Except for the financial charge, the other charges all concerned offenses against the *board* – not the Lord, the congregation, the community, or Scripture. As a consultant later told me, it seemed like the board was personalizing matters.

The next morning, I sent the following email to a church conflict consultant:

Things are moving at a rapid rate. Two board members met with my wife and a witness last night. They (a) added charges since last Saturday's meeting with me, (b) used the phrase "among other things" before the charges, (c) brought up something from 2008!, and (d) tipped their hand: my wife has not done anything against the Lord, the church, or the community. It's because of the way she talked to the board at a meeting, and she didn't do anything wrong, just spoke confidently. Someone on the board must have been offended but they had ten days after the meeting to address how they felt before we went overseas. Then they waited until we got back to share the charges. Unbelievable!

The board has not used Scripture in any of their dealings with me or my wife. They have not referred to the church constitution and bylaws. They are not aiming for restoration, reconciliation, or even repentance. It's all about destruction, shame, and vindictiveness.

The crucifixion has occurred. I am looking forward to resurrection morning!

In Jesus' case, the resurrection occurred only three days after the crucifixion. In our case, any resurrection would take much, much longer.

TAKEAWAYS FROM CHAPTER 2

For pastors and staff members:

- Avoid signing a prepared resignation letter on the spot. No matter how much you are pressured, you have the right to take a day or two and consult with your network (an attorney, a mentor, your spouse) *before* you sign any document. (You sought counsel before accepting the call; do the same if you contemplate leaving.) Too many pastors and staffers feel crushed by a prepared resignation request and wish to escape, but later *regret* signing that document. The board does not want to fire you or they would have done so already. They prefer to report that you resigned because it transfers the responsibility for leaving onto you – and it may be better for your career. But realize they may only offer you severance pay if you sign a resignation document immediately. (But if it's only a *token* severance, you may be giving up too much.)
- If the board is firing you because of wrongdoing, insist on having them document your offenses (unless you already agree with their assessment). It is possible that the board has manipulated, misinterpreted, or misrepresented whatever evidence they possess. If you agree that your offenses merit termination, apologize and make plans for your departure. If you believe they're wrong, and they won't rescind their decision, you can either resign voluntarily or appeal their decision to the congregation if your governing documents allow for that.
- Realize that your first reaction when confronted with charges may be to blame yourself for everything. It's difficult under stress to properly assess the accuracy of charges made against you. When you begin to think more rationally, you'll have a better idea how to respond.
- Build an emergency conflict network for times when you're struggling with church leadership. Over time, you will discover

who you can trust and whose counsel is most valuable. Place the contact information in your cell phone for quick access.

For board members:

- Make sure that every decision you make about a pastor or staff member is consistent with Jesus' instructions in Matthew 18:15-20 and Paul's teaching in 1 Timothy 5:19-21. If you ignore or leapfrog Scripture, God will not honor your decisions or bless your church.
- When correcting church personnel, aim to *reclaim* the person rather than just *remove* them (Matthew 18:15-16; Galatians 6:1). Removing a pastor or staff member should be a last resort.
- Address each offense as it arises as Matthew 18:15-16 and Ephesians 4:25-27 specify. It is cruel to store grievances and then dump them on someone all at once, especially if they've never heard any of the charges before and have not been given time to improve their performance.
- If you make charges against a pastor or staff member, deal with their *behavior* ("you failed to tell the truth") rather than pinning a *label* on them ("you're a liar"). Labeling a fellow leader can lead to shame and wound them for a long time.
- Make sure that the board is consistent in the way that employees are terminated. If you treat employees differently, it may appear that you have a personal vendetta against someone. Consider specifying the reasons for termination in a staff policies handbook *before* you need it.
- If your board is near an impasse with the senior pastor, think about bringing in a church consultant before matters get worse. An interventionist may teach both parties new ways of working together – or separating.
- If you've done all you can, and a pastor or staff member has not altered their behavior within a reasonable amount of time, then prepare a separation package in writing. Ask an attorney to review it before you present it. Be generous with the amount of severance you offer.
- If church members request a meeting with your board – even if you're uncomfortable with the people involved or the issues

they're raising – meet with them as soon as possible. Members have a right to meet with their leaders. If you fail to meet with them, it looks like you're hiding something or that you don't care about them – and it may come back to haunt you.

For the congregation:

- If you hear reports about problems inside your church's inner circle, suspend immediate judgment and refuse to take sides. If two people you love are struggling in their marriage, it's better to be on the side of the marriage itself than the person you know best. (After all, your friend might be guilty of offenses you know nothing about.)
- If a pastor or staff member suddenly resigns, assume he or she felt pressured to quit and is in great pain, especially if that person remains silent. Cut him or her some slack and assume they do not wish to abandon you or your church.

CHAPTER 3

HALLOWEEN NIGHTMARE

*D*uring the first week of the crisis, I asked the Lord for the names of Christian leaders who could help me interpret the conflict, and the same name kept sticking in my head. I knew a little about this person (I'll call him Wilson) because he had once sent me a letter commending me for an article I had written in a Christian magazine. I emailed Wilson and asked to speak with him right away. We finally hooked up on the phone early Friday morning.

Wilson told me that he had been up since 4:00 that morning doing consulting work and that he gets more calls in September and October for "church stuff" than at any other time of year. Since Halloween was the next day, could there be a spiritual warfare component to what we were experiencing, especially in the very hostile-to-the-gospel area where the church was located?

Wilson said that when the board met with the staff and told them why they had dismissed my wife that was a serious offense in our state. If the board had acted in a similar fashion in a secular organization, the aggrieved person could have sued them for millions of dollars. Wilson also asked if I was pastor of the church founded by Norman, and when I confirmed that I was – and that the communication between us had become sparse – he wrote: "Does not surprise me on Norman – and 'I have a hunch' that 'THEY' have dialed him in!" Wilson predicted that if the board resigned, thirty to fifty people would also leave with them, and those who were in touch with the Holy Spirit (especially those with the gift of showing mercy) would later tell me that they knew something was wrong but couldn't put their finger on it.

Later that morning, I had a conversation with someone (I'll call him Richard) who runs a Christian consulting firm. Richard immediately asked me about the personal and vocational lives of the board members. He believed that what was happening in their private lives had a direct bearing on how they were handling church matters. Richard stated that many boards are struggling with three primary issues in our day: they experience fear because God is not big enough for them; they struggle with stewardship because they believe the church is "all about us" and not a lost world; and they struggle with faith. Satan has figured out how to defeat us by using power as an aphrodisiac. Richard suggested that one way we could seek redress was through arbitration.

Laura sent me an email that Friday morning with a copy of the church membership roster and noted that a board member had requested the list at the beginning of October, a sign that the board was counting votes in advance of a possible public meeting. (Months later, I obtained a copy of the October 6 board minutes showing that the board had created executive minutes while we were overseas, presumably to discuss matters related to our situation.) My pastoral instincts told me that the board was trying to determine how many votes there might be against me if my job status was brought before the congregation, but the board discerned they lacked the necessary two-thirds majority to remove me from office. The experts were right: it was increasingly looking like the board targeted my wife as a way of eliminating me.

Kim and I decided to get away that Friday morning to clear our heads, so we drove over the hills to see a movie. While we waited outside the theater, Jerry called to say he had been in touch with Taylor and that the board once again had threatened to resign. When Jerry reminded Taylor that the board had agreed to meet with the pastoral advocacy group that evening, Taylor announced that the board would resign instead. (Had the board authorized Taylor to make that decision?) However, the board wanted to hand in their resignations to me personally. (Although the congregation voted board members into office, the bylaws stated that departing members should direct their resignations to the board itself, and I was the only member left.) When

I received this news, I sat down and wept. How could people I considered good friends and trusted leaders act like this?

After we returned home, Taylor wrote me and stated that the board wanted to meet with me the next morning at the church to submit their written resignations. He also said that the board would be available to help with the Halloween event if needed. He then asked me to email him or call him to confirm the meeting.

What a six-day reversal! The pastoral advocacy group's purpose was to meet with the board to *mediate* the conflict. They believed that if Kim's dismissal stood, the outreach ministry would be decimated and massive fallout would result. Sande observes that although Scripture clearly commends face-to-face meetings to reconcile people, it does not teach this is the only way to begin such a process:

> In fact, it is sometimes better to involve other people in resolving a conflict *before* trying to meet personally with someone who has wronged you. These people may act as neutral intermediaries who shuttle between you and the other person or as representatives who initially speak for you in joint meetings.[1]

Regardless of how the advocacy group members learned of Kim's situation, shouldn't church members have the right to meet with their governing board about such issues? The advocacy group was composed of some of the most influential people in the church (they had attended the church longer than most board members) and they didn't view themselves as a *pressure* group but as a *unity* group. They knew they had no official standing but wanted to head off a disaster-in-the-making. The board may have believed that no church members had the right to question them concerning a personnel decision (even though they'd have to account for it later). It's also possible they believed that I was using the advocacy group to get Kim reinstated, but I wasn't thinking that far ahead. I was spending most of my time trying to understand what was happening by contacting Christian leaders. While I *was* in contact with the advocacy group, they were making decisions independently of me, and several team members were now speaking directly with Richard, the consultant.

On Friday night, October 30, Kim and I met with the pastoral advocacy team at the home of Darrell and Jenny. We discussed the events of the previous week and spent time praying together. Although we were relieved that the "six day war" seemed to be over, none of us felt secure about what had transpired. One person wondered if we could trust the board, that maybe their request for a meeting the following morning was a trap. However, I was willing to go, even if it was a trap. As it turned out, the brief meeting the following morning would impact my life and ministry forever.

When I got home from the meeting, I checked my email and was astonished to find a resignation letter from Roger, the associate pastor. Addressing his letter to me, the chairman, and the entire board, he stated that the events of the previous week had affected him to the point where he could no longer fulfill his staff duties and that the Lord had directed him to make the decision. I fired back the following note to Roger:

> I want to ask you to reconsider your decision. The Lord has been working in incredible ways this past week. I have not been able to tell you what's happening because I didn't want to involve you. There has now been a satisfactory resolution to the issues that I believe will allow you to do your job here in a joyful way. I will call you tomorrow morning to discuss this with you. I need you and we need you.

The timing of the associate's letter looked suspicious, especially since the board had already agreed they would resign the following morning. But I tried to envision how difficult it must have been for Roger to hold things together the previous week. It's possible that a board member asked Roger if he was ready to become the lead pastor (even temporarily) if I resigned and that prospect might have frightened him. He also may have felt awkward being caught in the middle between the board and me, so without any warning he hastily cleared out his office and abdicated his job of two-and-a-half years. Yet how could he resign when his presence was most needed? The senior pastor and outreach director were wounded. The governing board had promised their resignations the next morning. And the biggest outreach event of the year was taking place the following evening. Since it was late that night, I resolved to call Roger the next day. Another unintended consequence of the board's imprudent decision, I thought to myself. Matters just kept getting worse.

The following day was Halloween. Because I was up all night in anticipation of that morning's meeting, I arose very early that Saturday and composed an email to consultants Richard and Wilson. Here's a sampling of the questions I asked them:

Can I appoint a provisional board through the end of the year? The sooner we regain stability, the better. If I have to wait and appoint a nominating team, that will take time and leave me exposed as the sole authority in the church.

If the associate pastor insists on resigning, how and when do I announce his resignation? The timing of it makes it look like he was in on everything but I think he's been traumatized.

How and when do we announce that the board has resigned? And what, if anything, are we allowed to say in public or in private about that?

For me to regain trust with certain key leaders, especially the staff, they are going to want to know what happened in capsule form. If I say nothing, they might assume that Kim committed some heinous sin or any number of things. Ideas?

The board was working on the 2010 budget. They have documents and keys. What do we say in today's meeting about those matters? And what, if anything, should Jerry and Darrell and I say this morning to the board?

I have more questions, but I'll start with those. Since I am in uncharted waters, I greatly need some guidance. Thanks!

Darrell and Jerry had agreed to accompany me to the meeting that Saturday morning at 9:00. We three made plans to meet in a coffee shop near the church beforehand, but Darrell called to tip us off that the board was meeting there instead, so we met in front of the church campus. I spent the half hour before the meeting on a conference call with Richard and Wilson, trying to envision all the possible scenarios that might emerge inside the meeting. As it turned out, we could not have anticipated the board's next move.

After asking the custodian to work away from the hallway, the three of us waited inside a children's room for the board. When they arrived, we all shook hands cordially, but one important board member was missing. Taylor got right to the point: the board was requesting mediation. They had contacted a former denominational official who recommended a mediator that lived several hundred miles away. While this may have seemed like a welcome sign, I was immediately skeptical because of what I had seen in our district in the past.

Over a nearly thirty-year period, I observed that whenever a major conflict erupted inside a church and district officials became involved, the pastor ended up resigning. Many pastors assume that their district leaders support their ministry until their church undergoes a major conflict, and then they are surprised to learn that officials nearly always recommend that the pastor resign, even if he is innocent of wrongdoing. As an official from another denomination explained, "Depending on a church's history, I usually come down on the side of a congregation, because it's harder for a congregation to mess up with a pastor than a pastor with a congregation."[2] But Rediger notes that too often, denominational officials offer only "pseudosupport" rather than ". . . true support in time of trouble. Some officials have come to believe it is more important to pacify a congregation than support the office of pastor."[3]

Time after time, I heard about a pastor who was treated unjustly by a small group in the congregation and the pastor resigned, feeling forsaken. In the midst of a serious conflict in another denomination, one pastor friend was told by his district minister that if he resigned, he would be recommended to other churches, but after he quit, no church demonstrated any interest in hiring him. In some districts, officials display a façade of spirituality but operate almost exclusively on the basis of politics and economics. Righteousness takes a back seat to keeping money flowing from churches to the district office. If you're a member of the "good old boy network," they might stand up for you, but if not, you're toast.

My friend Charles Wickman, founder of the Pastor-in-Residence program, relates the story of a pastor whose church grew from eighty to 370 in fifteen months, followed by the building of a new sanctuary, which was quickly filled. But a group in the church began losing influence and wanted to snatch it back, launching a major conflict. The pastor tried to follow his district minister's advice and be redemptive, but the official later demanded that the pastor resign, even though he had done nothing wrong. This pastor later learned that he was the 28th innocent pastor within a twelve-month period to be forced to resign in that district.[4]

So when I seemed taken aback by the board's request for mediation, someone asked me, "Aren't you for reconciliation?" I replied, "We're always for reconciliation. But we need to talk together and then we'll get back to you." (I had to run everything by our consultant first.) And then I promised to call Taylor later that day with our answer. After briefly discussing that evening's event, the meeting was dismissed.

After the meeting, Jerry and Darrell and I deliberated for a few minutes. It was the third time that week that the board had shifted their position. They had promised to meet with the pastoral advocacy group, but then cancelled at the last minute. They promised to meet with the advocacy group again, then cancelled and promised their resignations. Now instead of resigning, they requested mediation. After returning home, Darrell sent Jerry and me an email inquiring as to why the board was requesting mediation. Did it concern their issues with Kim or their rift with me? While the board had not made this clear, I assumed the mediation idea was focused on Kim's status because they had previously said I could remain as pastor.

However, what kind of reconciliation could we have sought? Our working relationship had been decimated. For weeks, they had been deliberating without my presence or input, creating an "us" versus "him" mentality. When I met with them the previous Saturday, there was zero flexibility in their position. Maybe the two board members who met with Kim and Darrell at the Thursday meeting were afraid that Kim was going to sue the board so they sought mediation to avert legal action. But how sincere was the board's request for mediation when they had already threatened to resign multiple times? Was the mediation process Plan B, a fallback position? Otherwise, why didn't they opt for mediation earlier in the conflict? However, if they had used a process that involved mutual interaction, they could not have controlled the outcome. Did they keep repositioning themselves in hopes of forcing our resignations?

In retrospect, bringing in a mediator *could* have been a positive move. Mediation would have slowed down the pace at which the conflict was progressing and increased communication between both parties. It would have reduced everyone's anxiety and given all parties a specific time and place to present their concerns – but it had to be the *right* mediator, someone both sides felt comfortable using. However, Paul Borden, former district executive with the American Baptists, offers this caution:

> . . . when the real issue of conflict is the control of the congregation (this issue is never the stated issue), those with the control will never give it up unless forced to do so. The nature and purpose of conflict mediation is to get believers to be reconciled, not deal with the control issues that cause congregations to remain dysfunctional.[5]

In other words, when denominational leaders recommend mediation to embattled church leaders, they know the process usually results in the pastor's departure. But from my perspective, the conflict was never about *personal* reconciliation. It was about the division of authority and control between the pastor and the board.

However, I believed that something else was happening. The board members were comfortable in a secular atmosphere, but there was not enough collective experience for them to navigate rough waters in a church. Had they included me in their deliberations, the week would have gone differently, but because they had marginalized me, I could not advise them. In fact, one of the casualties in a major conflict is the lack of communication between parties. The board was talking among themselves but not to me (even though they said I could remain as pastor), and I was talking to the pastoral advocacy group but not to the board (after all, they had asked me to stay away from the church campus that week). Most communication was being done via email which allowed both sides to have written records of the messages sent and received, but meant that real give-and-take conversations were hardly taking place. And even when both groups *did* communicate with each other, one side attributed the worst possible motives to the other side. A mediator could have been a huge help provided it was someone both parties felt safe with and trusted.

But as crazy as the previous week had been, it was about to get even crazier.

Kim was sitting in the large blue recliner in my upstairs study when I arrived home. I asked her if she would be willing to make a brief appearance with me at that night's Halloween outreach event. (If we didn't show up at all, that would alarm the entire church.) People might question why Kim wasn't leading the event as usual, but everyone would see that we were both okay, rumors to the contrary. When Kim asked me if the board had resigned, I told her that they had requested mediation using an individual recommended by a former district official. When Kim heard that news, she instinctively knew what it meant and began to reproach herself verbally for causing the entire conflict, focusing especially on the charge that she was "ungodly." After trying to get her to return to normalcy, Kim started heading for a dark place emotionally, forcing me to call the paramedics, who transported her to the hospital. Without going into detail, I believe that Satan had launched an all-out assault on us in an attempt to destroy our church and its impact in our community. After all, it *was* Halloween.

Those who hang around Christian circles sometimes hear the devil blamed for bizarre activities within an assembly. You'll hear phrases like, "Satan is really working overtime right now," or "This conflict is clearly the work of the enemy." While Satan *does* work inside Christian churches worldwide, how can the average believer tell when a conflict is the result of *satanic* activity or *human* sinfulness?

Based on my study of Scripture, I believe that Satan's activity can be detected when two primary factors are present: *deception* and *destruction*. Jesus' teaching about Satan in John 8:44 is the most compact statement about the evil one in all of Scripture. Speaking to Jewish leaders, Jesus said, "You belong to your father, the devil, and you want to carry out your father's desire. He was a murderer from the beginning, not holding to the truth, for there is no truth in him. When he lies, he speaks his native language, for he is a liar and the father of lies." Jesus says that the devil is both "a murderer" and "a liar." It's his nature to destroy and deceive. When church halls are filled with rumor and innuendo, Satan is at work. When there are attempts to destroy believers rather than redeem them, Satan is at work. When confusion reigns among believers, Satan is at work. When Christians begin to take sides against each other, Satan goes undetected.

Kim and I had seen Satan at work nearly twenty years previously in an area that has a large array of agnostics and atheists. We were launching a new church in a warehouse located at a busy intersection in a city with few impactful Protestant churches. Our leaders applied to the city for a conditional use permit but were turned down by the planning commission. When we appealed to the city council, some Christian leaders predicted that the council would uphold the commission's recommendation, but we called for times of prayer and fasting, and eventually won a unanimous 7-0 vote. Yet something freakish happened before that meeting. Our outreach pastor created a one-page flyer on a Macintosh computer asking churchgoers to pray for unity, our building, and God's will. When he printed the flyer, all the words were right-side up except the word "Pray" which appeared upside-down on paper even though it was right-side up on the computer screen! While the flyer frightened some attendees because it seemed to indicate demonic opposition, I believed the flyer signaled the way to victory: pray!

After our grand opening, our church quickly became the second largest Protestant church in the city, but we constantly sensed there were strong spiritual forces opposing us. For example, my family received a stream of obscene phone calls during the start-up phase. During our time there, my wife broke her foot, our son broke his ankle, our daughter broke her leg, and I tore ankle ligaments – all on the church campus. When our lease expired nearly five years after we started, the owner forced us out, and because we moved five miles away, we lost one-third of our attendees (those who lived in the opposite direction) overnight. Only then did I discover that some illicit activities involving drugs and sexual immorality had been occurring at the intersection where the church was located. When our church moved into that warehouse, light was invading spiritual darkness. No wonder Satan fought us so hard the whole time we were there! The devil often attacks a church because it is doing well and invading his territory.[6]

Twelve years later, darkness once again invaded light. Less than 5 percent of the people in our city went to *any* church on a typical weekend. There was little available land for churches, and most congregations had such tiny parking lots that attendees had to park on the street. For a city that size, it was surprising how small the Protestant churches were, and by 2009, only three evangelical churches of any impact remained. The church was located in a spiritually dark place, and yet we had grown over the years, winning many people to Christ and helping them mature as believers. At various times, the fire chief, a school board member, an assistant coach for a National Football League team, and an Admiral in the Coast Guard attended the church, as well as assorted attorneys, teachers, and military personnel. We had become a megachurch by local standards even though we were statistically a medium-sized church nationwide. Maybe this is why we became a special target of the enemy.

And yet one church leader constantly endured physical problems: Kim. She developed fibromyalgia after the stress of a previous ministry. When we moved to our new church home, we hoped her physical problems would subside, but in some respects, they were just beginning. She had such strange medical issues that one of her doctors began calling her an "enigma." Here is a list of the bodily challenges she endured while at the church:

- Taken to the hospital by ambulance one morning when she had chest pain and couldn't breathe. The diagnosis: pleurisy.
- Went to the emergency room the day before Easter with a migraine headache, which she has never had before or since.
- Had her gall bladder removed. After surgery, she returned home to recover, but woke up in great pain a few nights later and was readmitted to the hospital for seventy-two hours while doctors ran tests to determine the issue. Their diagnosis: the sutures used to stitch her up had come loose. She was taken back into surgery to have the sutures redone.
- Had surgery on her lower back the following year, just as we moved into a new house.

- Began to fall down a lot, sometimes in the middle of the street. This caused her to seek the help of a specialist. She developed two symptoms that in combination can signal a brain disease where the victims die a horrible death. One physician gave Kim a preliminary diagnosis verbally but didn't want to write down the name of the disease – but eventually did. When I looked it up online, the disease was more horrible in its effects than most forms of cancer, and I became concerned that she would soon die. Thankfully, one of her symptoms vanished after she discontinued using one of her medications, but it took several months to clear up the issue.
- Had hip replacement surgery three years later. While in the hospital, she developed compartment syndrome and was forced to stay ten days instead of the scheduled three. When she got out, she quickly developed a case of "slap foot."
- While Kim was passing out literature about the church during the city's annual parade, the wife of the board chairman accidentally slammed into Kim, who fell and hit her head on the street. Kim sustained a cut over her left eye which caused her to bleed profusely. The parade was stopped until paramedics took her to the local emergency room.
- Had spinal fusion surgery two years later.
- Had a knee operation seven months after that.
- Ended up spending five days in the hospital when she suffered great abdominal pain. After multiple tests, the doctors diagnosed her problem as gastritis due to inflammation of the colon. They assumed she had picked up a condition while in Kenya several months before. Kim left the hospital three weeks before our scheduled trip to Moldova. Most of our family and friends advised her to stay home, but she wanted to go so much that she went anyway.

Some of Kim's problems have genetic origins, some may be due to lifestyle choices, and some may result from other physical causes, but the sheer preponderance of the problems – and how her absences impacted our family and the church – may have been an indication that she had become a special target of Satan. (Three years later, she hasn't spent even one night in a hospital.) One of my seminary professors said that Satan attacks a church when it is united and engages in prayer and evangelism, and Kim has *always* loved to tell people about Jesus.

Satan's strategy seemed to be simple: stop outreach and missions by stopping Kim; stop Kim and you stop Jim; stop Jim and the church doesn't advance. McIntosh and Edmondson write:

> The pastor stands at the front lines of defense against the evil one. In addition to waging his own war against the devil, he is there when the devil attacks individual Christians, as well as when he attacks the church as a body. The pastor is in a position where he is targeted by the devil for all three reasons. The devil wants to defeat the believers in his church . . . defeat the church as a corporate body, and . . . defeat the pastor as an individual, thus destroying his ability to lead. Working on the latter can accomplish much for his dark purposes in the other areas as well. The understanding that pastors are special targets is borne out by research as well as the experience of many . . . . The devil wishes a pastor to feel defeated and has no compunction against kicking him when he is down. Times of discouragement can turn into times of disaster. The devil sees a vulnerable, discouraged pastor and focuses special attacks on him.[7]

As Kim entered the hospital that Halloween morning, we were in unexplored territory. My wife was known for her boundless enthusiasm and relational skills, but the events of the previous week and the board's hyperbolic charges had worn her down so she wasn't thinking clearly. Fortunately, I had called our daughter Sarah to come and assist me, and she arrived at an opportune time. (Sarah would be a huge help in the days to come.) Because I sensed that my wife needed to experience unconditional love, I called other family members and asked them to pray and, if possible, come and visit Kim even though I didn't know how long she would be hospitalized. Our son Ryan agreed to fly out the following weekend, and Kim's parents agreed to accelerate their timetable and stop by on a drive to Texas. I felt a little more secure knowing we would soon be surrounded by family.

But even though I wanted to visit Kim immediately, I still had several hours of work to complete that Saturday afternoon. From my home study, I called a church consultant who had been assigned to us by Richard's group. (I'll call him Paul.) Paul echoed what I had already suspected: we should not use a mediator recommended by the denomination because they tended to side with the church 90 percent of the time. He suggested that we use his group instead. (Of course, this might have been his way of redirecting business to his company, but with Kim incapacitated, I didn't have the time or energy to research alternatives.)

After speaking with Paul, I called Taylor, suggested we use Paul's firm for mediation, and explained my reasoning to him. (Taylor did not protest my suggestion.) If I was uncomfortable using the mediator recommended by the board, I had a perfect right to counter with another party. Faulkner writes, "Find someone trusted by both the minister and the church . . . . It is essential that the mediator be someone whom both sides trust. If an ally of either side is called in, matters could be made worse."[8] My call was brief and I received the impression that Taylor would relay my recommendation to the rest of the board. I also called the new executive minister of our district (I'll call him Steve) who had been a friend for more than twenty-five years. I told Steve that I couldn't preach the next day due to a family emergency and asked if he could find a speaker. For the first time in my life, I would have to miss giving a scheduled Sunday morning message. Steve called back later to say that he had secured a former pastor to speak. He also told me that someone from the church had called to tell him that we were undergoing major conflict. I hadn't told Steve the extent of the problem because I didn't want the district's involvement. Eventually, I would sit down and tell him everything, but this didn't seem like the time or place.

My email inbox was in perpetual motion, and during all the chaos, our children's director Shannon forwarded an email to me from the daughter of a board member, claiming she would no longer be able to work in the nursery "due to the sudden decision the board has made." Was this a harbinger of things to come?

With most of my calls completed, Sarah and I prepared to visit Kim in the hospital. I stopped by our mailbox and was surprised but pleased to see a copy of our city's monthly magazine which Kim had been anticipating for weeks. Eight months before, Kim had spearheaded an effort for our church to raise funds to build a well in a remote village in Kenya, and we raised the funds within three months. Then Kim and four other believers traveled to Kenya for the well's dedication. Kim had taken pictures of the event to the magazine hoping they would publish an article about the well project. This publication was sent to every home in the city and included a one-page spread of the dedication, complete with four photos, two featuring Kim (in African dress) and one including Kenya's then-vice president, Stephen Musyoka, who is a believer. There was a brief story accompanying the photos. How strange, I thought, that Kim entered the hospital within two hours of our receiving this long-awaited issue. Since this was Halloween, did Satan sense an opportunity to negate our church's humanitarian work by attacking the outreach director?

While Sarah and I drove toward the hospital in a neighboring city, I called Roger, who had resigned the night before. While we could barely hear each other, I wanted the answer to one question: had he met with the board while we were overseas? He assured me that he had not done so, and I believed him. I hoped his loyalties were with me, but I suddenly felt unsure how much I could trust him.

When we arrived at the hospital, I called Shannon and asked her to announce the next day that there would be an informational meeting after each service the following Sunday. According to our governing documents, any church meeting required an advance seven-day notice, and I was sure that meetings would be necessary, if only to announce Roger's resignation. I told Shannon that if anyone objected to her making the announcement, she should ignore them and make it anyway. She assured me she had the situation well in hand.

When Sarah and I arrived at the hospital, we both did our best to encourage Kim via telephone, but we had no idea what was wrong with her or how long she would be confined. My heart broke as I thought about how the events of the previous week had affected my wife. While we both remained convinced that she had done nothing to merit her dismissal, it felt like events were spinning out of control around us. Sarah and I finally left the hospital, unsure when Kim would return home. I felt so low I could hardly stand it. At this point, I didn't care about my job or my career. I just cared about my wife. Normally she would have been putting the finishing touches on the Halloween event, hoping to expose hundreds of parents and kids to the gospel and our church. But instead of serving others, she needed others to serve her.

As we later learned, the entire board showed up on campus right before Fall Fun Fest. They stayed for prayer, but rather than serving at the event (as they had promised the remaining staff), four of them left the campus and never returned. While one board member led the event, another sequestered himself in the kitchen making hot dogs and left before the event concluded, after which the two of them left for still another crucial board meeting. I have often wondered about the subject matter of that meeting. Did they meet to discuss my counter-offer of a mediator? Since Kim's hospitalization was highly classified, I doubt if the board knew why we hadn't attended the event, but our absence must have made them nervous.

Jerry and Angela graciously invited Sarah and me to their house for dinner that Halloween night. The Phillies and Yankees were playing in the World Series, and Sarah and I didn't want to spend the evening by ourselves. I confided in Angela (a former nurse) that Kim had gone to the hospital, later sharing the incident with Jane (also a former nurse) as well, although I chose not to tell anyone else at the time. After Sarah and I went home, I spent time online trying to discern what had happened to Kim. I couldn't be sure, but one thing I knew: I missed my wife terribly and prayed that she would come home soon.

My heart ached for her.

TAKEAWAYS FROM CHAPTER 3

For pastors:

- Realize that beyond human folly, Satan may be pulling the strings in your conflict. Gather a prayer team around you as soon as possible (Ephesians 6:18).
- During any conflict, be extremely careful as to who you trust with your thoughts and feelings. You will most likely be misquoted and misrepresented. Remember this adage from World War II: "Loose lips sink ships."
- Be cautious about inviting the denomination into your situation. While some officials may sincerely help you, district per-

sonnel may be willing to put *you* in the loss column as long as the *church* remains in the win column. Realize that your church represents future financial assets, while you do not. In congregationally-governed churches, the best a district official can do is to *recommend* you to a church rather than *guarantee* you'll secure one.

- The next time you hear about a pastoral colleague who is forced to resign his position, contact him directly, listen to his story, offer him support, and pray with him.

For board members:

- Once you begin a termination process, you cannot predict outcomes, guarantee consequences, or easily undo matters.
- If you want to bring in a consultant or a mediator to manage a dispute between you and the pastor, the pastor has the right to interview and approve any interventionist you might suggest. While one side can recommend a party, they should not impose that person on the other side.
- Make sure that neither anxiety nor anger drives your decision-making. Overreacting will almost always backfire on you.

For the congregation:

- Satan will constantly battle your leaders and your church, especially if you invade his territory through outreach. Counter his influence through prayer, truth-telling, and love.
- Refuse to spread the virus of anxiety. When conflict erupts in a church, you can feel the tension on the campus. While it's human to seek a quick resolution, some conflicts require patience and special expertise. Leave the situation in God's hands and refuse to let anyone draft you into joining their faction.

CHAPTER 4

RESIGNATION *EN MASSE*

*I*t was strange getting up the next morning and not attending worship at our church. With all the confusion swirling around, I forgot to tell one of the technical guys that a guest speaker was coming. When I called him an hour before the service, he didn't sound like the person I had known for years. After I briefly referenced the events of the previous week, he adamantly responded, "Jim, I don't ever want to talk about this again." I later learned that when Kim's name was removed from the website and her email account was closed down, this person had to carry out those assignments. While he *had* heard about Kim's situation, he hadn't heard from me in a week, but I didn't want to tell him why I wouldn't be at church that morning. I began to experience what it's like when friends start to turn on you.

It is the worst feeling in the entire world.

About 9:15 that morning, someone from the hospital called my daughter's cell phone and said that we could pick up Kim in one hour. We were overjoyed! Halloween was over and we were looking forward to a brighter day. After breaking Kim out, we drove to another city for lunch and grocery shopping. As we ate, I realized that I hadn't heard anything from Taylor for twenty-four hours. Would the board agree to use the consulting firm as a mediator? Or did they wish to make another recommendation? I suddenly felt incredibly tired. Having run on adrenaline for the previous eight days, I could no longer do so. Sarah drove us back home while I slept in the back seat of the car.

When we got home, I went to bed. It was good I did. Matters were about to go south. Late that afternoon, I received an email from a woman at church:

I was very concerned when I didn't see you at church today and it left me with a feeling that something was wrong. Even the outline for today's message seemed a little out of the ordinary. Sparse if you will. There was no mention of where you were, or Kim for that matter, before, during or after the service. After the service I asked one of the members of our church if everything was okay and although the person with whom I spoke was trying to maintain confidentiality they did tell me to pray and that the 'church is under attack.'

I checked the website for [the church] and it is down. I tried to reach someone in the office but I got the message that it is closed on the weekends.

I am worried and concerned first and foremost for you and Kim and secondly for our church. Without being too intrusive I would be grateful if you could please let me know if you are okay and if we still have a church.

While the board and I were tangling, there were undoubtedly many people like this woman who sensed that something was wrong and were deeply affected by it. I wrote her back:

Thanks for writing. Without getting specific, I planned to preach today, but something came up, and I had to get a guest speaker at the last minute. There are some issues, but I hope they will be resolved soon. Thanks for praying – and yes, we still have a church.

Jerry emailed me that afternoon to say that none of the board members or their children had attended services that morning. That must have seemed strange to the average attendee. The pastor, associate pastor, outreach director, worship director, and all the board members were missing – and without any explanations! Nobody discovered any resignation letters, either. Since none of us had heard from the board about our counteroffer, Jerry wanted the advocacy group to find out where they stood. As Paul the consultant said about the board in an email that afternoon, "So far, their position has been changing daily . . . punctuated by silence." Then Paul wrote me:

> Jim, I know that you are emotionally spent. But we must have your involvement to address the board. I'm praying for you. The people of your church love you and Kim. The advocacy group will provide a safe place for you to minister. You have a future in ministry . . . . May God Be Your Strength & Shield.

That Sunday evening – thirty-three hours after I last spoke with him – Taylor sent me an email. He announced in a letter that the entire board had resigned both their positions and their memberships. Their letter was addressed solely to me – although it continually referred to me in the third person – and most of the letter pointed out my short-comings, not Kim's, an indication that I was their target all along. It also contained false assumptions that could easily have been cleared up had the board spoken with me directly. For example, an entire paragraph was devoted to indicting me for not accepting their mediator. They accused me of negotiating in bad faith, claiming that they couldn't find mediation services listed on the consultant's website, although the transition team later found it easily. They also claimed that I had rejected their decision to dismiss Kim, when my real issue was their lack of process, which would have produced a different outcome. They were also upset that they hadn't heard from Kim without knowing what had happened to her. (I didn't want them to know about her condition because if the news had leaked out, it would have devastated Kim even more.) The letter lacked any admission of mistakes or olive branches for reconciliation, and is my final and lasting memory of them. Congregational systems consultant Peter Steinke notes that confrontational actions are increasing in churches today:

> The following conflict scenario is repeated regularly: friction between two parties intensifies; a series of painful exchanges follow; the sides deadlock; finally someone or some group requests or demands a person's removal or they threaten to

remove themselves. Any removal would bring relief to some but fuel resentment among others. Instead of being conciliatory or engaging in problem solving, people become polarized.[1]

After I forwarded the chairman's email and letter to the pastoral advocacy group, there was some rejoicing, but I was unconvinced that matters were over. As Paul the consultant wrote, "It is very uncommon for the entire lay board to resign." Because they resigned on a Sunday night, it would be a full week before I could verbally inform the congregation about this development. This gave the now-former board members seven days to share their story with churchgoers, allowing them to frame the conflict. While I was relieved that the board had resigned, I didn't have any pretensions that peace was at hand. Later that night, I emailed Paul:

> It just struck me that the board has consistently been meeting since October 24 without me, even though the constitution and bylaws say that I am a member of the board. I've just been told that they met after last night's Fall Fun Fest. How in the world can they justify what they are doing? They have not notified me of any of their meetings – not that I want to attend any of their nefarious meetings. What would the congregation think if they knew? What do you guys think?

Paul responded later that night:

> Constitutionally, the senior pastor is a member of the board of directors. In addition, the senior pastor shall be the leader of the church in all its activities. He shall be an ex officio member of all ministry teams. Meetings of the board that exclude you other than to discipline you or to evaluate your performance are unconstitutional.

The board told me I could stay as pastor, but then excluded me from all further meetings. They had chosen up sides and I had become the opposition. How could we ever work together again?

On a related matter, why did the board threaten to resign four different times in the first six days of the conflict? I have come to three possible conclusions:

First, *they feared a backlash after they announced Kim's departure to the congregation.* While Kim had made minor mistakes (who hasn't?), she was incredibly effective and immensely popular. At times in my ministry, I have had behind the scenes issues with popular leaders. While I've tried to address those issues privately, a pastor needs to be extremely careful how he handles leaders with a large following. Although no leader should have immunity, the backlash can result in a massive "train wreck." In that sense, the advocacy group may have done the board a favor by letting them resign *before* they announced Kim's departure.

Second, *the board had decided they no longer wanted to work with us.* Since the board perceived we were at an impasse, they chose to make a move that would end my tenure but extend theirs. Before we left for Moldova, I made plans to identify a few new board members for the following year because several current ones planned to leave their positions at year's end. But the minutes of the October 6 meeting (which occurred when I was overseas) indicate that *everyone* decided to remain on the board for the following year, possibly because they were confident they would stay as leaders and that I would disappear. Rather than talk things out, the board threw down the gauntlet and said, "We don't want to talk to you or work with you again. Either you leave or we will." It was a classic power play – a decision that a church insider later termed a "blood oath" – and almost a form of blackmail. They gambled that Kim and I would both resign to keep the board intact.

Finally, *the board felt chronic anxiety due to finances.* Due to the downturn in the economy, congregational giving was falling short of our budget, and the board was trying to negotiate terms for a new mortgage rate with our lender. We did have a large reserve fund that could carry us for a while, but we wanted to live by our donations. While I was concerned about the church's fiscal status, the board seemed obsessed with it. Steinke comments:

It is the chronically anxious individuals in the church family who are apt to conduct a 'search and destroy' mission. They will not hesitate to impose their wills on others. They make hostages of their gifts, attendance, and participation. They employ their stewardship as brinksmanship. Their ultimate threat is to run away from home – transferring or terminating their membership if an action is not rescinded, a person is not removed, or a demand is not satisfied. These tactics are effective in church families that place a premium on peace and harmony.[2]

Should I have called the board's bluff and asked for *their* resignations? Some pastors might have done so, but that's not my style, and the board knew it. That's why they threatened to resign together. They probably figured they were safe in making that proposal. (If I had asked for *their* resignations, can you imagine the fallout? And yet some pastors are thinking, "Good! Without a board, I can run the church the way I want!") But if Kim had resigned her position, and I had stayed as pastor, I would have been relegated to preaching and shepherding duties (like a chaplain) and the board would have seized nearly all decision-making authority. But when they did resign, they turned church governance over to the very person they wished to send packing.

The next morning, I sent emails to the staff, sending this one to the office manager:

It's all over, and it's turned out as well as can be expected. Please meet me at the church at 9 am and I'll explain. The Lord is still on his throne.

Paul read the board's resignation letter and concluded:

What the board did was inappropriate, very hurtful and wrong. It is appropriate for them to resign. But as humans we all make mistakes. We must seek to move forward learning from the past and owning any mistakes we made along the way. Genuinely forgiving others and forgiving ourselves is a long term goal. There will be much confusion, hurt and need for church healing going forward.

Wilson the consultant had a different take. He wrote:

> The 'Resignation Letter' was as good as I have ever read. It was 'Coached!!!!!'
> This 'Situation is Not Over' – Therefore 'Eyes & Ears Open and Mouth Closed.'

I drove to the church campus and greeted a few staff members, relieved that I would not see any board members there. When I entered my office, I found a large Clergy Appreciation card signed by people from the church – eight days after Clergy Appreciation Sunday. (The card had been in the board's possession.) On top of the card was a hard copy of the board's resignation letter. While that symbolism bothered me, my presence seemed to breathe new life into the remaining staffers. I later emailed an advisor:

> This morning, I called in three staff members and told them that (a) I was still the pastor and my wife was still the outreach director, (b) the board has resigned, (c) a provisional board will be chosen, and (d) we will be bringing in a consulting firm. As to (b), I didn't want them living in fear and confusion anymore. The fear and confusion already caused our associate pastor to resign and I didn't want anyone else to do so.

> I want to speak again to our (former) associate pastor and see if he can come back, at least for a couple months. But if I do, I'm going to have to assure him he's safe, and that involves telling him a little bit more than maybe you would like me to tell him. He resigned two days before the board did and I don't want people to think he was in with them. Maybe he was, but I don't think so. Today, my primary concern is getting some after care for my wife.

That night, after making sure that Kim was safe, I drove over to Jerry and Angela's home for a quick meeting with the pastoral advocacy team. Before the meeting, I received a message from a friend at church stating that her daughter had heard that Roger had resigned and Kim had been fired. The advocacy team had been keeping matters confidential, so I assumed this information originated with the resigning board members. (I later learned that the board went on a calling spree, telling select people that they had resigned and why.) Both sides had kept matters inside a tight circle, but now the dam had burst, and the news was spreading throughout the church. Since I could not manage the news, I focused on gathering leaders around me.

Because our church no longer had an active board, I needed help in governing the ministry – at least temporarily – so I quickly listed the five people I believed were the most spiritual, had the most stature, and would be most supportive. My list consisted of Alexander, the worship director; Darrell and Jerry, both former board members; Jane, the conflict expert; and Shannon, the children's director (who had a degree in political science). When I called Alexander that night, he quickly agreed to serve on the team, as did Darrell and Jerry. Jane turned me down initially, but when I persisted, she finally agreed. Although the consultant believed that one staff member on the team was plenty, I pushed for Shannon, and I'm glad I did. The group became known as the transition advisory team. In my view, knowing these five persons had agreed to work with me would give the congregation confidence in the days ahead.

As it turned out, I didn't know the church like I thought I did.

The following day, I arrived at the church office and announced to the staff members present that I was taking them out to lunch. We went to a popular place nearby and I was feeling better. Maybe I can stay as pastor after all, I thought, especially without having to fight the board all the time. Our mood at lunch was upbeat, and for a while, it seemed like old times. But after the meeting, I sent this email to Paul the consultant:

> I think . . . Roger was in on this. Today at our staff lunch, the staff said Roger was a good leader last week and left for home on Friday telling the staff he'd be back the following day to work on Fall Fun Fest. He resigned that night. What happened between his leaving for home and his resignation? The board agreed to resign.

Two days later, I sent another note to Paul:

> I went to church today and talked to our office manager and children's director. No one is emailing or calling in anger. Only one person has talked to either person about the situation in the past two days. My pastor's intuition (which can be fallible) tells me that only two members of the board are influential and I just don't think there's going to be a counterattack. We need to be ready for it, but the revolt was on the part of the board, not the church. If there was a counterattack, I can't even envision who would lead it, although I suppose the enemy always has available recruits.

Later that morning, a man in the church sent me this email:

> I see your side of the situation and I see the board's side . . . Without a quick resolution, I think you'll see a significant (50%?) attendance drop soon.

How did he know *my* side? I hadn't made any public pronouncements since the conflict began ten days before, and I hadn't spoken with this individual at all. But he obviously *had* spoken with an ex-board member or someone who knew their position, and the email writer seemed confident that up to half the church would leave over this conflict. That's a church split. What did he know that I didn't? The silence was beginning to torture me.

Because Kim was suffering from severe depression, I took her to a Christian counselor in a nearby city. My wife needed someone other than me to listen to her and assure her that she still had value. Kim's counselor had been a pastor's wife for thirty years and understood both church conflict and spiritual warfare. She diagnosed Kim with post traumatic stress disorder and recommended that she not work for a period of one year. The counselor told Kim that this entire tragedy was not her fault, even though some were saying just that. In her fragile emotional state, it was crucial that she place the blame outside herself for what had transpired over the previous ten days. The following observation from Christian psychologist Archibald Hart is fascinating:

I was born and raised in Africa as a European and was exposed to many primitive cultures when growing up. In more primitive groups the element of guilt is notably absent from depression. The tendency in these cultures is for blame to be externalized and placed on evil forces, ancestors, or one's enemies. People tend, therefore, not to blame themselves for their failures. Not surprisingly, this has important implications for their mental health. As one observes the transition to a western culture, blame gradually becomes more self-directed and a strong tendency toward guilt develops. Consequently, there is a much greater guilt component in the depressions of western culture.[3]

There would be plenty of future opportunities for Kim to assess what she had done wrong. Whenever she started to castigate herself, I would remind her of mistakes the board had made and tell her they were really after *me*, not her. While we couldn't entirely escape the situation, I was glad that Sarah could stay with us for a few nights. Sarah had obtained her undergraduate degree in psychology and was getting ready to enter a Master's program. Her strong presence and sweet words tempered with humor provided Kim with hope.

The Christian consulting firm that I was using wanted me to sign a contract with them so they would be paid for their services. Normally I would have sought board approval to hire a consultant, but being the only board member left, I made a unilateral decision to allocate the funds and hire Paul, although I did so in consultation with the pastoral advocacy group. (I sensed that my every move was now under surveillance.) Haugk has strong words for pastors who are under attack:

In times of active antagonism . . . use your authority to its limit. Failure to use the authority of your office represents more than just a private decision. In most denominations, because you derive the power of your office from the congregation, your refusal to act is the congregation's refusal. When antagonism interferes with the mission and ministry of the congregation, your anger should embolden you to use every ounce of your authority to end the situation . . . . At first you might feel terribly awkward using either your personal or official authority.

But exercising that authority may also make you feel like a
new person.[4]

Paul was scheduled to arrive via airplane on Friday around noon
and stay until late Sunday afternoon. I was so distressed about Kim's
condition that I felt like relinquishing decisions to others. I emailed
Paul:

I won't do anything rash. It is easy in the midst of accusations to absorb them all and tell yourself that your accusers
are right. What bothers me right now is that the board seems
to be getting their side of things out while I have to sit silent.
By Sunday, the damage could be irreparable. Will anyone even
listen to my side? And what if a petition begins to circulate to
get rid of me? One may already be circulating, although that
could be my paranoia kicking in.

Fortunately, Kim's parents arrived in town that Wednesday afternoon. When I was nineteen, Kim's father – a former Navy chaplain
and missionary to Saudi Arabia – returned to his home church in
Orange County to become their pastor, and I had already been hired
to work with the youth for the summer. I'm unsure what he thought
of me initially, but when I began to show an interest in his daughter,
he blessed our relationship just two months after we started dating.
He served two churches as pastor and then became a professor at a
Christian university. Since those early days, whenever I had a ministry
dilemma, he was only a phone call away – and here he was again, just
when I needed him most.

The two of us took a walk around our neighborhood and talked
through the ramifications of the board's resignation. Since they left,
it was almost eerily quiet. Had they walked away? Was that the end
of the fighting? Could I now lead the church in peace? Or was there
more consternation to come? I had no idea, but I didn't have too much
time to think about it. The transition team had scheduled its first official meeting that night. I invited my father-in-law to come along as a
consultant.

While I missed speaking the previous Sunday, I intended to speak
the following Sunday, November 8, and lay out a fresh vision for our

church's future, especially since our annual meetings were scheduled for later that November. The transition team wanted me to be strong and take command, yet due to the events of the previous eleven days, I wasn't sure I had it in me. But whenever I showed any self-doubt, the team chided me. The general feeling was that the board had resigned and was no longer a factor in the church's future. For some reason, I didn't believe that, but I lacked evidence to the contrary, and the silence still bothered me. After meeting for a few hours, we prayed and left for our respective homes.

Years before, Kim and I had vacationed on Coronado Island in San Diego, and down the street from our hotel was a theatre where a Christian drama group called The Lamb's Players presented plays. One night, we bought tickets for a play about a tiny church trying to survive called *A Divine Comedy*. The script was laugh out loud funny, the acting was superb, and the audience collapsed in hysterics. Since our church had a drama group, I recommended the play to our director and she obtained the script. It just so happened that three performances of the play were scheduled for that coming weekend. My prayer was that it would be a welcome diversion in the midst of a tense time in our fellowship.

After spending time with Kim's parents, and writing my message for Sunday, I decided to test the waters and visit the church campus that Thursday evening. Both the worship and drama teams were rehearsing for the upcoming weekend. It had only been four days since the board resigned, but I wanted to gauge people's reactions before I preached on Sunday. I normally spent Thursday nights working on my message at home, so people weren't accustomed to seeing me that night, but I could immediately sense that things were different. While some people greeted me warmly, others merely muttered a greeting, and some did not look at me, including the members of a family who had always been supportive. For the first time during my ministry, I sensed that people were uncomfortable in my presence. I had done my best to get along with everyone in our fellowship personally, but now I couldn't pinpoint who my supporters or detractors were. Only later did I learn that a copy of the board's resignation letter had been left in the worship center where it could be accessed by almost anyone.

The next morning, Friday, was a rainy day in our area. After telling Kim's parents goodbye, I prepared to pick up Paul at the airport. Right before noon, I received a call from Darrell, who had just spoken with George, a long-time attendee who was upset about the news concerning the board and associate pastor. Sure enough, George called me right as I prepared to leave for the airport. George was highly anxious about what the board's resignations meant for the church. I told him that I couldn't say anything right then but that we'd be sharing more at Sunday's meetings. But George wasn't satisfied. Before I left, he told me that an ex-board member had warned him not to allow his pregnant wife to attend Sunday's meetings because they wouldn't be safe. My heart leaped into my throat. This was the first I had heard that Sunday's meetings might get ugly. What better time was there to meet with a consultant?

I picked up Paul at the airport and drove to a restaurant in a city where it was unlikely we would be recognized. Paul and I got to know each other over lunch, and as it turned out, we had attended the same seminary. We tried to figure out why Sunday's meetings might get ugly but confessed that we didn't know. I then drove Paul to the church campus where he had already scheduled interviews with staff members. Finally, I went home to be with Kim, grateful that our son Ryan would be flying in later that evening. We both needed the support.

Later that afternoon, I sent Paul an email speculating about what any opposition might do in Sunday's meetings. My guesses: (a) circulate a petition so that 20 percent of the members could call a meeting to remove me as pastor (as the governing documents permitted); (b) have someone read the board's resignation letter; or (c) announce a lawsuit was being filed. Beyond that, I didn't really have any ideas. Rebecca, the office manager, sent me an email later that day:

> You asked me to let you know if anyone is inquiring about the situation here at [the church]. I received an odd phone call from George. He said he was going to speak with Roger and the board about what was happening. I didn't say anything to him . . . then he said he had to be 'ready' for Sunday. Not sure what he meant, but I thought you should know what just happened.

George was going to make Sunday a challenging day.

On Saturday, Paul asked me to write a statement I could read to the church at the beginning of both meetings the following day. I dashed off a two-page statement and submitted it to him. Later that afternoon, I met with the transition advisory team at Laura's house and we planned our strategy for the meetings. I would read my statement but take no questions. As the newly-appointed transition team leader – as well as an attorney – Alexander would then conduct the meeting. We debated whether he should take questions. If he didn't, it might look like a cover-up, but if he did, things might go south fast. Although she couldn't attend the meeting, Jane recommended that it was in everyone's best interests for the transition team to make a brief and pointed statement but not take questions.

My hope was that the congregation would accept my statement and trust me as their leader, but Paul made it clear: I was not to say *anything* after reading my statement. If I defended myself, someone could contact an ex-board member, ask if my statement was true, and come back and argue with me. We didn't want people caught in the crossfire of charge/countercharge.

That afternoon, I called Roger once more. I wanted him to know that I cared about him even though he had abruptly resigned. Those who had spoken with him claimed that he didn't want to get caught between the board and me, so he quickly fled. With my focus on Kim's health and the church's welfare, I hadn't thought much about Roger, but with matters coming to a head, I thought it was a good time to talk. I told him that I had selected a five-person transition team that would be announced the next day. While I did not identify the team members, I wanted him to know that I was still making decisions that would advance church unity. When the conversation ended, I told Roger, "I hope we'll always be friends." He agreed.

It was the last time I ever spoke with him.

That night, I prepared to attend the second performance of the play *A Divine Comedy* at our church. While Kim stayed home with Ryan, I walked to the church to attend the play and met Sarah outside the worship center. While some people were kind to me, once again, things didn't feel right. We howled at the play, which coincidentally had many parallels to our present church clash. Our people did a fabulous job producing it and deserved all the accolades they received.

As Sarah drove me home, we had to decide which route to take. Kim and I usually drove past the house of an ex-board member whenever we went to church, but it had became too painful, so we started using the longer route instead. Yet for some reason, Sarah and I decided to drive by that home about 10:00 that night, and we saw a parade of cars parked outside, including one that looked like Roger's van. Maybe those who gathered were celebrating someone's birthday, but it was also possible that former leaders were planning strategy for the next day's meetings. To this day, I don't know who attended that gathering or why, but a few hours later, it wouldn't matter anyway. When I arrived home, Alexander sent me an email indicating that he had just had a conversation with George (who had been in contact with ex-board members) and that George hoped there would be time for questions at the next day's meetings.

Years ago, I had trained myself to ignore most controversies that occurred before I spoke on Sundays. It was important that I focus on my message rather than be distracted by extraneous issues. While I gave some thought to the fact that George would be asking questions, I hoped that Alexander, an experienced attorney, would be able to handle matters wisely and that the silence of the previous week signified nothing of importance.

How wrong I was.

Early that Sunday morning, I reviewed the document that Alexander compiled for that day's meetings. Although there was some sentiment on the part of the transition team for not taking questions, Alexander decided he *would* take questions so it didn't look like the transition team was hiding anything. Because I was scheduled to deliver one of the most important messages of my life, I weighed in on his decision via email but then put it out of my mind. Here are several excerpts from the document that Alexander composed:

91

Q: Why did Roger resign?

A: In his letter, Roger says 'It is with a heavy heart that I submit this letter of resignation effective immediately. [My wife] and I have grown to love the people of [this church] . . .

After much intense prayer and thought, I feel that the Lord has led me to this very difficult decision. I will continue to pray for you all and the ministries of this church.'

We thank Roger for his dedicated service to [our church], will miss him and his family, and pray that God will continue to bless them in the years to come. He also mentioned, as Pastor Jim stated, that individuals can contact him if they'd like additional information.

Q: Why did most of the board members resign?

A: The transition team will look into this further. In their letter addressed to Pastor Jim, they say: 'It is through prayer and humility that we, the elected board of directors at [the church], resign collectively and as individual members effective immediately.'

The letter closes, 'With love for our brothers and sisters in Christ.'

There's additional text that is an evaluation of some members of the staff, but that information – like any performance appraisal – must be kept confidential. Most of you can understand that. If you work for a company and it releases your evaluation to the public, the company could face legal liability. It would not be legal or ethical for the company or other individuals to share that information, and the same is the case here.

In the meantime, we wish them God's best.

Q: Does the board have authority to terminate employees?

A: The transition team will look into this, but it appears the answer is 'no'. . . . There are two ways for an employee (other than the senior pastor) to be terminated. First, by written resignation. Second, where the senior pastor recommends termination AND the board approves it.

The transition team was as prepared as possible for that day's meetings. While we heard that they might get ugly, we had no idea why that might be the case. We were soon to find out.

Whenever our kids came to visit us, Kim and I would arrive at the church early and serve at the first service, and then our kids would drive over later and sit with us during the second service. But because Kim wasn't emotionally ready to attend church, Ryan stayed home with her. I encouraged Sarah to stay home as well, especially since there were indications the meetings might be unpleasant. But Sarah told me, "Dad, since Mom can't be there with you, I want to be there for you." After raising our kids to follow Christ, it was wonderful to have them minister to us during those distressing days.

My message that morning was based on Acts 14:21-28 and was a call for our church to make evangelism and missions a greater priority. I found a marvelous joke to begin the message and received a great response to it which helped put everyone at ease. After the first service ended, Jerry approached me and said, "A+." I appreciated his assessment, especially since I had to give the message a second time – but one hour later, I wouldn't *want* to give it again.

Since my father had been a Baptist pastor, I was accustomed to gatherings of the church called "business meetings." In a congregationally-governed church, this was the forum for making final decisions on issues like calling or terminating a pastor, approving the annual budget, and electing board members. While attending an independent church in my early teens, I attended business meetings for the same reason that spectators attended the gladiator games at the Colosseum in Rome: I wanted to see blood. No matter who came, or how well the meetings were managed, somebody always lost their temper – and that was the entertainment for the evening. The meetings were held after the Wednesday night prayer meeting, and I carefully observed what happened, even though I was too young to vote.

The meetings were led by a moderator who was assisted by a parliamentarian and were run according to *Robert's Rules of Order*, about which I knew absolutely nothing. Just when people began to share their true feelings, someone would call for the question or recommend that an issue be tabled until the next meeting. While the meetings were evidently necessary, they never seemed to be productive, rarely resulted in smart decisions, and sometimes caused division. When I finally became a solo pastor, our church had a custom of holding business meetings once per month, and they always made me nervous. (They had the same vibe as tense town hall meetings.) Several years later, during another such meeting, one board member yelled across the room at another board member's wife, and I couldn't tolerate that behavior any longer. In analyzing those meetings, I came to four conclusions:

First, *the meetings discouraged participation by the average member*. While *Robert's Rules* brought a semblance of structure to the meetings, only the moderator, the parliamentarian, and a few others really knew the rules, which gave them enormous power to shape the meetings to their advantage. Time after time, when a member wanted to speak, the moderator told them they were "out of order," which frustrated the speaker and prevented others from sharing as well. How could church members talk among themselves without wasting time on *Robert's Rules*?

Second, *the meetings were dominated by the same personalities*. While board members made proposals to the congregation, those who spoke at the meetings were usually members who felt powerless because they *weren't* leaders. Even if they couldn't get their way, they wanted everyone to hear their views, however cranky they might be. Over the years, I noticed that while a layman moderated those meetings, the pastor was expected to remain inconspicuous, surrendering his leadership to others. While that may have been the model at one time, I believe that pastors today should have a more prominent leadership presence whenever the entire congregation is gathered together, especially if he is truly the leader behind closed doors.

Third, *the meetings created anxiety because a proposal was usually followed immediately by a vote*. While board members usually had months to deliberate about an issue before bringing it before the church, members were asked to make an instant decision about a proposal they had heard about for the first time – and without as much information as the board possessed. The term I heard most frequently was that people felt "railroaded" into making an immediate decision. Imagine that during the next presidential election, you went to the voting booth, and the first time you learned about the candidates and propositions was when you opened your ballot. You'd feel violated because you didn't have time to think and pray about your decisions in advance. That's how many members feel at such meetings.

Finally, *those meetings were terrible forums for making decisions.* Inside a board meeting, members face one another when they speak and leaders can easily hear each other talk. But in a business meeting, it can be hard to see the faces of those talking, and people are constantly saying, "Speak up!" While it's hard enough for boards to arrive at consensus on some issues, multiply that times ten and you can see why business meetings often descend into chaos.

Because of the potentially volatile nature of such meetings, many pastors throughout America have either eliminated them altogether or have limited their number to one per year, usually an annual meeting for voting on board members and the next year's budget. (Some have even added worship times before any voting takes place.) These pastors schedule the meeting at a time when the congregation normally doesn't meet – like a Saturday or Sunday evening – so that only highly-committed members attend. While I respect those pastors, I wanted the maximum attendance at our meetings, so we scheduled them on Sundays after the second service because people were already on campus and it was convenient for them to stay a little longer. We enticed them by offering child care and a free lunch. I wanted broad ownership for our ministries and finances and tried to lead a ministry that was both informative and transparent.

Five years after becoming a pastor, I instituted some changes in those public meetings. Whenever we scheduled a meeting for members to vote on an issue, we first held an informational meeting the Sunday before. I usually led that meeting and received assistance from board members. We did not use *Robert's Rules* but presented common-sense etiquette for behaving at such meetings. We wanted people to hear proposals directly from their leaders (not indirectly from friends) and for everyone to hear about the issues simultaneously.

The leaders made a presentation – complete with written documentation – and then let people respond with questions or comments. I would gently remind people that while they were free to speak, they needed to be careful what they said and how they said it or they might regret it for years. No one was allowed to grouse about an issue privately but needed to use a microphone if they wanted to participate. If matters went south, the pastor and board had a full week to clarify issues, pacify a disgruntled person, or pull an item off the agenda before a vote. And you didn't have to be a member to have input at an informational meeting – just a regular attendee. When the meeting concluded, board members stood near the stage and participants were encouraged to question them or make appointments to speak with them. I believe you can trust believers to make wise decisions as long as they're given time to think and pray about them.

Then the following Sunday, we held a congregational meeting. (The term "business meeting" has negative connotations.) Although anyone could *attend* the meeting, only members could *vote*. We never permitted a voice vote. We discouraged questions because the issues had been thoroughly discussed the previous week. Members marked their ballots and handed them to pre-appointed tellers who tallied their votes. We used *Robert's Rules* simply to put a motion on the floor. Those meetings only lasted five to ten minutes. You can make a case for an informational meeting followed by a congregational meeting from Acts 6:1-7.

For twenty-four years, this system worked beautifully. The churches that I served previously went through some tough crises and yet everyone managed to stay together. Because people felt they could share their opinions – and leaders were non-defensive while hearing them – there was a visible unity in those churches. (Most people want their *say* more than their *way*.) Using the same process in *this* church, leaders had gone to the congregation multiple times for approvals concerning the building of a new worship center, and every vote was unanimous. But on Sunday, November 8, we misjudged the mood of the congregation and had two meetings (one after each service) when we should have had just one.

Unfortunately, our hard-won reputation for unity evaporated within a few short minutes.

TAKEAWAYS FROM CHAPTER 4

For pastors:

- During conflict, be open to the perspectives of advisors from outside your church as well as influencers from inside your church. They may see matters more clearly than you do.
- If your church has public meetings, give members adequate time to think and pray about matters before they cast any votes. Change your polity if necessary but do not insist that people make decisions when first informed about an issue. Anxiety breeds conflict.
- Realize that your family members may become targets for those who want to remove you from office. If a group leads a campaign to remove you, coach your family members with great sensitivity how to respond and encourage them to remain strong.

For board members:

- If you believe that a conflict is potentially serious (your church might split or there might be calls for your pastor's removal), contact a church consultant or a conflict manager sooner rather than later – and if it costs money, realize it's a necessary and wise investment.
- Avoid threatening to resign *en masse*. It looks like you're resorting to desperation because you can't get your way. (If it works this time, will you use this tactic again?) If your group does quit together, you will leave a leadership vacuum, throw your church into chaos, and force others to clean up your messes. It is better to resign as individuals when the church year is complete, or when terms of office have expired, or for more noble reasons. Once you resign and leave the church, you forfeit the right to impact future events.

- If you ever do resign, write a classy resignation letter rather than a vindictive one. Bitter letters burn bridges and have a way of being frozen in time.
- Personal and group anxiety will tempt you to take shortcuts whenever conflict erupts. Resist that feeling, prayerfully and patiently working through the biblical process instead.

For the congregation:

- When leaders leave the church, it is natural to want to know their reasoning immediately. Realize that you are entitled to know some things and not others but that you may eventually learn much of the truth if you exercise patience.
- If the remaining leaders won't reveal what is happening when people leave, contact those who have left directly. They will usually be receptive to explaining their actions. But because you're unable to hear both sides, do not take up their cause. Refuse to carry other's offenses!
- Do not forsake friendship with your pastor if he is under fire. Whether you think he's innocent or guilty, let him know you are praying for him and that you appreciate his ministry. There will be plenty of time later to form conclusions.

CHAPTER 5

HELL INVADES THE CHURCH

At the conclusion of the first service that Sunday, I announced that the first informational meeting would be starting in five minutes. I then read the following statement to the church:

> I have always said that [our church] is a generous and gracious church. I constantly tell people outside the church what a wonderful congregation you are, and I still feel that way. This is a very special church family. I love this church very much.
>
> Over the past two weeks, the leadership and congregation have been severely tested. You may think that I know everything that has happened over the past few weeks, but I'm not sure that anyone does.
>
> Several weeks ago, the board made a personnel decision. I am not at liberty to divulge the decision or the reasons behind it, but things are different at [our church] because of it. As it stands right now:
>
> - I am the senior pastor.
> - Roger has resigned, and he told me that you can call him if you have any questions.
> - Kim is the outreach director, but is on medical leave.

- Alexander is the worship director.
- Carl is the youth pastor.
- Shannon is the children's director.
- Rebecca is the office manager.

In addition, the other members of the board of [our church] have voluntarily resigned.

What happened? Why did this happen? While some people know bits and pieces, I have made three decisions to help us (a) figure out what happened, (b) ensure it never happens again, and (c) help our congregation heal.

First, I have appointed a transition team of five individuals who are trustworthy, godly, and wise. They are [I then listed their names and qualifications] . . .

The charter for this group is fourfold:

First, receive nominations from you, the congregation, on who our new board members should be. More on this next Sunday.

Second, finalize and present an operating budget for 2010.

Third, review the organizational and financial structure at [our church].

Fourth, analyze what has occurred over the past few weeks.

To help the transition team do just that, we have hired a professional church consultant named Paul from [consulting firm's name]. Paul lives in [I mentioned his state] and flew down on Friday. Paul will issue a report to the transition team and me and make recommendations for the future.

Maybe you have heard a lot over the past several weeks. Maybe you haven't heard anything at all. In any case, I ask that if you consider [church name] your church home, you will do the following four things in the days ahead:

First, pray for our church, our staff, and the transition team, that we will honor the Lord and make decisions that please him.

Second, feel free to talk with me or any member of the transition team if you have any questions.

Third, make sure you have all the facts before making any conclusions or decisions.

Finally, continue to attend our church and serve the Lord in the way you have been doing, to help advance God's kingdom at [our church] and in our community.

God bless you, and let's pray.

Reading the statement again months later, it accurately reflected all that I knew about the situation *except* what had happened to Kim. I knew that Roger had resigned, but I honestly didn't know why, and I knew that the board had resigned, but their stated reasons didn't make sense to me either. My statement let the church know that I was aware of the resignations and that I wanted to find out what happened and why. Steinke notes:

> In the early stages of a conflict, it is almost impossible to over-inform. As much information as possible is needed. Providing information tends to minimize the need for people to create information for themselves through gossip and embellishments of what they have heard from rumor. By communicating forthrightly, leaders also treat the members as mature adults who can handle whatever information is shared, not as children who need to be protected from bad news.[1]

Many people naturally assumed that as pastor, I knew what was happening behind closed doors and that I wasn't being forthcoming.

But I was caught in a double bind. On the one hand, part of me wanted to report the board's decision and get it out into the open, but on the other hand, any such announcement would have devastated my wife. Pastors know they cannot publicly report the extreme sufferings of parishioners without their approval, and I did not have my wife's blessing to report her condition to the congregation. So I did my best and reported that she was on medical leave. I'm sure some people that day assumed I was protecting my wife's job, but I was trying to protect her well-being most of all. According to my advisors, after the board resigned, her job status reverted to me, and I reinstated her with the provision that she could only return to work when she was healthy. In my heart of hearts, I was convinced she would never work for the church again, but I did not want to make any statement that would intensify her suffering – or give any detractors a premature sense of victory. But the biggest mistake I made was to encourage people to contact Roger if they wanted to know why he resigned. As it turned out, he was sharing certain things in his interactions with me but was telling others something different. I didn't find out anything was amiss until it was too late to reverse course.

When I was done reading my statement, I prayed and sat down in the front row. The transition team (except for Jane, who was away) stood on the stage behind Alexander, who began answering questions about the resignations. But our presentation was sabotaged because of George, who became relentless trying to discover why Roger and the board had resigned. Apparently one or more ex-board members filled George's ears with multiple reasons as to why they had left and shared restricted personnel information with him as well. As painful as the October 24 board meeting had been, it was five times more torturous listening to George's public accusations. Speaking in a somewhat anxious style, George stood and made the following claims in the meetings:

• I could take a leave of absence and Pastor Norman, the church's founding pastor and my predecessor, could be invited back to the church since he was available. (He lived *very* close to the church on weekends). When this idea was mentioned, I quickly glanced at Jerry, who was standing on the stage, and his eyes met mine. I had already told the transition team that there was talk of Norman returning as interim pastor – talk the team initially refused to believe.

- An investigation should be conducted as to why I didn't get along with the various youth pastors that we'd had since my tenure began. (Where did *this* come from? How was it even relevant?) Even though the board had never discussed this issue with me, I was prepared to handle that charge right then and there – and one of the departing board members knew full well what had transpired with several youth leaders in the past.
- The board had fired Kim and that firing should stand. (Yes, they had privately called for her dismissal, but they resigned before her termination was final and announced to the church. But how could former board members *enforce* a decision once they had left?)
- The associate had resigned for several reasons, charging me with nepotism. (This was the first time anyone had accused me of that charge in my presence in eight-and-a-half years. While I don't recall Roger ever making this claim to my face, this charge is tough to refute in a public setting because it *sounds* plausible.)
- The associate also claimed that church money had been mismanaged. (But he never said anything directly to me about it. By whom? When? How much? So hearsay somehow becomes a *fait accompli*?) No facts were given – only generalizations. If this claim was aimed at me, this was the first time anyone had made such an accusation in my thirty-five-year career – and those in the know were aware of how rarely but meticulously I handled church funds.
- The board had sought mediation to resolve the crisis, but I had rejected their proposal. (This was patently untrue. A group within the church had tried to mediate the crisis with the board on two occasions, but the board rejected their overtures, and I suggested another mediator to the chairman, but no board member ever got back to me until they resigned.)

I don't mind someone questioning my judgment. After all, pastors make dozens of decisions every week, and we're bound to get a few of them wrong. But George was questioning my integrity and insinuating that my character was corrupt. Even if he was just passing on charges, how proper was it for George to make those allegations without knowing if I had heard them before? My rights as a human being – much less as a Christian leader – were being trampled.

Since no ex-board member attended the meetings, George became their mouthpiece. While dominating both meetings, he lacked personal knowledge of his charges. Leas comments:

> It is difficult to be in conflict with partners who have left the scene. Sometimes people just drop out; they stop attending or participating in any church functions. But other times they stay at home and participate by telephone. Other people then come to the meetings bearing the grievances of dissatisfied persons who are not present to convey their views accurately and responsibly. This kind of behavior is difficult and annoying to deal with. Anonymous or relayed communications stay at the point where they began . . . . One bishop I know insists that the participants at conflict meetings only speak for themselves. He strongly encourages them to make 'I think,' 'I believe,' or 'I know' statements rather than remarks such as 'Some people have said,' or 'A lot of people are upset,' or 'I am speaking for those who have spoken to me and are afraid to speak out.'[2]

George became the unofficial congregational prosecutor and was parroting what former leaders had told him. How did George know the board members were telling the truth? He might have said, "Because these were good people." But wasn't I a good man as well, at least equal in integrity to each of them? George admitted as much when he told the congregation, "I'm a Jim fan." Besides, George hadn't witnessed me or Kim doing anything wrong *firsthand*. He was simply passing on what he had been told. But how did anyone know he was conveying their charges accurately? Those making accusations should have had the courage to be present but were nowhere to be found. Doesn't 1 Timothy 5:19 insist upon two or three *witnesses* to wrongdoing? In a court of law, without witnesses going on the record, the proceedings might have been concluded. But in a congregationally-run church – even with an attorney leading the meeting – chaos was just beginning. Leas observes:

It is understandable that someone who is hurt, not helped, or bored by what is going on in a congregation may choose to leave it. Indeed, it is understandable that one might choose to leave as a protest, hoping to influence the future policy or staffing. However, it is not appropriate that once having abandoned the responsibility of running and paying for a church's ministry, one should have equal weight in telling those who are maintaining it how to run it. The right to confront an organization's leadership comes with being responsible for its future. Therefore, it is important to consider members' current commitment when they advise what should be done in the future or complain about what has happened in the past.[3]

While the board said I could stay as pastor, George's defense of The Seven (the six former board members and the ex-associate pastor) became a public indictment of the way I led the church and staff. While no one called for my dismissal at those meetings, some people tried to convince others that I was the reason the leaders had resigned. Within a span of fifteen days, the guns that had been secretly pointed at Kim were now openly aimed at me.

The truth is that the congregation *needed* some answers as to why the associate and the board had resigned. Their departures seemed to indicate that something was seriously wrong in the church's top leadership circles. The former board members were speaking through George and their friends while I remained silent – an implicit confirmation that their charges were accurate. It seemed like I had done something hideous while The Seven were all angelic, and yet I was present at the meeting while they were not. It's easy to understand why the average attendee was confused that day.

How did I reply to George's accusations? Over nearly two-and-a-half hours, all I did was read the statement I had prepared at the start of both meetings. Some people pleaded with me to respond to the allegations, but I chose to maintain silence. Why didn't I say anything?

First, *the consultant had asked me not to say anything in my defense*. He asked me to remain silent, and I promised him I would, so I did. I *wanted* to defend myself, but with my accusers absent, how much good would it have done? Let's say that I tried to defend myself against a charge. All George or anyone else had to do was walk into the lobby, call Roger, share my defense with him, and bring back his response, even though I couldn't respond to him because he wasn't present. His leaving seemed to *enhance* his credibility in some people's minds.

Second, *I couldn't speak because I didn't have all the facts.* Although I wasn't convinced that Kim had misspent funds, no one permitted either one of us to see the exact amount she *had* spent. If I tried to defend her publicly, I could look foolish because I lacked accurate information. (For example, someone could have mass-produced a record of her spending and handed it out to the congregation without my seeing it first.) Three days after the October 24 meeting, I asked Taylor for written evidence of Kim's spending, but he referred me to the church's bookkeeper. I emailed her and asked for the information, but her reports were incomplete and confusing. And when Kim asked for the records when she met with two board members, they didn't produce anything, either. Here I was, pastor of the church, and I couldn't get my hands on documentation that the board used as evidence! It would take me another two-and-a half weeks before I received accurate information.

Third, *I had to protect two parties, and if I defended either one of them, it could make matters worse for everyone involved.* I had to protect the six people who formed the pastoral advocacy team because I had placed three of them on the transition team. If I tried to explain the events of the past several weeks, I might have been forced into revealing their names, and I didn't want to take that chance because the church needed their leadership. But I was also protecting Kim. If I defended her conduct without her being present, my words could be interpreted as real-live nepotism in action. She was so emotionally fragile that I wanted to keep her name out of the meetings without explaining why she wasn't there. So I quietly sat next to Sarah, who was forced to listen to the lovely congregation that she cherished become, in her words, "an alternate universe."

Fourth, *my own rhetoric could have escalated the conflict.* Most pastors possess strong personalities and are skilled at persuading large groups to see things their way. Because the average pastor could out-debate almost anyone publicly in *their* church, most boards would rather terminate the pastor privately than let him address accusations in a public meeting. (Of course, had I convincingly responded to all of the charges against me, my detractors would have created more.) While others *did* escalate the conflict, I can look back and feel good that I did not contribute to division that day. Richardson observes:

> The job of effective church leaders is to help keep down the level of anxiety in the emotional system of the congregation. When things are calmer, people are able to think more clearly about their options in the midst of stressful circumstances and develop a reasonable, workable plan of action . . . . They do not tell others to 'be calm.' They simply bring their own calmness to the situation.[4]

Finally, *I could not exonerate my wife by myself.* If she was to be cleared of the charges against her, that process would have to be led either by the transition team or a new board. No matter how much I defended her – either as my wife or as a staff member – an independent party would have to conduct a thorough investigation before she could be exonerated, so I had to remain calm and hope that my example eventually paid dividends. However, when the lead pastor of a church is wounded, the congregation becomes highly anxious. Steinke explains why such a scenario arouses opposition:

> I have seen three clergy whose children had been killed, two whose spouses died of cancer, and four who suffered other losses become the center of careless and irrational criticism. Conventional wisdom would lead us to believe that such circumstances would bring an abundance of compassion and tolerance. What happened, I believe, is that some anxious members needed the pastor to function at the same level as before the losses . . . . the anxious members needed their pastor to be strong, energetic, approachable, and the like. Needing security, the anxious forces reacted and focused negatively upon the pastor. The pastor in crisis jars the stability of the whole system.[5]

When a leader has every reason to be stressed but remains calm instead, people tend to admire that leader even more. Several years earlier, the infant granddaughter of a woman in our church unexpectedly died. During the opening minutes of the girl's memorial service, the deceased infant's father – who had been drinking – left his front row seat, charged me while I was speaking, pounded his fist on the podium, swore profusely, and then was quickly escorted from the room. The mourners were shocked. I paused before saying anything, made a brief comment, and then continued with the service. I am not sure how many paid attention to my subsequent words, but many people told me later how much they appreciated the calm way that I handled that unprovoked outburst. The way a pastor conducts himself impacts the whole church, and sometimes that means refusing to fight fire with fire.

While Alexander responded to some of George's accusations, George was allowed to speak far too long. He dominated both meetings with his revelations. While he had no official leadership role, the more he said, the more he seemed to sway the mood of both meetings. Since the accusations concerned my wife and me, and since I wasn't saying anything, those attending had to wonder if at least some of George's charges were true. As he thundered along, I wondered why someone didn't ask him to be quiet, but then I remembered a saying that my father-in-law taught me when I was a rookie youth pastor: "Laymen won't confront laymen." In my experience, this observation is a microcosm of congregational dysfunction played out in public. I longed for someone to act in the way that conflict expert Kenneth Haugk describes:

> I attended a meeting where a church member requested permission to speak after an antagonist had tormented the chairperson for 15 minutes regarding some trivial issue. The member addressed the antagonist and said, 'We've heard you complain about various pastors and other leaders for the last 15 years. Quite frankly, I'm tired of it. Please keep quiet so we can continue the meeting! Thank you.' Her straightforward comment was quite refreshing. The antagonist was so shocked that he didn't say another word all evening, and the meeting ended on schedule. Too often, lay people especially are unaware of the positive power in simply being themselves.[6]

Because lay people want to remain friends with other lay people (maybe they eat in each other's homes or serve together), they rarely confront each other about major issues, leaving that thankless task to the pastor by default. And if friends fail to confront each other, but a pastor does, it's easy for the offender to conclude that "the pastor is mistaken because he's the only one telling me I'm wrong." A friend later told me that some people didn't speak up in the meetings because they were hoping to hear from their lay leaders.

Toward the end of the second meeting, a long-time attendee finally said, "George, we've heard enough out of you today. Sit down." And George did. But by then, the damage had been done. The clinching blow was inflicted by a man I'll call Bert who had been my friend for more than ten years. Bert stood up and read the names of the board members who had resigned. He then concluded, "These are all good people. If they all resigned together, they must have had a good reason." Many of those present broke into spontaneous applause.

That's when I knew my ministry at the church was finished.

George wasn't the only one to make accusations that day, however. Someone stood and said that the board resigned because they had been threatened with a lawsuit. Ten days before, when Kim met two board members at the church, she became increasingly upset at the unfairness of the charges made against her. While some might be tempted to place the blame for this incident entirely on Kim, Leas explains why she may have responded as she did:

> The conflict management process should be slow, and accomplished so that all parties concerned about the outcome have a chance to affect both process and outcome. If the board moves too quickly or attempts an end run around individuals and groups, these persons will feel cheated by the process and ask for or demand another hearing, vote, or will take the dispute to another 'court.' Or, the people who lose will come back looking for revenge or redress.[7]

Even though I had asked Kim not to mention anything about legal action at that meeting, she told the two board members, "I could sue you because of what you've done." Should she have said that? No, and I told her so when she came home that evening. Christians should not settle internal disputes in secular courts. However, as leaders, the board should have anticipated the threat of a lawsuit and taken steps to protect the church before announcing Kim's dismissal. Had another staff member been the subject of termination, I would have insisted that the board seek legal counsel and contact the church's insurance company before taking any action. I am uncertain whether the board initially consulted with an attorney, but if they *had* sought counsel, why did they run? If they knew they were right, why did they leave? They should have been able to stand their ground with confidence. Maybe they wanted to cast me in the bully role so they could be perceived as victims – but shouldn't *someone* have called their bluff in that case?

When this accusation was made, I wanted to stand up and tell everyone, "*They* threatened to resign four times in the first six days of the conflict." While the board may have been concerned about legal action on October 29, I don't believe they quit solely for that reason. Besides, members of corporate boards are protected from lawsuits in that state, and we would *never* have sued the church itself. We *loved* the church. I believe that if Kim had let the board fire her, and the news had spread around the church, there would have been demands for the *board* to resign, and they had to know that was a possibility.

The most bewildering thing about both meetings was that nobody stood up and strongly supported us. I had been the church's associate pastor for eighteen months and its senior pastor for nearly nine years. Kim had been the outreach director for eight-and-a-half years. The associate pastor's tenure had been twenty-nine months, and yet some people chose to believe indirect charges emanating from him rather than defending two people they knew well. A few people stood and appealed for proper procedures, while others waited to hear directly from me, but I had promised I wouldn't say anything, and I kept my word. But while I did, my ministry of nearly eleven years slipped away in less than three hours.

Why were people reluctant to speak up on our behalf? Maybe it's because most people are averse to conflict. People avoid conflict in their homes and workplaces, even though those relationships are essential to their long-term well-being. By contrast, attending church

110

is optional for most people, and if they continually come to meetings and sense tension, they may choose to attend less often, stay home, or search for another church home. This is why it is imperative for church leaders to tackle conflict *before* it becomes public. Unaddressed conflict can harm a church for years to come.

I also believe that most people loved the board members and Roger – as well as my wife and me – and preferred not to take sides. In essence, the congregation had been informed that the board and associate pastor had chosen to divorce the pastor and his wife, and this news brought pain to everyone involved. I once read that the source of grunge rocker Kurt Cobain's problems was the divorce of his parents when he was eight years old. How many spiritual children are harmed by divorces between their spiritual fathers and mothers?

I am convinced that if one or two attendees had stood strong in those meetings, they could have neutralized the vocal minority, but no one spoke up and supported us. Why not? Psychiatrist Martha Stout writes about a time she chaperoned her daughter's fifth-grade class trip. On the bus ride home, one boy was picking on another boy who was developmentally delayed and friendless so he didn't know how to defend himself. Before any adult could intervene, a ten-year-old girl who stood four feet tall and was seated behind the two boys tapped the tormentor on the shoulder and said, "That's really mean. Quit it." Stout asks:

> What happens to us while we are growing up? Why do adults stop saying 'Quit it' to the bullies? Will this healthy little girl behave with the same kind of dignity and self-assurance when she is thirty years old and a foot and a half taller? . . . Sadly, given our present child-rearing practices, the odds are against it.[8]

While no church attendee strongly defended us, one person *did* confront the protesters. At the end of the second meeting, Paul the consultant walked to the front of the worship center, took the microphone, and forcefully told the congregation, "You have just destroyed your church!" I felt the same way emotionally, and I was glad he said what he did, although churches are incredibly resilient and have a way of surviving all kinds of crises. A better phrase might have been, "You have just severely damaged your church." The atmosphere that day became so toxic that Paul's words needed to be said. He addressed the following issues:

- Alexander told George in the meeting that church bylaws stated that staff members could only be terminated when the senior pastor made such a recommendation to the board. George believed that the bylaws had once stated something different. Paul told the assembled group, "It doesn't matter what the constitution *used* to say. It doesn't matter what you *think* it should say. It matters what the constitution says *now*, and the board did not follow the constitution." Although most judges won't take church cases, when they do, they look to see if a board followed their governing documents to the letter. Christian attorney Carl Lansing writes:

> Be shrewd, keep on top of your corporate structure, and be certain your actions are in compliance with those requirements. Overlooking the particular requirements of your nonprofit articles of incorporation and your bylaws, and failing to keep them current and in sync with the activities of your organization, can lead to serious trouble.[9]

- Paul also told the church that confidential personnel information could not by law be discussed in the meeting and that by doing so, the church had opened itself up to legal liability. There were charges made in the meeting that no one had any business saying in public. How did anyone know the charges were true? How many workers have lost a job and had the reasons for their dismissal paraded before their peers? And yet one or more ex-board members believed that since they had resigned, they were free to say anything they wanted. They so much wanted their decisions to be vindicated publicly that they ended up confusing and dividing churchgoers.
- Paul also defended my decision to choose a transition team and hire him as a consultant. George and some others believed that since I had chosen them, they could not be objective. But without a board or an associate pastor, Paul asked, what was I supposed to do? If I chose to lead the church unilaterally, I could be accused of running a dictatorship. The governing documents gave me authority to choose ad-hoc

committees. And I did not hire Paul so he would do my bidding. He interviewed staff members independently of me and wrote a report making specific recommendations to the transition team. No, I hired Paul because I needed experienced counsel and wanted the church to stay together, not to whitewash anything.

Understandably, I didn't feel like lingering around the church that autumn afternoon, and besides, I had to drive Paul to the airport. As we walked off the campus, my daughter Sarah asked Paul, "On a one to ten scale, with ten being the best and one being the worst, how would you rate those meetings?" Paul scored them a one or a two, among the worst he had ever seen. I told Paul that I didn't know how I could ever forgive George for the damage he had caused, and Paul fully understood. Two days before, Paul told me that he had been forced to leave his last church as pastor when someone sent a letter to every home claiming he didn't believe in several key Christian doctrines. Of course, that wasn't true, but that's how cruel some Christians can become when they are determined to remove a spiritual leader. The Apostle Paul's words in Galatians 5:15 are apropos here: "If you keep on biting and devouring each other, watch out or you will be destroyed by each other." After I dropped off Paul at the airport, I wondered what kind of future my family and the church had, but I knew we would not have a future together.

I arrived back home late that afternoon and told Kim, "We're moving." The secondhand charges, the surprising accusations from people we considered friends, and the lack of support all coalesced to make us realize that our services were no longer wanted. After updating several advisors, Kim and I realized that we were being forced to leave our beloved church family. While I was relieved that the tension of the previous fifteen days was ending, I was embarrassed that this kind of conflict was happening to me. After all, I had done my doctoral work on the topic of congregational antagonism, but when I wrote my dissertation, I envisioned working *with* the governing board to deal with *lay* antagonists. Because every board I had worked with in the past had supported me on those rare occasions when I was under attack, I never envisioned that the *board* would become antagonistic. When the pastor becomes the object of such an attack, he cannot manage the conflict effectively, either from a tactical or emotional standpoint. Regardless of a pastor's biblical knowledge or ministry experience, charges directed at his character wound him to the core – and in that wounded state, a pastor maintains a defensive stance and utilizes every ounce of energy just to survive. There is nothing worse than coming to church on Sundays without knowing who loves or hates you. It's intolerable.

We were determined to leave it all behind.

TAKEAWAYS FROM CHAPTER 5

For pastors:

- Whenever you're in a public meeting, exhibit a spirit of calmness through your demeanor, even if you feel turbulent inside. It is the job of church leaders to bring down the anxiety level so that issues can be discussed spiritually and rationally.
- Put together an informal group that can give you periodic feedback so you can constantly monitor and interpret the mood of your congregation. Sometimes pastors are among the least informed individuals in a church.

For board members:

- Know your church's constitution and bylaws. Comply with them completely. If you don't agree with some of them, institute changes using the process spelled out in your governing documents.
- Whoever moderates a congregational meeting must maintain control of it. While it can be beneficial for believers to share candid feelings, irreparable harm can be done as well. People may leave your church or stop practicing their faith over one out-of-control meeting. If you're in charge, do everything *you* can to make sure that never happens.

For the congregation:

- If you're ever in a public meeting where a pastor is being accused of wrongdoing, ask that the governing leaders follow the biblical process spelled out in Matthew 18 and 1 Timothy

5. If necessary, stand and read those Scriptures to the congregation. If the biblical process has not been used, recommend that the meeting be suspended until God's Word is implemented.

- Ask church leaders if the process they used to deal with the pastor was *fast* or *fair*. Insist on a fair process. Fair usually means slow. Fast can mean unfair. If people make accusations against the pastor, how many actually witnessed the pastor commit an offense firsthand? Is the pastor given the opportunity to respond to charges made against him in private first?

CHAPTER 6

POST-MEETING ANALYSIS

*W*hat would have been a better way to handle those meetings?

In my second pastorate, a man in his late seventies asked to come to a board meeting to complain about me. Jim had once been the board chairman but still led congregational singing. (This was before anyone was called a "worship leader.") One Sunday, we briefly disagreed about which hymns to sing at the next service. Jim said that he had always chosen the hymns and that I was trying to curtail his authority, so he contacted the chairman and came to the next meeting armed with seven complaints against me – grievances he had been hoarding for some time. (He must be given credit for coming to the board rather than spreading his discontent throughout the church, however.) Before Jim arrived, I asked the board to do two things whenever he leveled a complaint against me: first, ask Jim what evidence he had to support his claim, and second, allow me to respond to his complaints after he made each one.

Jim made his first complaint, after which the chairman asked him for evidence. Then I was asked to respond to Jim's charge. When Jim came to the meeting, he was confident he had a strong case, but when he arrived at the sixth complaint, he lost his zeal and never made the seventh one. (His complaints seemed more substantive when he was sharing them with family members than with the board.) The next morning, Jim called to tell me he was leaving the church, which made me sad. (When he died, his wife asked me to conduct his funeral.) But

I was proud of the board for allowing me to face my accuser, making him state his evidence, and letting me respond to his charges directly.

Had this process been required at the November 8 meetings, I might have been able to remain as pastor provided that I eventually responded to each charge in some fashion. How credible were George's public complaints when no one had first discussed them with me in private? Besides, the charges shouldn't have been permitted because my accusers had fled. Remember Jesus' words to the woman taken in adultery in John 8:10? Jesus asked about her accusers, "Woman, where are they? Has no one condemned you?" She replied, "No one, sir." Then Jesus told the woman that he did not condemn her either and that she should sin no more. Since her accusers had fled, only Jesus' verdict mattered.

I have heard pastors under fire quote 1 Samuel 24:6 as a way of keeping their critics at bay. While King Saul sleeps in the front of a cave, David – who is hiding in back with his men – creeps up and cuts off a corner of Saul's robe, even though David's men want him to murder Saul instead. But David tells them, "The Lord forbid that I should do such a thing to my master, the Lord's anointed, or lift my hand against him; for he is the anointed of the Lord." David speaks directly to Saul in verse 10 and utters a similar sentiment. I've also heard pastors quote 1 Chronicles 16:22 to silence critics: "Do not touch my anointed ones; do my prophets no harm."

These passages teach that God appoints and anoints leaders, whether kings or prophets. (Paul states in Acts 20:28 that the Holy Spirit appoints pastors/elders as well.) David knew he was the successor to Israel's throne but would only secure it in God's time and way. But when David agreed not to "lift my hand" against the Lord's anointed, he was refusing to remove him from office by *killing* him. (Israel didn't vote on anything.) Because the Lord selected leaders in the Old Testament, they could only be displaced by divine decree. But since members *elect* their pastors in congregationally-run churches, they have the right to *un-elect* them as well.

Besides, those Old Testament passages are trumped by 1 Timothy 5:19-21. Paul writes in verse 20, "Do not entertain an accusation against an elder [includes those who preach and teach; see verse 17] unless it is brought by two or three witnesses." Since spiritual leaders are constantly visible, people will sometimes make accusations against them, but Paul instructs Timothy not even to *listen* to charges unless there are multiple witnesses. In our case, if we deserved to be removed from our positions, why didn't others stand up and share sins they had witnessed us committing? But the only charges against us came from former leaders who had vanished. While this did not mean we were innocent, if The Seven were going to press charges, someone needed to do so in person rather than from the comfort of their home. Sadly, hearsay testimony was allowed to stand as fact. When a pastor is accused of public wrongdoing, there may be a multitude of prosecutors, but rarely is anyone appointed as his defense attorney.

Imagine how differently members of a spiritual community – including its leaders – would be treated if every church took Moses' words to Israel in Deuteronomy 19:15-21 seriously:

> One witness is not enough to convict a man accused of any crime or offense he may have committed. A matter must be established by the testimony of two or three witnesses. If a malicious witness takes the stand to accuse a man of a crime, the two men involved in the dispute must stand in the presence of the Lord before the priests and the judges who are in office at the time. The judges must make a thorough investigation, and if the witness proves to be a liar, giving false testimony against his brother, then do to him as he intended to do to his brother. You must purge the evil from among you. The rest of the people will hear of this and be afraid, and never again will such an evil thing be done among you. Show no pity: life for life, eye for eye, tooth for tooth, hand for hand, foot for foot.

Please notice four things about this passage:

First, *an accuser must be a witness.* Since George was not a witness to wrongdoing, he should not have been permitted to make public charges unless he had been assigned to be congregational prosecutor – which, of course, no one had done. Whether ex-board members had asked him to relay charges (which might insulate them legally) or he had volunteered to do so, George did something he may not have fully understood. Can you imagine standing up in a meeting and accusing your pastor of a litany of charges without ever witnessing any of his offenses yourself? Thompson notes that this section in Deuteronomy deals with "the false witness who has been a menace to society in every age and among many peoples."[1]

According to the sixth amendment of the United States Constitution, a defendant shall "be confronted with the witnesses against him." A witness cannot make charges against someone and then hide out as the accused undergoes a trial. The accused must be able to face an accuser in court so his or her attorney can cross-examine that person. Proverbs 18:17 says, "The first to present his case seems right, till another comes forward and questions him." Many Christians believe that this legal principle comes straight from passages like this one. The Roman governor Festus refers to this principle when he told King Agrippa about Paul: ". . . it is not the Roman custom to hand over any man before he has faced his accusers and has had an opportunity to defend himself against their charges" (Acts 25:16). When Christians ignore biblical principles for seeking justice, the process tilts toward the *political* and the most vocal members prevail. It would be a shame if secularists obeyed biblical principles in a greater way than believers.

Second, *one witness is not enough to establish guilt*. The Bible says there must be "two or three witnesses" to a crime because one person can misrepresent an event. When I was in high school, I was walking home from school one day with a friend when we saw a motorcyclist run a stop sign, hit a car broadside, and fly over the car, landing on the pavement. (He was okay.) While I told the police what I saw, my friend – who later became a police officer – saw things a little differently. We both saw the same accident and differed on some details, and yet several witnesses can give a more complete version of events than one witness ever could, and this protects the accused from personal vendettas. Both Jesus and Paul quoted from this passage when they mentioned the necessity of having "two or three witnesses" establish the facts in a confrontation (Matthew 18:16; 1 Timothy 5:19) – and Paul's words to Timothy deal *specifically* with Christian leaders. John Stott comments:

> In the Old Testament two or three witnesses were required to sustain a charge and secure a conviction, especially in regard to a capital charge. The same principle applies in New Testament times, in particular when Christian leaders are being accused. Indeed, two or three witnesses are to be required not

only before an accusation is sustained, but before it is entertained at all.[2]

Third, *every charge against an individual must be investigated by an impartial body*. Israel's priests and judges were to make a "thorough investigation" before charging someone with a crime or offense (Deuteronomy 19:17-18). A witness could not say, "I saw So-and-So commit a specific offense" and be instantly believed. Their charges had to be tested. But sometimes groups – even religious ones – are able to secure the verdict they desire. Sir Thomas More (a Roman Catholic), who served as chancellor under King Henry VIII, was arrested for high treason and confined to The Tower of London for refusing to support Henry's right to be head of the church in England. While More successfully beat back the initial wave of charges, he was finally accused by Richard Rich (the king's solicitor general) of denying Henry's right to lead the church based on a personal conversation in More's cell. More was later tried for treason, and based on the testimony of *one* man, a jury quickly pronounced More's guilt and arranged for his execution.[3]

Isn't there something inside us that recoils when we hear that a private conversation could result in a Christian leader's death? By the same token, how can the public accusations of one person result in the besmirching of a pastor's reputation without corroboration? Shouldn't an impartial body be appointed to "make a thorough investigation?" Isn't this what Paul had in mind when he told the church in Corinth (1 Corinthians 6:1-8) that they should handle their own affairs without involving secular courts?

Finally, *if the charges proved to be false, then the accusers were to receive the precise punishment the accused would have received.* What Brown writes about societies applies even more stringently to Christian churches: "Any society is sick if people within it will lie deliberately in order to inflict harm on others. The Lord is a God of truth; he does not deceive us by anything he says. Therefore, the word of those who belong to the covenant community must also be reliable and trustworthy."[4] Deuteronomy 19:18-19 states that "if the witness proves to be a liar, giving false testimony against his brother, then do to him as he intended to do to his brother. You must purge the evil from among you." Please note that the law of *lex talionis* (known as "an eye for an eye") specified the *limit* of punishment. In the case of criminal action, the penalty should fit the crime.

A veteran Christian leader recently told me about his church's policy when staff members are accused of wrongdoing. Two women claimed they had seen a staff member engaging in inappropriate behavior. Their claims came to the attention of this leader (who oversees staff) and he thoroughly investigated the matter. While he concluded that the staff member did not use his best judgment, the leader exonerated the staffer from serious wrongdoing. One of the women was dissatisfied with this decision and began to repeat her charges to others. This leader then contacted her and warned her that if she did not stop her accusations, he would initiate disciplinary procedures against *her*. Her accusations ceased.

This step is missing in Christian churches today. We have created a climate where people can make accusations with impunity because they assume that nothing will happen to them. These accusations are often passed around the church in the form of gossip and are believed *before* the accused leader knows about them or can respond to them. When the court of church opinion goes against that leader, he or she may be asked to resign. What a travesty of justice!

Christian leaders need to find ways to incorporate the principles embedded in this Deuteronomy passage (not necessarily the penalties) into church life so we can protect our leaders from false and malicious charges. Since we expect pastors to use the utmost care when they confront wrongdoing in others, shouldn't pastors receive the same respect? But this passage is a safeguard for *everybody*. Isn't this the way *you* would want to be treated if *you* were accused of a serious offense?

One of the most disconcerting things about those meetings is that *friendships* seemed to trump *principles*. The friends of The Seven were more upset that their friends were upset than that their pastor was treated biblically. Since The Seven were absent, their friends carried their offenses for them and spoke for them in both meetings. (Many who attended the first meeting also stayed for the second one.) I also received a strong sense that many members were willing to believe charges without any evidence. Those who liked Kim and me appealed for patience to learn the full story while those who liked The Seven defended their friends while indicting us. It's been my observation over the years that if churchgoers are forced to choose between their pastor and their friends in a conflict situation, they'll almost always side with their friends.

In 1 Timothy 5:21, Paul warned Timothy to make sure that he always used proper procedures when hearing accusations against spiritual leaders: "I charge you, in the sight of God and Christ Jesus and the elect angels, to keep these instructions without partiality, and to do nothing out of favoritism." To me, this is one of the strongest statements that Paul ever made. When a congregation meets to deliberate about the purported failures of its spiritual leaders, all of heaven is watching to make sure that God's leaders are treated "without partiality" or "favoritism," regardless of their popular standing. While it's a challenge for a church to be levelheaded when the possible sins of its leaders are being discussed, it's essential that a leader be evaluated by impartial processes, not mob rule. If you *like* a leader, don't brush aside charges just because he's your friend, and if you *despise* the leader, don't overlook evidence that might exonerate him. Leas comments:

> Most significant conflict in local churches is pastor focused. More often than not, the pastor is the issue under discussion. Even in situations where the pastor is not the presenting problem, as people begin to approach issues in the conflict, the pastor's leadership becomes embroiled with the other substantive issues being addressed. Whether the pastor as a person, the pastor's leadership style, or the pastor's position on issues, or all of these are at stake, the church needs to be very careful to make sure that its dealings with the pastor are fair and appropriate.[5]

In a court of law, an attorney would have defended us and made sure that due process was followed, but we had no such advocate during those meetings. Because a handful of former leaders made claims, some people believed them even though the claims had not been tested. But how would *they* like to have been judged in that manner?

On that Sunday, I believed that the best way to protect the church was for me to keep my mouth closed. I wanted to help the church, not harm it. I wanted to see it unified, not divided. I wanted the truth to come out, but to be shared with love. Sitting in my front row seat, I was extremely disappointed with certain people in our assembly. It was one thing for some attendees to support The Seven while failing to support me. It was another thing for Christians to neglect the biblical procedures that I had once taught them from Matthew 18:15-20 and 1 Timothy 5:19-21. A few people claimed that the meeting wasn't the forum for such discussions, that the church needed to trust the transition team and wait for their work to be completed. But when people become anxious and angry, they are inclined to shortcut processes. Steinke observes:

> People vary considerably in how they address emotionally challenging events. On the lower (immature) side, people are *reactive.* They blame more often; they criticize harshly; they take offense easily; they focus on others; they want instant solutions; they cannot see the part they play in problems. On the higher (mature) side, people are more thoughtful and reflective; they act on principle, not instinct; they can stand back and observe. They are *responsive.* Intent and choice characterize their behavior.[6]

To this day, I cannot forget George's accusatory language and the way those meetings so quickly descended into chaos. Those words and images will live with me – and many others – for the rest of our lives. When the second meeting mercifully came to a close (and it was three times worse than the first meeting), I carefully observed who came up to speak with me afterward. Not many people did, but I freeze-framed in my mind anyone who had the courage to tell me they loved us or were praying for us. The primary people who approached me were either new to the church or on its fringe. It was important for me to know who loved us unconditionally, and I was disheartened that more people didn't come up to me, although some had to be undergoing shock. But I did see George's wife give her husband a high-five as soon as the meeting was over.

What I didn't learn until later was how many people were too irate to speak. A friend told me that if he had spoken up, he would have become uncontrollably angry and later regretted what he said. Others were simply too numbed by the accusations to say anything at all. I felt especially bad for newcomers and new believers. As accusations were fired around the room, many unsuspecting people were caught in the crossfire.

I took my son Ryan to a major league baseball game when he was three years old. We sat on the end of a row in the upper box seats. Late in the game, two fans got into a fist fight within a few feet of us, and to protect Ryan, I cradled him in my arms and ran up the steps to the refreshment area until security broke up the fight. Had we stayed in our seats, Ryan could have been harmed because the fighters were oblivious to others. While I'm all for candor in public church meetings, mature believers need to protect the innocent who can be hit by stray punches. After those meetings, some parties were so frightened that they *never* came back to the church. I wonder if they will ever go to church again *anywhere*.

In her brief but poignant book *Crying on Sunday*, former pastor's wife Elaine Onley describes a similar public church meeting that deeply wounded her and her husband. Once again, she was shocked at how many people became part of the "silent majority":

> Time and again the majority is defeated – not because of the 'power and influence' of the minority, but because of the debilitating silence of the majority of God's good people. Comments heard again and again (and my reactions to them) are:
>
> 'I just didn't know what they were talking about or what was going on, so I just sat there.' (If you do not know, stand up and ask.)
>
> 'I really wanted to stand up and defend him, but I was raised not to get involved in conflict.' (Get involved.)
>
> 'I was so hurt and angry, but I was afraid to speak up.' (Do not be afraid; your courage alone could raise the voice of the silent majority.)

'There was so much I felt and wanted to say, but, then I didn't want to offend "The Group."' (Why fear offending them? They certainly do not hesitate to offend the person whom you called to serve as your minister.)

It is far better to offend or anger others by standing for what is right than to spend the rest of your days bearing guilt and remorse, knowing that your actions or words might possibly have turned the tide of an evil deed. Remember: it is never wrong to do right.[7]

Reflecting on those meetings nearly three years later, I have come to three conclusions. First, *I do not believe that most people who attended the meetings really knew what was at stake.* The *presenting* issue may have been the resignations of key leaders, but the *real* issue was that a small group wanted to remove the pastor. Every person who defended the board was unknowingly throwing me to the wolves. I'm not sure that even George knew what was at stake, and in that sense, I believe he was used to send me packing. Laney cautions:

Frequently church members will want to get rid of their pastor and will accuse him of preaching too long, neglecting visitation, or starting a new program without church approval. While these issues must be resolved, they are not biblical bases for church discipline. We must make sure that the discipline is for a definite *sin*, not just a difference of opinion, personal dislike or hurt feelings.[8]

A friend of mine who counsels pastors and consults with churches for a living believes that the only two sins envisioned in 1 Timothy 5:19-21 are heresy or immorality, neither of which was true in our case. A spiritual leader can obviously be removed for other sins – murder comes to mind – but in our day, pastors are often forced from office because of their personal style or ministry philosophy, and neither one is inherently sinful.

Next, *I believe that Kim and I not only endured criticism but also abuse.* The consultant indicated as much in an email he sent me after the meeting. For some reason, good Christian people suddenly lost their heads. August Lageman once served as the pastor of a church where he believed he had been abused. His words are worth repeating:

> Congregations often give inordinate power to the most vocal members. People act out – attention getting behaviors, sibling rivalries, seduction, scapegoating are all performed on the congregational stage. While dealing with these issues requires skill and patience, it does not necessarily follow that being a pastor includes accepting abuse. I once received from my district superintendent, after the congregation's annual meeting, an anonymous letter enumerating my faults. I was hurt and angry. As I struggled during the week with the topic for Sunday's sermon, I finally decided to preach on the letter. I was able to vent my anger and explain why I did not think an anonymous letter was the appropriate way to deal with the issues. A year later the congregation's annual evaluation listed the 'ability to deal with criticism constructively' as my major strength. The message I conveyed was clear: I would deal with criticism, but I would not accept abuse. Pastors educate congregations as to how they expect to be treated.[9]

Several years before, I *had* done this educating, summarizing the findings of my doctoral project by preaching two biblical messages on conflict resolution. But God's people can forget such teaching if they don't put Scripture into practice immediately and consistently.

Finally, *the meeting that day was not structured as a court of law.* If someone is permitted to make public charges against a pastor or staff member, then the accused should be protected by safeguards, just like in American jurisprudence. There should have been (a) evidence to support the charges; (b) witnesses to go on record; (c) someone appointed to defend the accused; (d) an opportunity for a defender to challenge the evidence and witnesses; (e) a knowledgeable judge to oversee the proceedings; and (f) the opportunity to appeal any verdict, among other procedures. Since it takes time to set up those processes, when charges began to be bandied about the room, someone should have ended the meeting because it was starting to resemble a kangaroo court.

While some mainline denominations have processes for certain trials already in place, most evangelical and congregationally-run churches do not. For this reason, when pastors are even *charged* with wrongdoing, there are always people who instantly believe the charges and insist that the accused be removed from office to relieve congregational anxiety. While Paul insists in 1 Corinthians 6:1-8 that believers should not take other believers to court in front of unbelievers, he also signifies that local churches should be competent to judge certain cases involving their members. He asks in verse 2, "Do you not know that the saints will judge the world? And if you are to judge the world, are you not competent to judge trivial cases?" Paul asks again in verse 5, "Is it possible that there is nobody among you wise enough to judge a dispute between believers?" Paul seems to be saying, "It would be better to have the lowliest Christian in a local church serve as a judge between disputing believers than the most competent secular judge imaginable." But this doesn't mean that Paul was recommending that incompetent churchgoers preside over cases! It would be far better to select and train believers who have excellent integrity and judgment for this role.

When he was a pastor in Michigan, Ed Dobson established a Committee for Restoration and Healing at the church that he led. Dobson writes that this group "at any one time is handling twelve to fifteen cases: threatened divorce, business disputes, interpersonal strife. I'm not on that committee. They resolve most situations without my input."[10] Although Dobson's chapter on this topic is only eleven pages long, it's filled with practical ideas about resolving disputes that most lay people and churches could implement.

So many of the safeguards that make our country's legal system distinct – you're innocent until proven guilty, the punishment should fit the crime, witnesses need to be cross-examined – supposedly are mentioned in Scripture. And yet, why do we find more justice in secular courts than we do today in churches? While decrying injustice *outside* the church, we tolerate injustice *inside* the church, often against pastors. Roman Catholics can take unresolved complaints to their own internal court system, and even priests accused of abuse are given canonical due process rights.[11] But because pastors in congregationally-governed churches are rarely protected by safeguards when they're accused of wrongdoing and lack a court of appeal, an increasing number of pastors are turning to the secular court system for justice. Churches could avoid this trend if Christian leaders created transferable models for resolving such disputes. But when pastors suffer abuse and character assassination, they are told by other Christians, "You can't use the secular court system. *That* would be wrong!" While pastors are expected to obey Scripture, those who make charges against pastors know they can say anything in public and *nothing* will happen to them. Are there now two moralities: one for pastors and another for lay people? How is this biblical? I addressed this topic on my blog in an article titled, "Who Will Stop Me?"

> Hi. I attend your church. You don't know who I am, but I show up nearly every Sunday and sit in the next-to-the-last row on the left side.
>
> And it's ironic that I attend your church at all, because I don't like the pastor. I don't like his sermons. I don't like his kids. I don't like the schools he attended and the hobbies he jabbers about from the pulpit. I just don't like *him* – and for that reason, I'd like him to leave.
>
> The right thing to do would be for *me* to leave the church and attend somewhere else. After all, at this point I'm not aware of anyone else who feels the way I do. But I don't want to leave. I want to stay. I want *him* to leave.
>
> There's a quick way for me to pull this off: start making accusations against the pastor. It almost doesn't matter what I accuse him of doing: sleeping around, embezzling funds, fuzzy beliefs, power plays – you get the picture.
>
> I can accuse the pastor of various misdeeds through (a) a whispering campaign ('Did you hear that the pastor was recently seen . . .'); (b) a letter sent to select church homes ('The pastor doesn't believe in the virgin birth!'); (c) a few strategic emails ('The pastor has been seriously overspending funds recently'); or (d) conversations with my friends ('Why does he continually refer to that TV show all the time?').

Having done this sort of thing before, I know that one or two of my accusations will eventually reach the pastor, and he'll be very upset. But I also know my accusations will reach the ears of the governing leaders as well.

And even if my charges are taken seriously, no one will come and talk with me. No one will ask me for the evidence that my charges are true.

The pastor's supporters will disbelieve the charges immediately. His enemies (among which I count myself a proud member) will believe all the charges and more. (We've just been waiting for someone to articulate them.) It's the group in the middle that I'm aiming for. I just need to pick off a few to accomplish my goal.

By this time, a few people will add charges to the ones I've already made. It almost doesn't matter what they are or if they're true or not. The board may choose to investigate the charges, but if they do, they will almost certainly not be traced back to me. And if anyone tries to confront me, I will just do what they do in politics: deny, deny, deny.

My first attempt may not be successful. The pastor may survive my little campaign. But if I keep making small charges here and there, the wind will pick them up, and when they get to the pastor, they'll start to wear him down.

And then one of these days, the pastor will resign due to burnout or stress, or a small group in the church will add to my accusations and formally drive the pastor out.

The pastor will be told by the leaders of both the church and the denomination that he needs to leave the church to preserve its unity, that the church needs to start with a clean slate.

But no one will do anything to me. I have ecclesiastical immunity.

Nobody will sue me. Christians aren't to sue other Christians according to 1 Corinthians 6:1-8, right?

Nobody will confront me. After the board deals with the pastor, they'll be too tired.

Nobody will finger me. In the unlikely event that the leaders launch an investigation to find out who started the rumors, they would probably speak with others long before they got to me. If I caught wind of their efforts, I'd quietly slip out the back door of the church, wait a couple months, and then return. Nothing would happen to me.

Nobody will ask me to leave. After all, I'm allowed to attend services at the church of my choice, right? And when the church calls the next pastor, if I don't like him, I already know what to do.

Who will stop me?

Nobody.[12]

If I infiltrated a church and began to spread rumors about its pastor, most of my accusations would eventually harm the pastor as long as I kept pressing and could assemble a handful of bitter people around me. Since most churches lack formal, written guidelines for handling such accusations, I could conceivably drive a pastor from office, and if I visited other churches, I might even knock out some megachurch pastors along the way. Sounds diabolical, right?

Exactly.

When are Christians going to wake up and realize that all attempts to *destroy* pastors (rather than *disciplining* them) originate from Satan and not God? We are dealing with pure evil and can't fight it by looking away or trying to hush up matters. We have to discuss it openly and institute solutions or we're going to witness more pastors and churches decimated in future days. While the devil would prefer that Christians not know about or discuss this problem, it's crucial that we name it and expose it to the light.

I received a few emails at home after the meetings. Alexander, who helped me draft the church's governing documents seven years before, wrote me late that night to say that someone had contacted an ex-board member about their right to terminate an employee. Alexander quoted from the bylaws and then wrote:

This means there are two ways to end the employment of a staff member (other than the senior pastor): resignation or upon a recommendation of the pastor and subsequent approval of that decision by the board. If there were three ways, then the second to last sentence would have said: 'The employment of staff may be ended upon the submission of a written resignation to the board, upon recommendation of the senior pastor with the approval of the board, and by action of the board.' But that is not what it says. There is no power of the board to terminate unilaterally.

By the way, I wanted to check my conclusion with someone else, even though I have been a lawyer for 22 years. Another lawyer, who has practiced for over 30 years and is a senior partner of one of the largest law firms in the [region], reached exactly the same conclusion.

A prominent community member later sent me this note:

I have to admit that I was overwhelmingly saddened by the response and questions of one of the members at the information meeting between services two weeks ago. What he said and the anger with which he spoke made me weep in church. I could hardly come back in for the second service. Even worse, one other member who was crying like me said it was because she didn't trust the gentlemen selected and standing up front to do more than a cover-up job. I spent a good part of that day reading Bible passages that deal with conflict in the church of believers. In no way did what happened that day at church align with any of St. Paul's instructions regarding conflict in the church. Take very good care and please know that you are in my prayers.

But the best note of all came from an unexpected source:

> Dad,
>
> I just want to make sure that I let you know how proud I am of you right now. I am so impressed how you handled yourself today during each meeting. You really are an amazing man to be able to sit and take all the junk that was thrown at you. How you were able to keep calm and in control of yourself and your emotions is truly amazing to me. I know that you asked me today if I still love you after all this and I just want to say that after today I love you *EVEN MORE* than I did before. I have such a new level of respect and appreciation for you. And I can say with a full confidence that you are a man after God's own heart.
>
> I love you Dad and am proud and honored to have you as my father.
>
> Love,
> Your daughter Sarah

My church family may have been slipping away, but the events of the previous few weeks had drawn me even closer to my own family. At least I knew *someone* who really loved me.

TAKEAWAYS FROM CHAPTER 6

For pastors:

- Teach your congregation the wisdom of the process that Moses recommended in Deuteronomy 19:15-21 long before it's needed. Try and encapsulate that passage's principles in your formal documents, and make sure those documents are consulted if a conflict surfaces.
- Realize there are people in every congregation who do not like you and will say derogatory things about you in public if given the chance. Do not let this wound you severely. Your Savior

was treated the same way and yet was innocent of any wrong-doing. It usually says more about them than about you. (If they feel that way, why do they stay?)

For board members:

- If your pastor is under fire – either privately or publicly – he will be unable to manage any conflict directly and will require your assistance. If you support him, call a meeting, gauge the magnitude of the opposition, examine the validity of the charges, and begin the process of addressing the conflict in earnest. If your support for him is soft, ask one or two board members to speak with him privately *before* making any final decisions on his status.
- Long before you need it, make sure that your church has a written process for resolving disputes involving the senior pastor. If you lack the time or expertise to create such a document, check and see if churches you know might have one already.
- Never allow complaints about your pastor to be brought up in a public meeting if the pastor has not been confronted with the issue in private. Matthew 18:15-20 says to take matters to the church only at the *end* of an attempted restoration process, not at the *beginning*.
- If you leave your church and/or resign your membership, resist attacking the pastor publicly or you will be attacking the church as well. You strove for unity when you were on the board. Continue to strive for unity after leaving it or you will confuse and harm many people.
- If you choose to leave the church, then leave it for good. Do not invite friends from your former church to try out your new one. Do not try and influence matters in the church you left. Turn around, walk away, and find another fellowship.

For the congregation:

- Resist the urge to criticize your pastor publicly. Once you do this, you'll feel obligated to defend your allegations and even ratchet up your criticism so you won't lose face with others, but you may look foolish if any of your accusations are later proven to be false.

- Never destroy a leader's reputation in a public meeting. You will be doing Satan's work for him. Assume that leaders are innocent until proven guilty. Trying to destroy a leader ultimately harms you, your relationships, and your church.
- If you do speak in a public meeting, ask God to give you the courage, wisdom, and grace needed to influence your church family positively. One person *can* make a difference!
- If you cannot wholeheartedly support your pastor, it would be better for you to leave the church than to join forces with those who wish to remove him from office (which may haunt you for the rest of your life).

CHAPTER 7

UNDERMINED

7he next morning, I drove to the local Walmart and purchased boxes. I had no idea where we were moving, but I knew we had to pack and get ready to leave. Over the next few weeks, I constantly put boxes together, packed up belongings, and stacked them in the garage. I had heard about this kind of thing happening to other pastors, and considered myself fortunate that it had never happened to me, but now that it had, I felt humiliated. I sent Paul this email:

Thanks for your words at the meeting yesterday. It was the only defense I was afforded all day. We need a 'soft landing' right now. The transition team will be meeting tonight. I plan to spend very little time with them, just trying to separate me from the church. The sooner we leave, the quicker someone can come in and try and heal things.

We already have places we can live for a while as refuges when we leave. We'll be okay. I just need to know who I/the board should talk to from here. Thanks, Paul, for helping us this past weekend.

Paul's response:

> God bless you brother. After yesterday's meetings, I agree with your assessment. This has become an abusive, unsafe environment for you and Kim. I'm praying with a very heavy heart. I now believe that you should immediately go on medical leave (or unused sabbatical time) and that someone else should fill the pulpit for you. You must finalize your severance agreements with the TAT (or new board). One final thought: You will not always feel this way. I believe that there is a future for you in ministry.

Later that day, Paul sent me this note:

> Despite our best efforts, things seem to be rapidly going from bad to worse. In addition to the events of yesterday, I have reason to believe that preparations may be underway to recruit . . . members to forcibly remove you from office using the constitutional process.

Why did Paul feel that way? It's because several people called the church office that morning to ask for a copy of the membership roster. A woman we had always assumed was a supporter wanted to circulate a petition to establish an independent, congregationally-elected committee of five to investigate "any and all reasons" for the resignations.

The petition was viewed differently by various parties. Paul believed that the petition's intent was to remove me as pastor. A transition team member believed the petition was designed to discover why The Seven had really resigned. A friend later told me that the petition's aim was to dig up dirt on us. Since I had already decided to resign, the petition didn't threaten my job, only my reputation. But how would circulating a petition help at all? Because the congregation had become anxious, people wanted their pastor either to alleviate their discomfort or assume the blame. They unknowingly searched for a scapegoat, a concept also known as the "symptom bearer" in family systems theory:

However, the symptom bearer is not necessarily the 'sick' member of the congregation. The congregation as a whole is the carrier of the illness. Congregations can easily get caught up in blaming someone for all their troubles. The rest of the people then take no responsibility for their own part in the condition. A beginning sign of health is when persons stop blaming others and begin to take responsibility for their own involvement in the situation that is producing the anxiety.[1]

Fortunately, Alexander eventually talked down this woman from pressing the petition idea, although by that time, I was told she had collected the signatures of twenty members. In an email to a transition team member, Paul added:

My report is not materially changed by the concern over a possible constitutional ouster campaign. Jim and I have communicated yesterday and today that sadly this is the direction things need to go. However, the *urgency* of processing this for the protection of both the Meyers and the church became higher after yesterday . . . . Why take the chance? How much more should Jim and Kim endure? My concern is based upon people requesting constitutions and bylaws. And then, requesting a membership list.

In his final report to the transition team, Paul made the following points:

The dissidents in Sunday's meetings or potential petition campaigners should not be allowed to be in any leadership role for at least two years. The former board members have acted so extremely and destructively, that they should not be allowed to re-enter the fellowship of [the church] without time and genuine repentance for their inappropriate actions. (Their renewed presence will most likely prevent the deep wound from healing.) Former Pastor Norman, whose name has been interjected into this situation on several occasions, should not be allowed to become interim pastor. He should not be interacting with [the church] or its people during this difficult time.

(Steve [the new district minister] should be asked to help guard against inappropriate or unhelpful contact on Norman's part.)

Provided the evaluation of the transition advisory team finds no significant wrongdoing by Jim or Kim, it is suggested that they both voluntarily resign in order to: protect them from further attacks, protect Christ's church and best protect their future ministries. (They both have given so much for Christ and his church. I believe that God has a future for them in ministry.)

While Paul did not interview the former board members or associate personally (something he would have done as a conflict manager), he did witness firsthand the forces that attempted to harm us at the previous day's meetings, forces that originated with those departing leaders.

Would I hire Paul again? In a heartbeat. Because he had been a pastor for many years, and had a broad knowledge of church polity, he was able to enter our situation on a Friday (after receiving copies of our governing documents) and write a report on Monday that recommended a specific course of action. Denominational leaders are most concerned about the church. The consultant was just as concerned for the church as he was for my wife and me. He'd *been* there.

It was especially enlightening for him to witness the informational meetings firsthand. He knew *exactly* what was happening (the opposition was trying to force my departure) and he recognized the tactics involved. Although he wanted to keep a low profile, the explosiveness of those meetings forced him to walk to the front of the worship center and ream out the congregation – something I never would have done! While I understood why some felt he was a "homer," once he sized up the intentions of the antagonists, he did his best to shelter Kim and me from further abuse while offering beneficial guidelines to the transition team. I recommend that churches in similar situations hire seasoned consultants, although they can be expensive.

Where can you find them? In our case, I typed the name of a consultant I remembered into a search engine and spoke with him the next day. That consultant's organization then assigned Paul to our church, and he was hired. I would also contact other pastors, seminary professors, parachurch leaders, and Christian counselors to see who they might recommend. And Tom Harper has formed an organization called the Society for Church Consulting. They have a directory that recommends consultants who have been certified by their organization. You can find them at www.churchconsultation.org.

The transition team scheduled their first official meeting for that Monday evening. I was invited to attend the meeting after team members became organized. During our time together, I was concerned for the members themselves. At the previous day's meetings, while standing on the stage, they became targets because they stood with their pastor publicly. Some attendees vilified them as friends of mine who were biased even though they were people of great character and integrity. Since most people in the church were there because they liked my preaching or leadership in some way, wouldn't almost *anyone* I had chosen been a friend? Or was I supposed to identify my adversaries and place some of *them* on the transition team?

I believe that a few people knew in advance that I had chosen that team and that they came to the November 8 meetings prepared to discredit my choices. I had only told one person outside a tight circle: the associate pastor. Did he share that information with my detractors who in turn disseminated it to church friends? When I announced the names of the transition team, it wouldn't have mattered if I had chosen John the Baptist or Andrew the Apostle. Because those team members were connected to me, they were automatically considered suspect.

But the ex-associate wasn't the only person whose role in this conflict I suspected. Nearly twenty-two years before, Norman, the church's founding pastor, met me at a district Christmas event and invited me to meet him for lunch near his church, which I did several weeks later. As we shared our ministry wounds together, we formed a bond that lasted for years. Norman and I later met with a group of pastors every month for lunch, and we enjoyed a Christmas get-together with our wives in his home most Decembers.

Over the years, Norman had asked me to speak at his church a few times. When he was making plans to retire, he invited me to become his associate pastor and succeed him if matters worked out. I initially balked at his overture and sent him an email listing five reasons why it would be good to work together along with five objections. When he addressed the objections, I relented and flew to meet with the search team, which had already combed through eighty-five resumes. After preaching at the church, the board eventually issued me a call, and six months later, our family moved to the community surrounding the church. Although I preferred to see a succession plan in writing, I came to the church by faith and helped shape the transition. (I felt more matched to the church than any I'd ever served.) Ten months into my tenure, I received a 95 percent affirmative vote at a special election to call me as senior pastor after Norman retired. After we served eighteen months together, I became the church's second lead pastor upon Norman's departure. With a few minor exceptions, I felt the transition went smoothly.

Norman attended a Sunday service at the church about a year after his retirement, and as we were going to lunch, he relayed that he was hearing good things about the ministry. I reminded him that wouldn't always be the case and hoped he would support me regardless. Not long afterward, I visited Norman and his wife in their new city, taking them to lunch and spending the night in their home. Several years later, when they visited our community, Kim and I invited them to our house for dinner. I assumed we would remain good friends and colleagues. Although Norman had moved out-of-state, I wasn't worried about him undermining me. When the two of us worked together, I had his back whenever someone complained about him, and he had mine. I assumed that arrangement would continue unabated.

But the night I attended the transition team meeting, Paul confirmed that Norman was involved in the conflict and had advised the church board. By listening to people's complaints, he validated them which emboldened them to take further action against me. I have reason to believe that a small group was hoping that Norman would return to the church so they could have their beloved former pastor back – nearly eleven years after his departure. The man who asked me to be his successor provided counsel for my detractors, which helped to hasten my exit.

When a pastor with a long tenure leaves, some members fail to grieve his loss adequately. Whether he led them to Christ, baptized their children, or counseled them through crisis, some believers have room in their hearts for only one pastor. Steinke writes:

140

Common to many church families is the unworked grief that surrounds the loss of an endeared pastor. Unable to let go and move ahead, some family members remain too emotionally attached to their Jacob or Esau. Regardless of the means of the pastor's exodus – replacement, retirement, forced resignation, or death – there is separation anxiety. Not resolved or managed, the anxiety turns into rejection of the new pastor, withdrawal from the family, or fervid attempts to fuse with the newly assigned or called pastor.[2]

Research from The Alban Institute indicates that a new pastor who comes to a church after the long tenure of the previous pastor almost always becomes an intentional or unintentional interim ("the sacrificial lamb"). The style of the long-term pastor has been so imprinted on the church that his departure produces conflict.[3] Fortunately, the congregation had gotten to know me during the eighteen months that Norman and I served together, and after he left, I constantly let the church know how grateful I was that he believed in me. While I knew a few people would never fully accept me, most churchgoers handled the transition with maturity.

Those few people at the church who knew of Norman's involvement told me it was irrelevant, possibly believing that any problem between us was simply an interpersonal clash. But I wondered to what extent ministerial guidelines had been ignored. Since few lay people know that such codes exist, let me share two examples describing the relationship between a predecessor and his successor to demonstrate the consensus around this issue. The following guidelines are directed toward a departing pastor and come from the United Methodist Church:

Make no disparaging remarks about the work or life style of a predecessor, successor or other ministers . . . . The former pastor shall avoid all conversation and communication with church members about the new pastor, as well as problems and issues regarding the former church. If approached, the former pastor needs to tactfully explain that ethics do not permit such a discussion.[4]

And these guidelines come from the Presbyterian Church USA:

> The former pastor best honors their ordination vows by exer-
> cising self-restraint regarding the business and spiritual well
> being of the congregation: he/she may maintain *friendships*
> with members of the congregation, but must avoid spoken,
> written, or electronic conversations regarding policies, prac-
> tices, people, or programs of that congregation insofar as they
> might be perceived as attempting to influence decisions or rela-
> tionships within that congregation. Under no circumstances
> may the former pastor make public (or likely to be made
> public) statements or offer opinions critical of the interim or
> new pastor or pastoral staff.[5]

When a pastor leaves a church, he offers that congregation and
their new leader the gift of neglect. While he may pray for the welfare
of the church and its pastor, he should not interfere with the way the
church is governed, or chooses its leaders, or spends its money. If he
does become involved, the church may splinter into camps, some following the former pastor while others follow the current one. While
the ex-pastor may never witness the division that his interference
causes, his involvement may negate much of the good that he did as
pastor – but few churchgoers have the courage to say, "Knock it off
and go away." Besides, those denominations that provide a code of
ethics usually don't enforce them. While it may be torture for a former
pastor to keep his mouth shut, that's his divine assignment. (John the
Baptist *never* interfered with Jesus' ministry.)

When some pastors leave a church, they cut off all ties with former
parishioners and refuse to interfere in church life so everyone can move
forward. (One pastor I'm familiar with has announced that when he
retires, he's moving far away so the next pastor can lead without any
intrusion.) But other pastors stay informed about their former church and
maintain friendships with people there, and some pastors even remain
as members. With permission from the current pastor, an ex-pastor can
even return to conduct weddings or funerals or do guest speaking. But
the longer a pastor led a church, the harder it is for him to break away
from it. It's part of who he is. Yet after a pastor departs, his friends need
to censor their conversations about anything negative that is happening

inside their fellowship. If they want to complain to someone about their current leaders, they need to speak with the appropriate parties *inside* their church. The *last* person they should share with is the former pastor. In fact, before a pastor leaves a church, the board should give him a code of ministerial ethics and tell him that they expect him to abide by it. Then if a governing leader suspects their former pastor is unduly influencing current churchgoers, he can contact that pastor and remind him of his professional obligations. If a pastor interferes with a former church, the chances are poor that his role will be revealed or that anyone will correct him. Such pastors operate in the dark and assume that their sabotage of a successor will never come to light. Since most denominations lack a way for one pastor to file a grievance against another pastor, we have to trust God to right any wrongs.

I always supported Norman in public. In fact, I invited him to speak at the dedication of the new worship center four years before and read a letter of commendation to the congregation. I then presented him and his wife with a plaque honoring their achievements, and composed the text myself. The plaque was hung in a hallway in the building constructed during Norman's tenure. While I will always be grateful for the opportunity he gave me, I will never understand why he thought it justifiable to assist my detractors in their efforts to remove me from office. Several years before these events occurred, I removed my ordination certificate from its frame to look at the signatures on the back of the pastors who had voted to recognize my call to ministry, and I was surprised to see that Norman's signature was one of twenty-three that day. He was present as I officially *entered* ministry – and nearby as I officially *exited* ministry.

After spending an hour with the transition team that Monday evening, I told them that I was placing my career in their hands and needed to separate myself from them so they could work independently of me. But I trusted them and thankfully, they justified my trust. After praying with them, I ventured out into the autumn air, aware that my days at the church were numbered.

Alexander called me after the meeting to say that he didn't see how I could remain as pastor. The Seven had made so many accusations against me that some of them stuck in people's minds. He also told me that the associate pastor ultimately harmed my standing. If he had stood with me, I could have survived the board's resignations, but because he aligned himself with them, I could not stay. Alexander also recommended that Kim and I avoid coming onto the campus for a few weeks until a new board was elected, and we honored that request (with one exception) even though we were entering ecclesiastical purgatory. In addition, he told me that I could not serve communion with any credibility in the minds of some members. That statement hurt me a lot. I loved serving communion, as most pastors do, and considered it a great privilege to lead people into focusing on Christ's death for us. It suddenly dawned on me that I had performed my last baptism, child dedication, wedding, and funeral as well.

But I was most bothered by the fact that I couldn't preach anymore. When the board met with me on October 24, they told me that I was a gifted teacher. But now the outcries of The Seven and their allies meant that I couldn't preach until my final Sunday, which was the most devastating blow of all. The penalty seemed so severe that I may as well have committed spiritual felonies.

Laura sent us the following email the next morning:

> I want you both to know how much I appreciate you and your dedication to the Lord . . . and your friendships. I have spoken to some of our members and they do support you as our pastor and the meeting the other day does not necessarily represent the body . . . so whatever you decide to do know that you are loved and have many friends . . . One or two voices do not represent this body . . . remember that! God is now in control . . . You fought the good fight . . . . And I hope and pray you are staying at [our church].

Before we went to Moldova, we assumed that everyone supported us except those few we knew who stood against us. But after the November 8 meetings, we assumed people *didn't* like us unless we heard some explicit expression of love. Maybe we weren't interpreting matters correctly, but that's how we felt at the time.

I don't ever want to feel that way again.

On weekdays, Kim and I devoted ourselves to packing our possessions, while on Sundays we didn't know what to do with ourselves. The Sunday following the November 8 meetings, we didn't attend church anywhere because we felt too exhausted. We read Scripture and prayed together and then rested for the remainder of the day. That's how we spent the next few Sundays as well. Going to church *anywhere* suddenly felt very dangerous.

At the November 8 meetings, I had invited people to contact me if they had questions, and some began sending me emails wanting to know what was happening. For example:

> Please explain to us what is going on. There is much gossip going around. We just want the truth.

And this one:

> I am wondering if you can shed some light on why the board and Roger resigned over activities at [our church]. I have not heard anything from others at church and will feel better hearing it from a source vs. hearsay. If you don't mind emailing the situation, I would appreciate it.

Because I knew that any emails I sent would likely be forwarded to others, I was extremely careful with my replies, although I did answer everyone who wrote me. I had to wait for the transition team to complete their work, for a new board to be chosen, and for Kim to meet with the bookkeeper before I could say anything of substance. Every fiber of my being wanted to reveal the whole story to select individuals, but I had to wait for other events to transpire first.

Several friends provided us with updates, and the biggest news concerned the composition of the new board. My charter for the transition team was to receive board nominations from the church body. However, because some in the congregation were skeptical of the transition team, those leaders just wanted to get a board in place and move out of the way. But someone devised a selection process that made me wince. At a public meeting, members were allowed to nominate *themselves* from the floor to be board members. Eight individuals did just that. Then the following Sunday, the congregation was told to vote for six names, and the top six would become board members. This procedure did not incorporate any vetting process (other than verbal and written testimonies and public answers to a few questions) and meant that people who weren't biblically qualified, were emotionally dysfunctional, or had criminal backgrounds *might* end up as official church leaders for the next one to three years. I sent the team leader an email expressing my concern about this process.

After the names of the eight nominees became public, I visited the church office to vote. (After all, I was still a member.) If you couldn't attend the meeting that weekend, you had to go to the office and cast your ballot in the presence of the office manager. When the results of the election were made public, the new board consisted of three men and three women. Two of the male board members knew about the conflict firsthand, so I later shared my story with the remaining man. Since the three new female board members hadn't heard my version of events, I scheduled a meeting with the woman I knew best who had pleaded with me in an email to reveal my story *before* she was elected. Her conclusion after we met: you are our pastor, and we want you to stay. But I told her that I couldn't stay.

And yet, I began having second thoughts about leaving. Since my primary adversaries had left the church, who was left to lead any opposition? If I struck a deal with the new board, maybe I could stay, although I didn't know about Kim's position or health. Evidently there was some talk about Kim resigning and giving me a larger salary so we could survive financially.

One night, I spoke with two transition team members about my chances of remaining as pastor. I was told that 95 percent of the people were behind me, meaning that 5 percent opposed us. (That was the same percentage breakdown when I was elected pastor.) But I was told candidly that if I stayed, I had to be prepared to fight, and it might take five years to defeat the opposition. Five years? I had no idea they were that determined. Had they covertly opposed us for a long time? Or was their opposition triggered by the resignations of The Seven? While Kim and I both knew a handful of people who didn't like us, we assumed they didn't have much influence, and they didn't seem to have any natural leader. Before the conflict surfaced, I was unaware of any substantive complaints about me from churchgoers except for one person who ironically claimed that the board always complied with my wishes. Maybe *some* people approached the board to complain about me, but I was unaware of any discontent with my ministry. In fact, as far as I knew, my struggles were with the board as an entity, not with any of the individuals on it.

One pastor friend urged me to stay and defeat the opposition. He told me that several pastors who had experienced an involuntary exit attended his church and were miserable because they couldn't find new ministries. If my wife had been in better health, I might have taken time off and returned with renewed strength, but because she was so brittle emotionally, I decided that we could not endure any more conflict. (And the church needed healing as well.) While we overwhelmingly had the numbers on our side, the opposition seemed more determined – and much more vocal – than our supporters.

When I first became a pastor in my late twenties, I was appalled at how many pastors in our district were forced to leave their ministries because they were opposed by a handful of antagonists. As a rookie pastor, I met on a monthly basis with the district minister and other area pastors for lunch, and whenever I heard about a pastor who was forced to resign, I wanted to know why it happened and how he was faring, especially since I had become friends with some of those pastors. The dominant impression I received was that each minister resigned because "he had it coming" and that lay leaders reluctantly handed out the treatment he deserved.

For example, one pastor in our district told his congregation in frustration that they "didn't give a damn" about a certain issue, but because the pastor used the word "damn" in a public meeting (not a church service) some leaders believed that he had disqualified himself from service. But I wanted to know *why* he used that language. When I first entered the district, this pastor took a special interest in me, and if he became so incensed that he used emphatic language inside church walls, then maybe some detractors pushed him over the edge. Another pastor friend was forced to leave his church because his daughter had been falsely accused of an offense and he resigned to protect her. (The truth came out sometime later.) But in district circles, we rarely heard about unhealthy *congregations*. Instead, the implication was that if a pastor was forced out of office, you could trace his departure to something *he* did or said wrong. The very *presence* of conflict indicated his guilt. It's like saying, "Caiaphas is furious; the Pharisees are incensed;

Pilate is anxious; the mob is unruly. Who is responsible? It must be the fault of that man hanging on the center cross."

So early in my career, I learned how district leaders viewed pastors who experienced a forced exit. The pastor was usually blamed for whatever conflict occurred. Upon hearing the news that another colleague had resigned, I would call that pastor and ask him why he left, and every man was transparent enough to tell me. Then I'd ask, "How many other district pastors have called to express their concern?" The answer was *always,* "You're the only one." As I recall, in my first several years as a pastor, seven colleagues were forced to leave their churches, and every one told me I was the only minister who called, which broke my heart. I later did a study of pastors in our district and discovered that out of sixty pastors that had departed, fifty were no longer connected to the denomination. I felt so strongly about this issue that I wrote an article for our denominational magazine titled "Who Cares for Lost Shepherds?"

Why don't pastors demonstrate more concern for their colleagues who experience forced exits? Maybe pastors have enough happening inside their own churches to reach out to peers, or they wouldn't know what to say to a colleague, or they don't want to become embroiled in another church's issues. But my guess is that most pastors don't want to associate with anyone they perceive as a loser. If you're forced out of a church, the perception is that you must be incompetent, immoral, or ignorant of church politics. There is something wrong with *you*, not the church, and if you were smarter, you wouldn't have such problems. For example, I recently heard a seminary professor refer to a leadership structure he utilized when he was a pastor, stating that he never really had a major conflict with a congregation over two decades of ministry. Translation: If you handled matters *my* way, you wouldn't have *any* conflict.

But this sentiment seems arrogant to me. Jesus wasn't crucified because *he* was unhealthy but because the political and religious leaders of his day were spiritually rebellious. Paul wasn't chased out of European cities because anything was wrong with *him* but because his hearers were hostile toward the gospel. (Were all Paul's problems with the churches in Corinth and Galatia *his* fault? Doesn't he usually place the responsibility for church troubles at the feet of the whole church rather than single out certain leaders?) It's popular to say, "If the team isn't winning, fire the coach," but some pastors have led their churches to growth and yet are forced to leave because the pow-erbrokers feel less significant as the church expands. While a small percentage of pastors deserve termination, the great majority who are involuntarily sacked have done nothing worthy of banishment. Goetz recommends that denominations keep better records of forced exits to identify repeat-offender churches and suggests that denominations discipline churches that slander or abuse their pastors.[6]

Most pastors simply aren't tough enough to handle a conflict when they're the target. I once had dinner at the home of a professor from my seminary and asked him why pastors aren't taught "street smarts" in school. He said that the accreditation committee required academ-ically-oriented core classes and that most practical ministry matters could only be addressed through electives. Although I *did* take an elective course on conflict management in seminary, there were only eight students in the class.

While the lack of "street smarts" training may contribute to the way pastors wilt in conflict situations, most pastors are attracted to ministry because of their tender hearts, which are easily broken when they sense they're being unfairly criticized. Although politicians are content with merely winning elections – even if they prevail by a slight majority – most pastors feel wounded when even one dissident raises his voice. This is why it's imperative for lay people to be trained and empowered in conflict management. When a pastor is attacked, he cannot manage the conflict either emotionally or tactically. He needs additional help from inside the church.

According to Charles Chandler, 77% of all pastors are *feelers* on the Myers-Briggs scale, while 23% are *thinkers*. When a "feeler" is asked to leave his church, he feels crushed and may choose to leave quickly. (Do "thinking pastors" tend to fight back more often against attempts to force their resignations?) Nearly all the pastors I know who have undergone a forced exit have regretted that they did not share their stories with people they loved. In the process, many people who remained in that congregation assumed the pastor was at fault and broke off all contact with him. Friendships built up over the years were demolished within a short period of time.

I was determined that was not going to happen to me.

TAKEAWAYS FROM CHAPTER 7

For pastors:

- If you're leaning toward resigning, ask several people to be honest with you about your standing in the church. Be prayerful. Seek counsel. Think it through. Do not cut a deal fast just to alleviate your anxiety. A hasty exit may harm your health, your family, and your career.
- Put together a support group of pastors (preferably from various denominations) and meet with them regularly. If you ever need their assistance, they'll already be in place.
- Do your best to get along with your predecessors but realize you may be able to do little along official lines about their machinations.

For board members:

- If you mistreat your pastor, it may haunt you and your church for years to come. If you treat him with class, even if you don't think he deserves it, the Lord will reward you.
- Christian leadership requires that you consult Scripture before injecting corporate practices into church life. Master and implement those passages that discuss handling charges against spiritual leaders (Matthew 18:15-20; 1 Timothy 5:19-21).

For the congregation:

- Love your pastor in a practical fashion. When he preaches well, write him a note or send him an email and tell him so. Let him know you're praying for him. One sincere compliment may lift your pastor's spirits for weeks.
- Defend your pastor when he is absent. Insist that anyone who criticizes him either talk with him directly (if it involves a personal offense) or speak with him or a board member (if it involves church policy).

CHAPTER 8

LEAVING MINISTRY

*A*fter the November 8 meetings, I knew we couldn't stay at the church and would soon need to move from the area. But The Seven weren't going anywhere. While they had left the church, they still maintained their homes, jobs, and friends. Soon after we left, the interpretation of our departure would be scripted by The Seven and their allies, not by us. We didn't want the church's future or our legacies tarnished by baseless charges, so as the occasion arose, Kim and I arranged to share our version of events with selected friends in private settings. Sometimes it was in a restaurant, or over the phone, but we believed that it was important to tell our story. Since we couldn't have a public trial – and we would have welcomed any fair process conceivable – we were forced to defend ourselves. Some Christians believe, "You don't have to defend yourself. The Lord will defend you," but that's not always how real life works. Didn't Paul defend himself before magistrates on multiple occasions in the Book of Acts? Isn't the entire book of 2 Corinthians a defense of Paul's apostleship and ministry? In fact, aren't the Four Gospels both evangelistic and apologetic documents? No one at the church volunteered to be a truth squad for us. If our side of events was going to get out, *we* had to do it, at least initially. And if we didn't, then Satan's version could tarnish the *church* for a long time.

One pastor friend told me that when he was forced to leave his last ministry, he told the church that he would vigorously pursue a defense of his character and ministry – and it didn't hurt that an attorney friend remained within the congregation. Bill Hybels comments:

Some people say a pastor should never defend himself, but obviously I think differently. When the apostle Paul felt that the church of Corinth was not understanding his role, essentially he said, 'Excuse me. Pardon what I'm going to do here for the next few minutes, but I'm going to tell you the price I've paid to carry out my apostolic calling.' And Paul proceeded to recount his shipwrecks and beatings for the sake of the gospel. I see that as a way of defending himself. Sometimes we have to do that to keep our heart pure.'[1]

When being publicly criticized, a pastor must determine *how* he will address his critics. While I wanted to openly and honestly address people's concerns, I lacked a healthy way in which to do that. As I discovered firsthand, if a pastor says nothing, some people will believe his critics. If he stands in the pulpit and defends himself against the latest rumor, he will appear hypersensitive. Pastors sense they're walking through a minefield during such times.

I knew that after our departure, we would be accused of various offenses because we weren't nearby to clarify matters, and it happened true to form. For instance, I was blamed for not supporting someone's pet social cause, for the lack of success in someone's ministry, and for hiring my wife as a staff member (even though that arrangement produced significant growth). When you're not present to rebut charges, a mythology forms about what really happened, and as the mythology hardens, no amount of reality can overcome it. Many people – even Christians – prefer to believe falsehoods rather than face uncomfortable truths about their friends or themselves. In fact, most believers evaluate a leader on the basis of how much they *like* him or her rather than how *effective* that leader really is. As this anonymous poem puts it:

There was a preacher whom I used to like. I thought that he was great.
His sermons were wonderful – as long as I liked him.
His speech was passing fair – as long as I liked him.
He lived a clean life – as long as I liked him.
He was a hard worker – as long as I liked him.
He was the man for the job – as long as I liked him.
In fact, I was strong for him – as long as I liked him.

But, he offended me one day. Whether he knew it or not, I do
not know.
Since that day, he has ceased to be a good preacher.
His sermons are not so wonderful – since he offended me.
His speech is of no account – since he offended me.
His faults are more prominent – since he offended me.
He is not a hard worker – since he offended me.
He's not the man for the job – since he offended me.
In fact, I am trying to turn everybody against him and get rid
of him – since he offended me.
It's really a shame he's changed so much.

One person that I wanted to meet with was Steve, the new district minister. I had known Steve for two-and-a-half decades and appreciated his pastor's heart. One November afternoon, we met for lunch and I shared my story with him, and he listened well and seemed supportive. Pastors usually have mixed feelings about trusting denominational leaders. Because pastors confide in few people, they are glad when someone offers them a listening ear, but when district officials know too much about a pastor, they might not be inclined to recommend him to a prospective church someday. In his study of forced exits among pastors, LaRue states that "respondents are divided over the helpfulness of their denominational supervisor. Equal numbers found this individual to be 'very' supportive (23%) and 'not at all' supportive (23%)."[2]

Pastors usually don't confide in people within their own churches because many of their problems concern others within that church (like staff, board members, or antagonists) and they don't want their feelings circulating. As pastors eventually discover, we have four types of confidants: friends outside the church, ministry colleagues (pastors, missionaries, and professors), Christian counselors, and our wives. (LaRue's survey surprised me when he stated that only one in five pastors who have experienced forced termination sought out a Christian counselor.[3] I would have guessed the percentage was much higher.) But since psychologists cost money, our colleagues are busy, and friends may live far away, our wives receive the brunt of our struggles. For this reason, if there is a job harder than being a pastor, it's being a pastor's wife. In his study of forced exits, LaRue claims that "the best source of support for nine out of ten married pastors comes from the pastor's spouse."[4] But where can she go when *she* needs support?

After the conflict went public, Kim and I consulted with two counselors. Although they can be expensive, even a few sessions with one can be enlightening. Many pastors and staff members who experience an involuntary exit choose to swallow their pain and move on with their lives, but inevitably, the hurts of the past end up surfacing in unhealthy ways. We wouldn't think twice about spending thousands of dollars to deal with a serious physical issue. Why then are so many pastors reluctant to consult a Christian counselor over emotional and mental issues?

One of the biggest clouds hanging over Kim concerned the charge that she had overspent funds from the outreach and missions budgets. Since we had not seen documented evidence of her alleged offenses, she could not defend herself effectively. She just knew that the figures that were initially relayed to me were incorrect. Finally, one month to the day after the October 24 meeting, Kim met with the church bookkeeper to sort through her recent expenditures. (They had to wait until all the bank statements arrived.)

One of the revelations from their meeting concerned funds that had been wired to Moldova in October after our mission team left for Europe. Because our team didn't want to carry a large amount of currency into a Communist country, two church staffers sent money to a bank in Cahul, a city near the village where we were staying, and I was present when a pastor friend collected those funds. While Kim had authorized the wiring of a specific amount, the staffers sent an additional $2,000 – much more than should have been sent. Evidently someone chose to send along additional funds, but Kim did not know about or approve this action. The bookkeeper told both Kim and me that the board never asked her about the funds, but this expense was undoubtedly added to her budget overrun. But wasn't this really a "team foul?" How could anyone blame Kim for wiring too much money when it was simply a misunderstanding? And how could anyone fail to contact her or the bookkeeper to discover the truth? If a prosecutor had made a similar error, his whole case might have been thrown out of court. If you're wrong with one calculation, couldn't you be wrong with others?

Kim was overjoyed as she reviewed her spending. While she could not exonerate herself, the transition team or the new board could. As it turned out, Kim's combined budgets through 2009 showed that she had exceeded her allotted amounts by a small sum. (This specific information was never shared with the congregation.) While I would have preferred that her budgets be in the black, was barely ending the year in the red worth throwing a church into consternation?

Feeling better, Kim asked me that same night if she could read the board's resignation letter, which I had purposely kept from her. I forwarded it to her computer, but after reading it, Kim was so distraught that she wanted to take legal action against The Seven for violating her rights. Once again, I told her that wasn't an option for us. Besides the time and expense of a lawsuit, Christians who sue each other are not viewed with favor in the larger Christian community. And yet, at times that seemed like the only way to receive justice.

A few days later, the Lord gave me an idea. I told Kim that each of The Seven was going to settle their accounts with her immediately. I offered her a specific dollar amount per leader if she would consider the matter settled, and she agreed. As I gave her the first amount, I told her, "Okay, So-and-So is now settling with you." Kim then went shopping, and with each item she bought, she thanked the board member who had made it possible. One day, she mentioned someone's name and said, "Thank you for my shoes!" While this was only a cosmetic solution to her anger, it allowed me to tell her, "Let's stop thinking about legal action. They all settled with you, remember?"

We both suffered from another condition that created great anxiety: we no longer knew who to trust. While we were grateful for those few people who sent us cards or emails or flowers and said they were praying for us, we wanted to know if our church family, whom we had tried to love unconditionally, would love us that way in return. The answer was yes in some cases and no in others. Since we were asked not to come onto the campus for a few weeks, we had no way to assess directly how specific individuals felt about us anymore. We both knew the identities of those who opposed us. (Most pastors and their wives do.) And we surmised that most people were confused about the charges they were hearing and didn't know what to believe – but it hurt us that *anyone* drank the Kool-Aid.

Three years after our departure, many people still do not know why we left. A pastoral colleague shared a possible explanation with me. As charges circulated against us, people knew us so well that they refused to believe them. Instead, they said, "No, that can't be it. It must be something else." I've heard several guesses as to why we left, and they aren't even remotely true, so I can only wonder what kind of mythologies people believe. But by this time, most people will believe whatever they want. There isn't much we can do to change anyone's mind. We have to leave our reputations and our legacies with the Lord.

On Thanksgiving evening, Kim and I began to discuss an issue with a realtor friend that we wished to avoid: the selling of our home. We had owned our home for six-and-a-half years, the second house we'd ever called our own. While I didn't mind leaving the area, I wished we could take our house – which looked like a rustic cottage from the outside – with us. But we couldn't stay. When we lived in one well-populated area years before, we could visit malls and restaurants without running into anyone from our church for months, but in this community, we would see people we knew practically every day. Besides, four former board members lived within a mile of our house, and we preferred not to bump into them.

One morning, Kim and I made the mile-and-a-half trek to the local grocery store and ran into a couple from church that we knew supported us. When they expressed concern for us, we began telling them how we *really* felt about the conflict. Although we spent only five minutes with the couple, Kim and I were both appalled at the rage inside us. We couldn't seem to restrain ourselves concerning the unjust treatment we had received. How could we stay in that community without experiencing healing first – and how could we be healed if we stayed in that community?

The first Wednesday in December, I was invited to meet with the new board. Steve, the district minister, was also present. The board listened as I assured them I did not want to recriminate against anyone. Someone asked if I would take questions, and I agreed. The first question was, "Are you going to try and reconcile with Roger?" I told the questioner that I was not aware that *I* needed to reconcile with *him*. (In my mind, we had always gotten along well both personally and professionally.) After Roger resigned, I had two telephone conversations with him, and my last statement to him was, "I hope we'll always be friends" after which he uttered the same sentiment back to me. But at the November 8 meetings, I discovered that Roger had been collaborating with the former board. I told the questioner, "I assumed we were friends. But he turned against me. He needs to reconcile with me." This was not a perspective the board had yet heard. When pastors leave their churches abruptly, how many false charges are later made about them without anyone refuting them?

I fielded other questions and then showed the board an anonymous note that had come in the mail that day. The typewritten note demanded that Kim and I resign with the word RESIGN in capital letters. I just laughed when I saw it because this attempt to scare us was so pathetic. On occasion, I have been so upset with someone that I *felt* like sending them an anonymous note, but I desist when I remember how cowardly that behavior is. How can the recipient respond to the writer? And how can anyone accurately weigh the complaint or complainer? But the note's timing signaled that there were people who would do or say *anything* to see us leave the church.

Finally, I told the board that Kim and I had chosen to resign. Three board members already knew that was my plan, but my announcement took the others by surprise, and for the next few minutes, there was a lot of weeping and hugging. One leader told me, "You're the only pastor I've ever known." Even in my weary state, God gave me the grace to minister to those leaders one last time. After the meeting, I ordered two books for each person focusing on the board's role and asked that they be charged to my account. When the new members joined the board, they may have assumed they would be working with me, but the Lord had other plans. After I spoke in-person to the new board, I lobbied for Kim to address them as well. The following week, she finally did. Here is her account:

I wanted a voice. No one allowed me to have a voice during the whole time. My counselor finally told me, 'We're going to give you a voice.' Because I hadn't been to church for weeks, I was afraid of being at church on our last Sunday. My counselor told me, 'You need to go – just pretend you're an ambassador of grace and love.'

I finally met with the board. I went in and we just talked. Then the board prayed for me for about fifteen minutes. Each board member prayed for me, and it felt good. I wasn't sure they believed my viewpoint because the new board members were friends with the old board members, but at least I got it done.

The transition advisory team was working on their report as to what caused the conflict, and during their investigation, they contacted Roger and all six ex-board members. Fair enough. However, the team failed to interview Kim other than to ask her a single question via email. Before a trial in a court of law, Kim might have given a deposition, but in this case, her account of events was considered irrelevant. I spoke to various team members, trying to discern why they didn't interview the principal player in the conflict. They said they already knew Kim's side but had not yet heard the side of The Seven. Maybe the transition team didn't want to make Kim feel any worse emotionally, but once again, she felt like she no longer mattered.

Several months after our departure, the new interim pastor met with Roger and the ex-board members to hear their stories. The interim claimed publicly that he had interviewed all parties relevant to the conflict, but he never spoke with Kim. (If he didn't interview her because she had left the church, then why interview The Seven who had also left?) Kim long suspected that a few male leaders didn't think she should be a staff member because of her gender, and when she wasn't interviewed by the interim pastor, she once again felt unimportant. The interim's failure to interview Kim made me wonder if we were both being cast as convenient scapegoats. After all, the former board members still lived in that community, but we had moved hundreds of miles away. If people chose to blame us for what happened, how would we even know about it?

One evening in early December, I was told that an ex-board member was circulating still another charge against us, one that could easily be refuted. (I later heard *another* charge bandied about concerning a practice that I had openly been engaging in for years, but *now* it was wrong.) This development told me that ex-board members felt free to make additional charges against us because they didn't have to convene and record decisions in the official minutes. They could say whatever they wanted without facing us directly and hope that some churchgoers would believe them. These charges also told me that The Seven were not going to stop criticizing us simply because *they* had left the church. Since we didn't know who was making these claims, or how many people heard them, there wasn't a fair way to address them. If we were accused of a specific offense, and we successfully answered that charge, two more charges would appear. It's like playing that Whack-a-Mole Game at Chuck E. Cheese. As each mole springs from its hole, you smash it on the head to pound it back into its hole, but several additional moles instantly emerge. Painful as it was, Kim and I knew we had to leave our beloved church behind. Addressing the latest rumor, the bookkeeper sent me an email the following day, calling it "ludicrous" and stating that "whatever people are saying or thinking just isn't true." She assured me that none of the former board members had ever contacted her to inquire about any misspending. If her statement was accurate, the board chose not to use their single best resource for interpreting expenditures. It still baffles me how they could assume the worst about us when we had been known quantities in the church and community for nearly eleven years.

It wasn't long before a new board member scheduled an appointment to discuss separation agreements for us. I was glad we were even having the discussion. Leas observes that "if differences with the pastor end in a dissolution of the relationship, consideration should be given to the pastor for length of service, opportunity to find other work, need for retraining and financial need."[5] By contrast, one of my pastor friends, who served his church for nine years, received only two week's pay and a plaque after he was forced to resign, and he quickly lost his medical insurance. Only four in ten pastors who undergo a forced exit receive a severance package, and even then, it's only equal to three months.[6] Goetz writes:

> Another suggestion is for denominations to encourage churches to provide forced-out pastors with a standard severance package worth six months of salary .... Not to care eco-

nomically for forced-out pastors, it seems, is to muzzle the ox when it is on its knees. Plus, larger severance packages might cause churches to pursue reconciliation rather than termination.[7]

I have heard some professionals recommend that a departing pastor receive one month's salary for every year he served his church. I wrote on my blog:

While some board members might exclaim, 'I would never receive severance pay like that at my job,' please realize the following facts about pastors:

- They are ineligible (in most cases) for unemployment benefits.
- They and their family members will suffer tremendously. It is common for the older children of a terminated pastor to stop attending church and even leave the faith. The wives of terminated pastors go from being somebodies to nobodies overnight. If the marriage has already been strained by ministry, the couple might head for divorce.
- The terminated pastor is sometimes in so much pain that he turns to alcohol, drugs, or illicit sex.
- They will lose almost everything dear to them by being terminated: their careers, their income, their church family, their local friends, their house (if they have to leave the community and sell), and their reputations – in other words, they will lose their life as they know it. (This is why pastors often hang on in a church long after they should leave.)
- They will be stigmatized as a 'loser' in much of the Christian community. As a veteran pastor told me when I first entered the pastorate, if a pastor resigns with no place to go, it's the 'kiss of death.' If he applies for another church position, his resume will most likely go to the bottom of the pile because he was fired from his previous church. The Christian world is very small and word gets around quickly.
- They will often suffer constant depression, great anxiety, and feel like God has abandoned them.
- They will be shocked to discover that most of their ministry colleagues will turn away from them.

- The terminated pastor usually has to rebuild his life and ministry, and that takes time. The separation package allows for the pastor to pull away from ministry so he can take stock of his life and begin the healing process. If the pastor is given a token severance package, the pastor and his family will feel that he has been 'kicked to the curb' and it will take them a long time to forgive those who hurt them.

We talk a lot in the church today about *social* justice. This is *ecclesiastical* justice.

If a board cannot or will not give the pastor a generous separation package, then it needs to think twice – or ten times – about letting him go. Getting cheap here borders on being unchristian.[8]

Uncomfortable as it was, I shared with the leader what I felt was fair. Those funds would allow us to move from the community and become established elsewhere so we could discern the Lord's next assignment. I also asked that the board provide funds to foster our healing. After consultation, this leader informed me that our requests would be granted with minor exceptions. All I had to do was fall on my sword and submit a resignation letter to the board which would be read the following Sunday. Here is my letter:

December 6, 2009

Dear Michael,

This letter is to notify you that I am resigning the office of senior pastor of [the church] effective December 13, 2009. Kim is also resigning her position as outreach director effective the same date.

Over the nine years that I have served as your senior pastor, the Lord has done many amazing things in our midst. We have seen a steady increase in church attendance. We have seen people come to faith in Jesus and be baptized. We have reached out to our community in various ways with God's unconditional love. We have built a new worship center together on our property. We built a well in a remote village in Kenya. And we sent four missions teams to Moldova. I will always look back with gratitude for the partnership we have enjoyed together. We love you and will miss you very much.

In my humble opinion, [our church] is the best church in [our city] because of you, the congregation. I have told everyone I know that you are a gracious and generous church. You were already this way when we came here in June 1999, and my prayer is that you will continue to demonstrate these qualities in the days ahead. As Paul wrote to the church at Philippi, 'He who began a good work in you will carry it on to completion until the day of Jesus Christ.'

I encourage everyone to stay at [the church] and pray for the new board you selected and for the staff who remain. They will need your encouragement, support, and love.

May Jesus Christ continue to be glorified, worshiped, and preached in and through [this church]! Keep building Christ's kingdom!

Even though I was privately fighting my emotions, I learned the following adage years ago: "The way you leave is the way you will be remembered." Kim and I wanted to be remembered for the way we loved the Lord and his people while trying to expand his kingdom. If we engaged in blistering public attacks on those who harmed us, it would negate much of what we had accomplished. It was better to ignore the mistreatment in public and thank people for the privilege of serving the Lord in their midst.

While I had read my own resignation letters in previous churches, neither of us wanted to read our letters this time. We were concerned that someone might shout "Amen!" or applaud, so the new chairman read the letters instead. We were later told that the congregation was shocked and that the atmosphere afterward resembled a memorial service. Because Kim and I wanted to attend worship that morning as far away as possible, we made a forty-five minute drive to a church in another city. When we walked up to the worship center, we ran into a family who had once attended our church but had moved to a new community. When we briefly explained that we were moving, the husband instantly offered to help us load our things into a moving vehicle. (Up to that time, I had no one to help us move.) Thankfully, the Lord was watching out for us.

What would be the best way to describe my departure? In the past, there have been only two categories in Christian circles to describe the way a pastor left: either he resigned voluntarily or he was involuntarily terminated. However, Hoge and Wenger use *three* categories to describe why a pastor leaves a church: "involuntary leaver" (a pastor forced out against his will); "voluntary leaver due to pull factors" (a pastor leaves for a new occupation); or "voluntary leaver including push factors" (a pastor isn't forced to leave, but push factors were clearly present). Concerning the latter option, these authors state, "The minister in such a situation ponders the pull and push factors and makes his or her decision based on the influence of both."[9] Using their terminology, my situation could best be described as "voluntary leaver including push factors." It's quite a mouthful to share with others, but it does lead to fascinating discussions!

When I appointed the transition team in early November, I hoped they would create a process for selecting a new board and write a report as to what caused the conflict. As it turned out, the team chose not to publish their report. LaRue states that two-thirds of the churches that force out a pastor don't reveal the real reasons for his departure to the congregation.[10] However, Faulkner believes that members have a right to know such information and will create their own facts if they don't have it.[11] (Full disclosure eliminates church leaders from telling people, "If you only knew what we know.") All five team members still valued us as friends, so I assumed they hadn't discovered any major offenses. If the report had been issued, I'm certain that people on all sides of the conflict would have found reasons to disagree with its conclusions. Since I didn't have anything to hide – what people were saying about me was far worse than reality – I would have welcomed its publication, but I respect the judgment of those who decided otherwise.

As if matters weren't bizarre enough, I received an email from a new board member on November 30 informing me that Carl, the youth pastor, was now planning to resign. Carl had reported directly to Roger but now wanted to leave the church as well. Was he weary of all the conflict? Was he upset that his supervisor had resigned? Whatever the reason, maybe the tension in the hallways became too much for this intelligent young man. Several staffers told me that after the conflict became public, Carl isolated himself from the other staff. The damage inflicted by unresolved conflict spreads deep, far, and wide.

Because December 13 would be our final Sunday, I didn't want Carl's resignation to clash with our departure, for both of our benefits. So I drove to his house unannounced and spoke with him in private. I updated him about the conflict and encouraged him to let us have our farewell separate from his, and suggested that after January 1, he could resign and complete one full year of ministry. He seemed to consider my idea, but as it turned out, Carl's resignation *was* read to the church on our final Sunday, and sadly, most people forgot about him. His departure meant that the top ten leaders all resigned within six weeks of each other.

My theme on our final Sunday was "Go for It!" My outline was simple. I told my church family that I wanted to "thank you, remember you, encourage you, and challenge you." My tone was positive and upbeat. I asked Kim to compose something that I could read to the church on her behalf, and I read this note in the middle of my message:

Dear Church Family,

It was ten-and-a-half years ago Jim and I accepted the responsibility of pastor and wife at this church. It has been an honor to serve you in that role. Supporting and loving my husband is very important to me. I have been proud to serve alongside Jim and to be his partner in loving and meeting the needs of the people at this church. You, as the congregation, have been so wonderful to our family. We will never forget you and will always see you as our extended family. Thank you for loving us.

In March 2001, eight-and-a-half years ago, I joined the staff at our church as director of outreach. This was a wonderful privilege and a big responsibility. Together, we have been taking risks to reach people in our local community and abroad.

I believe that outreach is the passion of the church. People are dying every day without Jesus and searching for meaning in life. But we have the good news of Jesus and the answer to life.

Because of you, our church has reached out to many, many people through special events held at our church and off campus . . . . Because of you, guests who come for the first time feel welcomed and accepted. They have the opportunity to join small groups or become involved in ministries. Thank you for letting people know that they matter to God! Continue spreading good rumors about the church! Invite your friends, co-workers and neighbors to the church so that they may hear the good news of Jesus Christ.

Thank you for sharing your enthusiasm and generous funds to spread the good news abroad. Because of faith, a well was built in Kenya. Because of faith, a pizza house was built in Moldova. Six short-term mission trips were accomplished to build up the churches in Moldova and Kenya. May you continue to spread the gospel of Jesus Christ.

Last of all, I thank you for your perseverance in ministry, and for each volunteer that gave of their time to see the church become stronger each Sunday. Continue to serve our Lord Jesus Christ with joy and stay strong against the devil who wants to discourage you.

And then I said this about Kim:

I am married to a woman who dreams dreams and sees visions. Quite frankly, she thinks so big that I often get exhausted just listening to her talk. We'd go out to eat and I'd want to talk about our kids or our next vacation and Kim wanted to talk about going to Kenya or the next big event at the church. But I am so glad for the way the Lord made her.

After recounting some of her many accomplishments, I concluded:

> All of our staff members work hard. But Kim usually went above and beyond the call of duty. There was a time we used to watch *CSI* together on Thursday nights, but Kim usually didn't make it home because she was meeting with someone or finishing a project. She often went out on her day off to take someone a meal. She has the biggest heart of anyone I've ever known and touched the lives of everyone she met in some way. I have always said that her tombstone is going to read, 'She made people feel special.' Kim, you have been a gift from God to me and to those who know you. Thank you for who you are and all you have done. I love you!

This was the only time during our ministry that I recall complimenting Kim like this in public. In fact, I usually let other people lift her up when she did well so I didn't appear to be biased. However, it was fitting that I listed a few of her many accomplishments on that final Sunday. During the first service, no one responded after my recitation, but during the second service, Kim received a standing ovation, public recognition for her faithfulness and productivity over many years. Since Kim hadn't attended a service at the church for nearly three months, the ovation told her that she was still greatly loved by many in the congregation. While it was a healing moment for her, it probably ticked off those who felt otherwise.

During my message, I told the congregation that this was my final day as pastor and that I did not want people to call me and complain about church matters in the future. I mentioned that any interim pastor wouldn't be better or worse than me, just different – and the same would be true of any new senior pastor. While I was trying to tell the congregation that it was unethical for me to interfere in church affairs anymore, some took my words to mean that they would have to break off all contact with me, although that was *not* my intention. While we still have friends in that church, we hear from fewer of them as time goes by. Sadly, when we lose contact with someone, I wonder if they've turned on us as some others have.

After both services, some people came to the front of the worship center to say goodbye and have photos taken with us. Had I remained as pastor, the campus would have felt unsafe to Kim. If you've ever been dismissed from a job, imagine how you'd feel about returning to that place on a regular basis. Kim recalls that last Sunday:

> I will never forget Jenny and Darrell and our daughter Sarah meeting me in the patio area and telling me, 'We're going to shield you from any enemies.' I felt protected. I felt like they were lifting me up by their elbows.

> The services were packed like usual. Some of the people who came were people we had impacted when we first came to the church. Some were bawling their heads off. I looked out and saw people we wanted to say goodbye to but couldn't. I remember two people who told me, 'This is not right.' They felt just awful.

> During the second service, people clapped for me – after all these years. After both services were over, I was saying goodbye to people, and I saw two women, one of whom had greatly harmed us. Without my saying anything, I was escorted off the stage and told, 'It's time to go.'

In our case, churchgoers were not given enough time to say goodbye to us so they could begin the healing process. While I offered to stay a few weeks and help with the transition, I sensed that some influential individuals wanted to hustle me out of the church. While I understood their thinking – the sooner Jim leaves, the more quickly we can begin to heal – the church lacked any kind of *pastor*. There is a reason why many church documents require a pastor to give at least a thirty-day notice before departing. Over the years, many people view their pastor as their spiritual father. They see him every Sunday at church. They seek his counsel in person, via email, or over the telephone. They ask him to baptize them, visit someone in the hospital, or dedicate their infant to the Lord. The whole pastor-parishioner relationship is built on love and trust, and before a pastor leaves a church, he will want to spend sufficient time saying goodbye to certain individuals. If I had been allowed to stay thirty days after my resignation (through the end of the year) rather than the seven days I was given, I believe I could have helped church healing accelerate. But my departure left a huge vacuum, and without a shepherd, some people remained in pain and eventually left the church. As in thousands of similar cases, there was not enough time between our resignations and our final Sunday for any of us to say goodbye adequately. Church consultant Loren Mead writes:

> Emotions we have about pastors are often highly charged. Pastors trigger feelings – good and bad – in those they work with in a congregation. Remembering experiences with past pastors is quite likely to touch levels of people's lives that are not touched by anyone other than a family member, parent, or sibling. Losing a pastor can be a hard emotional blow, triggering all the emotions of grief – it is not strictly a rational exercise.[12]

To their credit, the new board made provision for the congregation to contribute toward a departing love gift and to sign a large farewell card. Kim and I were deeply touched by those who wrote us a note. One woman even gave us her tithe for the month. Most people only had a few days to decide how they wished to say goodbye. But as we discovered shortly after our final Sunday, some people didn't even know we had resigned. The day before we left town, Kim and I ran into a woman from the church that had been on vacation. She was shocked to hear of our departure and began to cry. She didn't have any time to process what had happened.

Some people that I valued as good friends never communicated with me in any form after the November 8 meetings. After seeing them on Sundays, serving with them and counseling them, they suddenly vanished. It took years to develop those relationships, but it only took a few hours for some to end. Some of these friends were present on our last Sunday but did not speak with me and probably never will again. Whenever Kim and I experienced a crisis, we turned to church friends rather than family members because our church family was readily available. While we would have to do unspeakable things to be ostracized from our families, unfounded allegations of wrongdoing prompted some in our church family to turn their backs on us. While I viewed many churchgoers as both parishioners and friends, some people simply viewed me as their pastor, easily replaced by the next one.

Then there were those wonderful people who loved us unconditionally. Some were convinced we were completely innocent. Others may have believed we were guilty of minor offenses. Still others may have been confused by everything being said but chose to stick by us anyway. And some were caught in the middle between the affection they felt for the pastor and his wife and the respect they had for The Seven.

Kim and I reviewed our friends on Facebook and "unfriended" anyone we suspected stood against us. We didn't want them to be privy to our plans or our feelings. While some might have advised us to delete our Facebook pages altogether, we needed to feel like we still had friends. Looking back, I'm glad we both kept our Facebook pages. When we finally moved away, it was a way for us to connect with people we still valued.

Kim and I have always been as inclusive as possible whenever we've thrown a party. If we invited the young couples or the seniors to our home, we'd invite every name in the directory. We planned a final get together at Laura's home on our last Sunday, but we only invited friends who still believed in us. If someone explicitly told us they supported us, we invited them to our party, but we didn't invite anyone whose loyalties we questioned. While our attitude might seem uncharitable, the betrayals against us had been so painful that we could only associate with people around whom we felt safe.

The night after the party, Kim and I read the cards and letters that people had given us. We were grateful for each person who chose to express their thoughts to us. We wept as we realized that we would never see most of our church family again this side of heaven. For the past fifty days, we had been forced to think almost exclusively about those who had rejected our leadership. (It's hard to think about your allies when an angry army is pursuing you.) But now it appeared that everyone had laid down their arms. For a brief time, we could think about the past ten-and-a-half years and thank God for all he had accomplished through us.

How I wish that the good feelings we felt that night could have been permanent.

TAKEAWAYS FROM CHAPTER 8

For pastors:

- If you do resign, try and give multiple reasons for your departure. Make your letter brief, positive, classy, and uniting.
- It is *not* divisive to tell selected friends the truth about your situation in private. It *may* be divisive to plan or approve any counterattack.
- Be open to consulting with pastoral counselors. They have heard similar stories and can give you insights and help you assess your options.
- It's difficult to release a ministry that you've built, and it's especially sad to leave a congregation that you love so much. But we have to learn how to let go and turn the reins of leadership over to Jesus. Isn't it *his* church to begin with?

For board members:

- During a major conflict – no matter what you do – expect that some people will resign their offices, while others will leave your fellowship.
- If your pastor leaves without a new job in place, offer as generous a severance package as you can. Trust that God will eventually replenish those funds.
- When a pastor leaves the church, be as classy as you can on his final day. Arrange for refreshments. Ask people to bring or sign cards. Let people show their appreciation through an all-church departure gift. Give him a great sendoff! These expressions of love do not signify that you *approve* of all the pastor's actions but that you *appreciate* his efforts and wish him well in any future endeavors. If you don't arrange for such a time, you will short-circuit the grief process for your congregation. You don't have to *feel* love to *give* love. The way you say goodbye to *this* pastor will carry over to the *next* one.

- If possible, allow the pastor to have a minimum of thirty days to say goodbye to the congregation. Pastors feel violated if they cannot have this time, and many churchgoers will remain unduly attached to their ex-pastor if they are not given time to grieve his loss.

For the congregation:

- Realize that if the pastor resigns, he may not want to leave your congregation. Try to be gracious and understanding toward him. He does not want to abandon you.
- Arrange for some photos to be taken of you with the pastor on his last day. Over the years, Kim and I have greatly treasured pictures with believers we cherish.

CHAPTER 9

RECOVERING

*T*hroughout my ministry, I have been blessed to serve with many splendid board members. Whether they were called elders, deacons, or just "members of the board of directors," I have always worked well with governing boards. Whenever I was attacked by antagonists, the entire board supported me, especially the chairman. I suppose I came to expect this support.

In our last ministry, one man in particular stood with me whenever I was under fire: Robert. A pastor's son, Robert had once experienced a sickening church split. Reluctant to join the board initially, Robert became chairman for two years, and I enjoyed working with him because he was thoughtful, fair, and wise. I valued his judgment, and when he told me I needed to rethink an issue, I listened. Robert let me know that he always had my back, and he kept his word. On those rare occasions when someone became upset about a leadership decision, Robert would explain the board's position and calm the person down – and he would inform me when those incidents occurred. I trusted him fully and continue to trust him to this day. Had Robert still been on the board – or even in the church – I am confident matters would have been handled in a more biblical and sensible fashion. In fact, if I had been serving with *any* of the boards from the past, I believe matters would have been handled with greater patience and wisdom. Robert believed that if there was a conflict between the pastor and the board, it was his job as chairman to mediate the conflict, not side with either party. Every pastor needs a Robert who will tell you the truth to your face but support you when attacked from behind.

In the spring of 2009, Robert retired from his profession, and he and his wife sold their home and purchased a house near the ocean. They also bought a second home near family in the Southwest. Robert was one of the first people I contacted after the October 24 meeting, and we regularly discussed the latest developments. Somewhere along the line, he invited Kim and me to stay at their second home until we discerned our next assignment, which took enormous pressure off of us. While we knew we had to leave the community, we had no idea where to live, and we didn't want to be a burden to anyone. Robert's place was about thirty minutes from members of my own family. Kim and I had lived nearby years before and knew the area well. The Lord was already starting to provide.

The day before we left our community, Kim and I took one last trip to the large city near our home. While Kim shopped, I waited outside and heard a rendition of "Silent Night" broadcast through loudspeakers. Instantly, I became distraught. For the first time in a decade, I wouldn't be leading a Christmas Eve service. (We always ended the service with "Silent Night"). But more than that: for the first time in our lives, we did not have a church home.

The week before Christmas, we jammed our Honda Accord with possessions and drove to our son Ryan's house. We had no jobs, no prospects, no church family, and no house to call our own. Half our belongings were in a moving POD near our new home and half remained at our old place. For the first time ever, our kids didn't visit *our* house for Christmas. When we attended a Christmas Eve service at Ryan's church, I became extremely distressed, recalling how many wonderful such services we had enjoyed in our former church. After my father died, I remember how empty our family felt during each holiday because he wasn't present with us. Now that I had been severed from my church family, I felt a similar emptiness.

We enjoyed Christmas Day at our son's place, but had to repack our things into the Honda the following day. Kim and I finally left for our new temporary home late that afternoon, and as we turned onto the freeway, she began to sob uncontrollably. When we finally arrived, we thanked God for a safe place to stay while we recuperated from our nightmare. Neither one of us really knew how complicated those recoveries would be.

We knew that we would eventually have to forgive those who hurt us to make progress in our lives, but we weren't ready to do that initially. The wounds were far too fresh. Kim and I constantly tried to figure out the motivations of those who injured us because their actions seemed opposed to the gospel. Whenever we got in the car or went out to eat, we would talk about what happened. Even when we sensed that our loved ones were sick of hearing from us, we still rehearsed the injustice, trying to make sense of events that didn't make any sense.

One Sunday, as we drove toward a new church, Kim and I briefly discussed past events, and by the time we pulled into the parking lot, she didn't want to attend worship. So we drove into the country and talked matters through until we came to a temporary resolution and returned home. Because our emotions were so unpredictable, we chose to isolate ourselves from everyone but close family and caring friends for many months. Such feelings make you feel like you're abnormal, and to be honest, many believers act like there is something wrong with you if you express them at all. Thank God for Christian leaders like the always human Charles Spurgeon:

> A child of God is not expected to be a stoic, for God's grace takes away the heart of stone. When we endure trials, we feel the pain. Do not ask to be made hard and callous, for this is not how grace works. Grace makes us strong to bear trials, but we still have to bear them. Grace gives us patience and submission, not stoicism. We feel, and we benefit by the feeling. There are some who will not cry when God chastens, and there are some who will not yield when God strikes. Do not be like them! Be content to have Job's suffering heart (Job 1:21). Feel the bitter spirit and the anguish of soul which racked that blessed patriarch.[1]

If some kind of clear, corrective process had been used by the former board, we both would have cooperated with it and stayed at our former church. But no such process was ever suggested. We continually beat ourselves up trying to discern what we had done to deserve such mistreatment. We replayed events repeatedly, trying to compile timelines that made sense.

About a month after moving, I received a call from a new board member asking if we could give redacted copies of our separation agreements to them so they could show the old board we did not intend to pursue legal action. I instinctively agreed. Although I hadn't yet forgiven them completely, I didn't want them fearing that a lawsuit would be delivered to their home or workplace. After redacting the agreement myself, I sent it to a new board member who distributed copies to the former board. Maybe this small gesture could begin the healing process.

Like most pastors, I have preached on forgiveness many times. People struggle most with forgiving friends, relatives, or work colleagues who have severely violated them. Sometimes the offenders are believers, sometimes not. On occasion, a Christ-follower will even become angry at an entire entity such as a company or a church. While it's challenging to forgive *individuals* who have hurt us, it's even more daunting to forgive an entire *group* or *population*. Yet that's what Jesus did from the cross when he cried, "Father, forgive them, because they don't know what they're doing" (Luke 23:34). This classic statement during our Lord's greatest torment has inspired generations of believers. Let me relate three truths about this verse to our situation.

First, *Jesus did not directly forgive those who placed him on the cross.* He did not cry out, "*I* forgive them . . ." No, he asked his *Father* to forgive them. As Jesus stated in Mark 2:8-11, he had the power to forgive sins unilaterally, but on this occasion, he asked the Father to forgive on his behalf. Why did Jesus do this? Did he ask the Father to forgive because none of his attackers had given evidence of repentance? Was it better for him to delegate the forgiveness of monstrous offenses to the Judge of All? Whatever his reasoning, there is nothing wrong with me asking the *Father* to forgive someone's offenses. I can do as Jesus did and say, "Father, I ask that *you* forgive them for this particular offense." After all, the Father is a perfect forgiver while I am an imperfect one.

But some Christians point out that Scripture commands believers to forgive each other directly. For example, Paul writes in Ephesians

4:32, "Be kind and compassionate to one another, forgiving each other, just as in Christ God forgave you." Paul adds in Colossians 3:13, "Bear with each other and forgive whatever grievances you may have against one another. Forgive as the Lord forgave you." If we returned to our former community, and we could arrange to sit down individually with those who harmed us, we could tell each one personally, "I forgive you for hurting me." But when you're hundreds of miles away, and you might never see those people again, how do you express forgiveness? Do you speak into the air and say, "I forgive them for this particular offense?" Do you tell the Lord that you forgive them? Do you send those who hurt you an email or a card and tell them, "I have now forgiven you?" (They might counter with, "For what? We didn't do anything wrong.") Do you verbally direct your hurt to an empty chair, imagining that one of your antagonists is sitting there? How does a believer forgive people without speaking to them directly? And how completely can you forgive someone who denies any need to repent? Greenfield addresses these issues:

> When I was pressured to retire early in my last pastorate by the machinations of a small group of antagonists, I wrote each one a lengthy personal letter describing how I felt about what they did to me, my ministry, my marriage, my family, my health, and my future. I tried to be honest without being harsh. I felt they needed to know that they had hurt me deeply. Not one of them wrote in response, called me, or came by for a visit. Not one said he was sorry. Therefore, I had to move on with my life, shattered though it was, and start over somewhere else.
>
> For my own sake, I needed to forgive them even though none said he was sorry. I tried to do that even though it took me a long time. I wrote to each one that I was forgiving him of his mistreatment of me, knowing it would be a process rather than something instantaneous. I had to do it for myself. I did not expect reconciliation, but I did need to be free of my resentment . . . . I could not afford to put my future happiness in the hands of those people who made me so miserable by their abuse of me.[2]

Second, *Jesus called on the Father to forgive "them."* Who does the term "them" refer to? In context, it refers to the Roman officials and Jewish leaders who conspired together to execute an innocent man who also happened to be divine. Jesus lacked the wherewithal to mention the names of each offender, so he classified everyone together. In our day, governmental and religious leaders don't agree on almost anything – and they agreed on little in Jesus' day, either – but Jesus would never have been crucified unless both groups worked in concert (Luke 23:12). Jesus' example from the cross indicates there will be times when his followers must forgive (a) federal, state, and local governments; (b) spiritual leaders of all stripes; (c) those who have violated us yet remain anonymous; and (d) individuals that hide inside a larger crowd.

Does this mean that Kim and I could say, "Father, forgive them" and rest assured that the Lord knew the identities of our offenders? Or did we have to forgive each person by name for each offense they had committed against us? Neil Anderson believes that for each person we need to forgive, we say, "Lord, I forgive (name) for (offenses)."[3] I understand this recommendation but remain puzzled why Jesus did not use this formula on the cross. Is there only one way for me to express forgiveness? And once I have expressed it to the Father, must I express it directly to those who have wounded me?

Finally, *Jesus asked the Father to forgive those "who do not know what they are doing."* Jesus says there are people who do wrong and yet think they are doing right. They are "well-intentioned dragons."[4] On this occasion, some people believed that executing Jesus on a Roman cross was the right step for the government to take. But Jesus' words signify that they missed his true identity, violated their own procedures, and failed to discern their real motives.

Kim and I kept repeating this phrase for the first few months after our departure: "Father, forgive them, because they don't know what they're doing." If someone asked, those who harmed us would probably say they knew *exactly* what they were doing. But as I told the board at the October 24 meeting, they really *didn't* know the forces they were unleashing, which subsequent events have borne out. But just like Jesus, we *had* to forgive them, the sooner the better. During a conflict, people may act confidently, only to realize years later that they sinned grievously. Leas observes:

Over a number of years I have learned a great deal about conflict from my personal experience and from many congregations with which I have been privileged to work as an outside consultant. Through many successes and failures I have learned that when people differ from one another, when they are upset with one another and when they are frightened, they do not handle themselves or their situation well. I have learned that no one knows how to make others be good or to handle themselves in a way that is just right so that the conflict will go away and everyone will live happily ever after.[5]

However, several issues made us pause before we forgave our former friends. For starters, the greater and deeper the losses, the longer it takes to forgive completely. We hadn't just lost our jobs, but our incomes, our friends, our reputations, our lifestyles, and possibly our careers as well. In Kim's case, she lamented the loss of a house that she dearly loved. (We had recently remodeled the kitchen, installed wood floors, and repaired extensive water damage, but the house was seriously underwater financially when we listed it for sale.) Although it took us ten months to sell the house in a short sale, I was ecstatic (because we were free from the financial obligations surrounding the house) while Kim wept (because that house represented stability). In addition, moving from the area meant that we no longer lived in proximity to our daughter Sarah. The losses seemed to keep mounting. Wickman observes that "the pain of a forced exit is a wound that never fully heals."[6]

In addition, at least eight leaders/friends turned against us, and those same people attacked my wife to harm me. It's hard enough to forgive one person who betrays you, but *eight Christian leaders*? It's almost too much to bear. Yet if we *didn't* forgive them, we'd be emotionally chained to them for a long time, and we wanted to be free. Anderson writes:

If you don't let offenders off your hook, you are hooked to them and the past, and that just means continued pain for you. Stop the pain; let it go. You don't forgive someone merely for their sake; you do it for your sake so you can be free. Your need to forgive isn't an issue between you and the offender; it's between you and God.[7]

Five months after leaving our former church, Kim and I took the step together. We bowed our heads and asked the Father to forgive each person by name who hurt us. This was unilateral forgiveness and signified that we no longer held their offenses against us and wished them well in the future. When a pastor experiences a forced exit, forgiving offenders unilaterally is the only realistic option because he can forgive them privately without having any personal encounter with them. In individualistic Western cultures, unilateral forgiveness has become the norm because broken relationships are the private property of the disputants rather than the community.

However, conflict expert David Augsburger states: "In more collective cultures – traditional cultures, the biblical worldview, the contemporary two-thirds world – the understanding of forgiveness is that it is not a private act of intrapsychic release but instead a truly social transaction of interpersonal reconciliation."[8] Using this paradigm, forgiveness is a mutual transaction, the kind that Jesus envisions in Luke 17:3-4: "If your brother sins, rebuke him, and if he repents, forgive him. If he sins against you seven times in a day, and seven times comes back to you and says, 'I repent,' forgive him." Augsburger comments:

> The first sets the offended person free by releasing all resentment, all claims for recognition of the injury by the offender, all demands for repentance and restitution . . . the second is a mutual recognition that repentance is genuine (repentance by one or both parties) and right relationships have been restored or achieved.[9]

The challenge for a believer is both to forgive an offender unilaterally and to strive for relational restoration. Sande writes:

> When an offense is too serious to overlook and the offender has not yet repented, you may need to approach forgiveness as a two-stage process. The first stage requires *having an attitude of forgiveness*, and the second, *granting forgiveness* . . . . Pray for the other person and stand ready at any moment to pursue

complete reconciliation as soon as he or she repents. This attitude will protect you from bitterness and resentment, even if the other person takes a long time to repent. Granting forgiveness is conditional on the repentance of the offender and takes place between you and that person (Luke 17:3-4).[10]

Before we left the church, a person I respected wrote me and lamented the fact that I did not agree to the board's offer of mediation. Although the consultant advised that I counter with another mediator, I realize this allowed people to say, "See, he doesn't want reconciliation – he just wants his way." But around the time I resigned – when I had zero authority – I told a key church leader that I'd be willing to admit I had made some minor mistakes if some of The Seven would agree they had erred in some fashion as well. Reconciliation could not occur unless those who attacked us could admit they had made *some* mistakes, although if even one person did that, they might feel disloyal to their group. My hope was that my overture might begin some kind of healing process, but I don't know if my offer was ever passed on to the former leaders. My concern was that if we launched a healing process, Kim and I would be re-prosecuted (a prospect she couldn't have handled) rather than forgiven in any meaningful way. As far as I know, the sentiments the board expressed in their resignation letter are still the way they feel today. Since reconciliation seems unattainable, unilateral forgiveness is the only viable option.

Throughout this process, family and friends encouraged us to "let go" and "move on with your lives," but it hasn't been easy. People wanted us to move on due to their own anxiety or because they sensed our pain and felt that enough time had elapsed for us to heal. When some pastors are forced to leave a church, they "shake the dust off their feet" and quickly put the conflict behind them – but I found that impossible to achieve. My analytical brain could not rest until it had uncovered the truth about our situation. The first few months in Arizona, I was still angry, but as the months wore on, I was more puzzled than anything. Why did the board do what they did? Based on the destructive aftermath, it didn't make sense to me.

When Kim's youngest brother was eighteen, he was killed by a drunk driver. Kim had never experienced the death of a close loved one before and it really shook her up. However, she had to engage proactively in certain actions so that healing could begin. We visited the spot where her brother was killed. We drove to his gravesite. Kim flew to be with her family several times as they pursued a civil suit against the driver. We briefly joined Mothers Against Drunk Driving. After the driver was sentenced – and she got off *too* lightly – Kim was finally able to release the injustice, but only after a judge issued a verdict eighteen months later that signified closure. I operated on a similar basis. After six months, I still had unanswered questions about what happened, so I contacted several friends – some of whom still attended our former church – and inquired about certain details. Some interpreted my puzzlement as bitterness and chided me to let things go. While I understood their counsel, I *couldn't* move forward until most of my questions were answered. A mentor told me that these situations rarely make sense and that we must learn to live with the ambiguity, but I needed to probe specific details before I could move ahead. After consulting over the phone with Christian counselors who specialize in helping wounded pastors, I was finally able to release most of my feelings after eight months. Writing this book has also been therapeutic because I've been able to rid my brain of trouble-some issues and regain perspective – and I've learned that anger is part of the healing process.

You can't short-circuit these feelings. It's like trying to hurry up grief after a divorce or a loved one's death. You have to drink the cup of suffering dry. You can only put it all behind you when *you're* ready, not when *others* want you to be ready. Although we enjoyed marked improvement in emotional health after the one-year mark, we chose to move to be closer to Kim's new job. The move cost us time, energy, money (we lost a deposit on a rental), and possessions (we broke a few things), and the moving event triggered negative emotions that we thought had disappeared: "Why will this be the fourth house we've lived in over the past fourteen months? Why do we have to haul all our possessions around *again*? Will we ever be able to buy a house and return to the life we once knew?"

In his book *Forgive & Forget: Healing the Hurts We Don't Deserve*, Lewis Smedes describes four stages of forgiveness: hurting, hating, healing, and coming together.[11] Shawchuck and Heuser summarize these steps:

The first stage of forgiveness . . . is *hurt*. During this phase one may feel completely assailed by pain, be numb to it, or be minimally aware of it. Whatever the case, it is vital to explore the places where pain may be dwelling and experience it.

Hate is the second stage, marked by feelings of rage; it is during this phase that we continue to wish that the person(s) who harmed us would suffer at least as much as we are suffering. It is important not to rush through or minimize these two stages, but to allow time and space for a complete catharsis.

The third stage is *healing*. Healing happens naturally if grieving and anger run their course. The following are characteristics of this stage: a genuine ability to wish the best for the one(s) who sinned against us, taking responsibility for our part in the conflict, and gaining deeper insight into God's forgiveness of us.

Beginning again is the final stage, marked by a readiness to come together again with the one(s) who offended us and finding a new freedom to move on.[12]

If Smedes is correct, then the ability to forgive and look toward the future follows a loose progression rather than a strict timetable. Kim and I were not purposely holding on to pain so we could feel victimized or powerful. We genuinely wished to release it, but the first few times we tried, we weren't successful. Unilateral forgiveness is vastly inferior to genuine reconciliation.

In the end, Kim's spending was examined both by the transition advisory team and the new board (a total of nine different people). Neither group concluded that her spending merited a harsh punishment, nor did they reinstitute any of the non-financial charges made against her. (Since those offenses were against the ex-board, they were non-transferable.) One of those nine leaders wrote us before we left the church and said:

It is unbelievable what has happened to you and our church since you returned from Moldova! My heart is so sad to think that except for next Sunday we won't hear you preach again, Jim.

Please know Kim that not only will we . . . miss your bubbly enthusiasm and fabulous outreach, but the City . . . and our missions program will never be the same. I am so sorry that you had to go through this tragic experience.

My total frustration is that what happened did not need to occur!! I so wish the board had approached the process and timeline in a manner that would not have hurt you both, the church or them.

Two weeks after our final Sunday, the new board chairman announced to the congregation at the end of a worship service that the board had done an investigation and that there was no evidence of wrongdoing on our part. (One witness said that the place went silent.) Although Kim and I were both grateful for this verdict, we didn't find out about it for *eight* months. (Had we known earlier, it might have accelerated our healing.) But when we did hear about it, we wondered, "Then why did everyone have to go through so much pain?"

One year after we resigned, I sent the following letter to the six people on the pastoral advocacy team:

Dear _____,

As 2010 draws to a close, I want to thank you for something you did in the fall of 2009.

I've been reading a book called *The Wounded Minister: Healing from and Preventing Personal Attacks* by former pastor Guy Greenfield. The fourth chapter of his book is titled 'The Minister's Greatest Enemies: Passive Lay Leaders.' Here are two extended quotations from this chapter:

'So why is it that when a minister is under attack by an antagonist or a small group of "uglies," some of those who are usually friends and supporters become thunderously silent, meek, and mild, and passively allow the attacks to continue unabated? I longed for the day when representative leaders of the silent majority would rise up and say to my antagonists, "Enough is enough. Stop this nonsense or leave the church. If you don't stop it or leave of your own accord, we will expel you ourselves. You have no right to batter our minister and drive him away." But those words never came. No advocate stood up to the critics to challenge their criticisms, even though most of them knew that the criticisms were full of outright false accusations and half-truth innuendoes. In the face of evil, silent friends are no friends at all.'[13]

But you did stand up to the attacks. You were not silent. You spoke up on our behalf. You defended Kim and me even though some of our friends flipped on us – for good. You did your best to stand behind us even though it cost you – and only God knows how much. Greenfield goes on:

'There were critical times when attacks would come and I would try to contact my supporters for advice only to find them either out of town on business or unavailable at work. They did not have time to "prepare a defense" for me when the attacks came at official board meetings or church business meetings. The antagonists had plenty of time to plan their strategy, organize their supporters, hold secret planning meetings with their friends, and spend numerous hours telephoning people to get out the vote for key meetings. My supporters were like a National Guard unit being called up to fight a full-time, seasoned, and well-armed military unit.'[14]

But unlike most pastors' supporters, you were there for us. You made time for us. You responded to emails. You took my calls at strange hours during the week. You attended hastily-called meetings even though you led busy lives. It felt like you dropped everything for us. And you stood by us even as we watched some others walk away.

If this is painful for you in any way, I don't want to hurt you. On behalf of Kim, I just want to thank you. While we all learned some things through the crisis of 2009, I learned that you are the kind of person I want when I'm in a foxhole undergoing enemy fire. And while I hope you only enjoy peace and harmony in the churches you attend in the future, if more attacks do come, I know you'll be ready to stand down the antagonists.

So thanks again for your support, your prayers, and your encouragement to Kim and me. But most of all, thanks for your friendship.

As Christians go, you are one in a million.

Happy New Year!

A team member responded:

Thank you so very much for your kind words. It was our pleasure to stand beside you in the heat of battle. It didn't matter what others thought (of course we thought they were wrong anyway). You and Kim had given so much and deserved the respect and kindness that you never got from your critics. The way the board acted everyone lost, especially the two of you.

How I wish I could clone those six people and send them to every church and pastor under attack! But since that isn't feasible, my prayer is that their story will empower and embolden lay people in various churches to intervene with the governing board or with other antagonists to ensure that any action taken against a pastor is done biblically and with due process. If they had not come alongside us when they did, I have no idea how we would have survived.

Eleven years before these events occurred, I attended an annual event called CareGivers Forum in Colorado Springs. The Forum was composed of individuals and couples that ministered to pastors and their spouses who had been wounded in ministry. While some ministries specialized in intensive counseling, others focused on retreat centers, and still others featured consulting or conflict management. That weekend, I met Charles Chandler, who had just founded The Ministering to Ministers Foundation in Richmond, Virginia. Charles had undergone his own forced termination and shared perspectives that were new to me. So when our conflict erupted, I contacted Charles right away. His counsel was invaluable, and I was excited when he invited Kim and me to a Wellness Retreat sponsored by his ministry. Kim and I attended the retreat in Tennessee the month after we left our church and the time was extremely beneficial. Although the days were long, Charles and his presenters were top-notch and told the eleven of us at the retreat that "they can take your job but they can't take your calling." Upon leaving, Kim and I realized that while we had suffered more mistreatment than any other participants, we had also experienced a "softer landing."

I have been told on good authority that it takes pastors one to three years to heal after an involuntary termination. While I don't consider myself an expert – more like a survivor – here are five steps that helped our healing along:

First, *we didn't force ourselves to attend church services initially.* We didn't have an aversion to church like some pastoral couples do after such an experience, but we were still in pain because Kim wasn't serving and I wasn't preaching. We missed a few Sundays over the first three months but have hardly missed any since. While we needed to find a church where we felt safe, some we visited felt dangerous. It took us six months to find a home church.

Second, *we took time to grieve.* If Kim felt like getting angry, I let her express herself. If I felt like crying, she encouraged it. Almost every memorable occasion hurts during the first year away from your former church: Super Bowl Sunday, Easter, Mother's Day, Father's Day, Thanksgiving, and Christmas Eve. If our marriage had already been strained, the ugly emotions that we felt could have ended our relationship, but because we've always allowed each other to be human, our relationship grew stronger. In fact, Kim told me several times, "You're once again the man that I married." (Can becoming a pastor alter someone's personality?) One day, I asked a man who has counseled many pastors, "How do you know when you've been healed?" He told me to look for three markers: grieve your losses, forgive your adversaries, and become involved in a local church again. That's solid counsel.

Third, *we both saw a counselor.* We sought referrals from several churches and finally settled on a woman who really cared about us. She and her husband had been involved in a parachurch ministry years before and had left involuntarily as we did. The counseling gave us a place to share our negative feelings and receive the assurance that we were normal people who had experienced an extraordinary tragedy.

Fourth, *I began to write about what happened to us.* I've been working on this book for three years. People have asked me, "Isn't it difficult to rehearse the pain?" There *are* times when my intestines get tied in knots, but on the whole, writing has been therapeutic. It's how I figure things out. I'm able to take events and conversations and perspectives that have crowded into my mind and release them by recording them. While I've had rough days, I recommend writing as a way of clearing out your brain. There is catharsis through the written word. One year after leaving, I also started writing a blog concerning pastors and conflict. All these thoughts have been rattling around in my head for years, and now I have an outlet for sharing them.

Finally, *we began dreaming about the future.* We initially went out together every week and reviewed our future options. Could I pastor again? If so, would I be a senior pastor? An associate? An interim or transitional pastor? If not, could I teach in a seminary or Bible college? Could we go overseas as missionaries for a year or two? We came to believe that God was calling us to begin a non-profit ministry whose mission is "preventing and resolving church conflicts biblically" – but we had no illusions that it would be easy.

My wife and I recently visited the city where our former church is located, but we felt uncomfortable being there. We wish we felt the freedom to set foot on the church campus again, but we can't ever envision going back. (A friend asked me, "Why would you *want* to go back?") It's ironic that we feel free to visit every church in the world *except* the one where we enjoyed our greatest ministry effectiveness. I've been told that people would be glad to see us if we did visit, but we wouldn't want to attract undue attention or intrude on someone else's ministry. While we have separated ourselves emotionally from the church as an institution, we will always love its people. But I suppose the real barrier to any visit is that the church we once loved and served with joy now feels unsafe. Just as Paul and Barnabas sailed away from each other in the story found in Acts 15:36-41, so too many pastors and their churches reluctantly withdraw from each other, never to meet again this side of heaven.

The threat of forced termination is every minister's worst nightmare.[15] Pastors feel this way because they have a "total institution mindset" about their churches, which results in feeling powerless when they think about leaving. Writing to pastors, Boers says that "if the local congregation is our life, then the stakes will seem all the higher. If we feel a threat of losing our position, it is not just our job that hangs in the balance but our whole world, our 'total institution.'"[16] Wickman comments, "From years of experience I say, for a pastor to recapture his heart lost in a forced resignation is difficult, almost beyond description."[17] My desire is for both pastors and lay leaders to learn and utilize biblical ways of handling disagreements so that differences can truly be resolved. And if it's best for all parties that a pastor leave a church, my prayer is that both the pastor and the board will work at handling matters with truth, grace, justice, and dignity.

TAKEAWAYS FROM CHAPTER 9

For pastors:

- If you're forced to leave your church, God will not abandon you. While your life may be different – you may be in survival mode for a while – the Lord promises to care for his children.
- If you haven't done so already, take time to forgive each person who has hurt you. Name each person along with their offenses. Forgive as Jesus has forgiven you.
- Realize that the anger and pain you feel after experiencing a forced exit is real (so don't deny it) but also temporary (so you will eventually heal). Expect some rough days, especially on national and Christian holidays.

For board members:

- If you want God to bless your church, make decisions primarily on the basis of Scripture rather than business, economics, or politics.
- If you are having trouble with your pastor, have you confronted him biblically?
- If the pastor has involuntarily left the church, have each of the board members forgiven him for any offenses he may have committed? You may need to make this a group exercise.

For the congregation:

- If you can send your former pastor and his wife an email or call them after they've left, you have no idea how much that would mean to them, even if they do not reply.
- As God brings your former pastor and his family to mind, ask God to help them to heal. It has meant a great deal to us whenever someone has told us they're praying for us.

CHAPTER 10

MISTAKES I MADE

My intent in the next two chapters is to analyze the factors that I believe led up to the events that devastated so many people. In so doing, I will take responsibility for those areas in which I made mistakes, and I certainly made some. It takes wisdom to properly assess responsibility whenever two parties separate. For example, when a husband and wife divorce, whose fault is it? If it's a celebrity couple, the mainstream media likes choosing a hero and a villain and they follow that template throughout their coverage. But if God handed down a decree that objectively assessed the couple's responsibility, maybe he would assign the husband 60 percent of the blame while faulting the wife for 40 percent. But the wife shouldn't focus her energies on his 60 percent when she's 40 percent guilty. She should take ownership for her blunders *first*, and only *then* address his offenses. Isn't this what Jesus was teaching in Matthew 7:1-5?

> "Do not judge, or you too will be judged. For in the same way you judge others, you will be judged, and with the measure you use, it will be measured to you. Why do you look at the speck of sawdust in your brother's eye and pay no attention to the plank in your own eye? How can you say to your brother, 'Let me take the speck out of your eye,' when all the time there is a plank in your own eye? You hypocrite, first take the plank

out of your own eye, and then you will see clearly to remove the speck from your brother's eye."

So in keeping with Jesus' instructions, I'm going to take the plank out of my own eye before I attempt to remove specks from the eyes of others. We all have a tendency to demonize our enemies while exonerating ourselves during a conflict, but most of us play some role, however small it may be. By taking responsibility for my part, I hope to help others avoid making the same mistakes that I made.

My first mistake is that *I didn't pay enough attention to the composition of the church board.* Since I was eighteen, I could recite the biblical qualifications for spiritual leadership backwards and forwards (1 Timothy 3:1-7; Titus 1:5-9). I noticed who managed their families well, could explain and defend Scripture, and had their lives under control. Like most pastors, I was always on the lookout for such people. I ran every prospect's name through the lens of Scripture and consulted with the staff and board before asking anyone to serve.

When it comes to choosing leaders, I believe that a pastor can choose the *perfect* person, the *best* person, or the *only* person. The *perfect* person is the prototype, someone who is uniquely suited by maturity, experience, temperament, and giftedness to serve in a specific ministry. The *best* person might not be optimal for a position but stands out among all possible candidates. But on rare occasions, you're reduced to recruiting the *only* person available when having someone is better than having no one. Ours were not the *perfect* board members or the *only* people available, but they were among the *best* our congregation had to offer at the time. While I believed that each person we asked to serve on the board was biblically qualified, I failed to take into account overall board chemistry, making four mistakes.

To start with, *I ignored the fact that everyone on the board was younger than me.* Over the course of my ministry, some board members were older while some were younger, but this time, *every* board member was younger, which may have been why they all banded together against me. Since no one person felt comfortable speaking with me directly, leaders redirected conversations about their concerns to each other, and then the board spoke with one voice when I came to meetings. There wasn't anyone of stature like Robert with whom I could easily relate. While board members were well-versed in business practices, most were relative novices in church leadership, and half weren't involved in any significant ministry outside their board duties. We needed at least a couple of older, more experienced leaders on that board for balance.

Next, *I didn't provide the board with enough training concerning their roles and responsibilities from a biblical perspective.* I did a good job offering such training in past ministries, and we had several all-day board retreats years before in *this* church, but that last year, the training stopped. This could have been done at a weekend retreat or through a study time before each monthly meeting, but I kept putting it off. The last few times I had scheduled a board retreat, the event was cancelled because not enough board members could attend. And whenever I scheduled training inside a board meeting, the time was largely pre-empted because someone would claim "we've got to hurry the meeting along because we have a packed agenda." Although I outlined a training curriculum, I was not proactive enough in implementing it, and must bear responsibility for that decision.

In addition, *I spent more time developing relationships with staff members than board members.* Our staff met for several hours once every week, and those meetings were highly productive. We shared how God was working in our lives, prayed with each other, and took time for ministry training. Once every quarter, we spent an afternoon doing something fun together. We got to know each other as people, not just staffers. But the board did not operate as the staff did, partly because they met monthly, but also because I wasn't in charge of board meetings. Consequently, while I had great personal relationships with staff members, my relationships with board members tended to be more businesslike – but *they* got along with each other very well.

Finally, *I realized too late this wasn't the right group for this stage of our church's life.* The board was composed of people who were all involved in business to some degree. We should have had a more diverse group – maybe a military officer, or a teacher, or a blue collar worker, or a former pastor rather than just a group of likeminded individuals – but few others in the church were biblically qualified. Because this group shared a common mindset, they coalesced quickly. If I could do it over again, I would only approve people from various walks of life who were fully committed to an outreach-oriented church.

In addition, they were cautious individuals who were not prone to taking risks. I felt like I had to prove myself to them continually, like I didn't have any credentials or experience. For this reason, I was continually frustrated by my inability to understand their thinking, and I'm sure the feeling was mutual. Looking back, even though church bylaws stated that we needed a minimum of five members, I should have insisted that we only select members who were behind the church's vision and their pastor's leadership, even if that totaled less than five.

My second mistake is that *I assumed that board members were fully behind the church's outreach orientation.* For the first five years of my ministry, we fulfilled our mission and vision statements well. They provided the impetus for spiritual and numerical growth as well as a new worship center. We were an outreach-oriented church that wanted to serve and reach its community for Jesus Christ. But after we built that worship center, I struggled to put into words the direction that God wanted us to go.

The problem was that the church was landlocked. A church growth expert told me that a church can only accommodate 100 to 125 people per acre of land, and we were jamming hundreds onto a one-acre campus that could fit only so many people. The children's rooms were filled on Sundays. The parking lot – which we shared with the entire community – was usually crammed with cars. We were often maximizing the property. The campus was invisible from the street and sandwiched between three surrounding buildings. City government had announced its opposition to churches moving into the few remaining undeveloped sites, so selling the property never seemed viable. While I dreamed of starting a church to reach a younger demographic, it was difficult envisioning where it could meet.

Since building or moving seemed unrealistic, I sensed that God wanted us to add a third service. While on vacation, Kim and I had visited North Coast Church in Vista, California, home of the multi-venue approach to ministry, and I thought their model could work at our church. Because no one in our area was reaching a younger demographic, and many young couples at the church preferred edgier worship music, starting a third service seemed like the best option for reaching more people. North Coast offered worship services to believers with a variety of musical tastes, so I researched their model, presented it to the board, and proposed that we send two teams of leaders to both Saddleback Church and North Coast to experience firsthand how those churches were handling their worship options. The board agreed with my proposal and chose to finance the trips from our reserves. Ten leaders attended the two trips, including two board members, three staff members, and me. Since adding a third service required logistical changes and additional funds, I sought written input from everyone who attended the trips to broaden ownership for my proposal.

The programming team that planned our services was excited about the prospect of a third service, as were most staffers. We believed that as we stepped out in faith, God would provide all that we needed. In the summer of 2009, we set a temporary date for starting a third service within one year. It would give us time to cast a vision, recruit personnel, and research final costs. With the programming team and staff behind the idea, we needed a green light from the board – and because two members had gone on the trip, I assumed it was a slam dunk.

I met with the board on a Saturday morning and assembled a PowerPoint presentation with photos showing how both churches handle their various services. I assumed that I just needed to cast a vision and demonstrate that this would be a great idea for our church and community. After some discussion, the board unanimously *rejected* the idea of a third service. They believed that we didn't have the money (even though we had a six-figure reserve fund) and suggested that we might resume the discussion the following year. The dunk was blocked.

I was stunned. When I got home, I told Kim, "That decision was made before anyone even entered the room." When I told the programming team that the board had rejected the third service proposal, several members became very upset, and when I told the staff, most of them were disappointed, believing that the board lacked faith. While I did my best to explain the board's position to both groups, it was difficult to hide my dissatisfaction. Planning a third service would have energized our church, enthused our younger believers, and emboldened our community witness. If I had been working with the board that approved the worship center project years before, my proposal might have sailed through, but this was a different time and group. Until that moment, I didn't know how far apart we really were.

After the board's decision, I became demoralized because I could no longer see any exciting ministry challenges before me. Looking back, that day was probably the end of my ministry in that church, even though I stayed four additional months. Although Kim and I wanted to take risks for Christ and his kingdom, the board's mindset had changed over time and we couldn't adapt to caretaker roles. Wickman describes the results of ten studies done over a dozen years:

> The conclusion: the primary stressor experienced by pastors, leading most often to forced resignation, is VISION CON-FLICT, the ugly pastor/pew rift over how the life and work of a particular church is to be understood and acted upon. It is primary in the terrible phenomena of pastors-at-risk and forced resignations.[1]

My third mistake is that *I got ahead of the board on a fundraising project*. When Kim and I first came to the church, there wasn't much emphasis on missions, and only the youth took short-term trips. But in 2006, I was invited to visit Moldova during a sabbatical to teach a course on marriage to Christian leaders who had enrolled in a three-year training program. Kim and I had a marvelous time there. She then led a team there for the next three years, and she also visited Kenya twice. This emphasis on missions was exciting to our congregation, especially when the missionary family we supported in Moldova visited our church and the pastor we supported in Kenya later did the same. Since we had a limited ability to grow the ministry on our small campus, we could at least advance Christ's kingdom in other cultures.

After our church had begun to financially support a pastor in Kenya, our missions' team decided to build a well in the village where he grew up (six hours outside Nairobi) because people were walking six hours each way to get water. In early 2009, the team arranged to bring Pastor Peter to our area for several weeks, and while he was here, the team wanted to launch fundraising for the well. Laura paid to do a feasibility study to see if there was water underneath the village – and there was.

Pastor Peter was scheduled to speak at the church in early March. Laura wanted to sell bottles of water after services as a way of launching the fundraising effort, and I enthusiastically approved her idea while

I was away on vacation. My thought was, "Peter's *here*! Let's do it!" But I inadvertently authorized the effort without informing the board or seeking their input. (Up to this time, the church had no formal fundraising policy. In a sense, I as the pastor was the policy. On those occasions when we raised money for a mission trip, I received board approval, told the church about the trip, and people donated funds promptly.)

While the congregation never sensed anything was wrong, I voluntarily admitted at the next board meeting that I had stumbled and we worked to straighten matters out. But this may have been the beginning of my struggles with the board. Although I should have handled the fundraising sequence better, the church gave generously to the well project, and we raised all the funds within three months. But the board did not share the congregation's joy in the well's construction. They seemed to look strictly at its cost and felt that people diverted their giving from the general fund to the well project – which they did not. (I checked.)

My fourth mistake is that *I failed to acquire sufficient authority to manage staff*. When Roger was hired in May 2007, then-chairman Charlie told me he wanted Roger to meet with the board as a non-voting member. Although I expressed objections (I'd had a bad experience with a similar arrangement before), Charlie insisted that Roger attend meetings. (In retrospect, I should have registered my objections more forcefully.) How could I discuss Roger's performance while he was present? He worked for me, not for the board, and I worked for them, not for him. This was not due to any insecurity on my part (I welcome differing viewpoints) but because such an arrangement blurs the lines of accountability.

At first, the associate and I seemed to be in sync at meetings, but he gradually began siding with the board on critical issues, especially anything that concerned finances. I had a great relationship with both parties until Roger began attending meetings, and things slowly went south after that. I finally told Taylor that our governing documents did not allow the associate to sit on the board, so Roger was no longer invited to meetings, but the damage had been done. In fact, the associate became so aligned with the board that I believe they began looking to him as their pastor. When he was hired, he told me that the associate should be an "extension of the senior pastor," but he ended up becoming an "extension of the board" instead. Since they were business people, and he agreed with them on business matters, he became their "business pastor." Since I was more concerned with spiritual matters, I became the "spiritual pastor." In the end, the board chose to work with the *business* pastor and eliminate the *spiritual* pastor.

I believe that in most cases, church boards should only be composed of the lead pastor and elected board members. When a staff member sits on the board, this arrangement makes him or her feel equal to the senior pastor in decision-making authority, even though most staffers report directly to the pastor, not the board. At the most, staffers can attend a meeting, make a report, and then leave.

Whenever *any* staff member made a mistake, I would address the issue at my first opportunity. I preferred persuasion to coercion, but if the staffer didn't cooperate, I had few options. I lacked the authority to fire staff, and they knew it. Although I never let misbehavior slide, staff members knew there were limits to my authority and that they could form alliances with board members to gain ecclesiastical immunity.

In some churches, a staff member will complain to a board member about the senior pastor and the two will form an unofficial alliance. So if the pastor ever comes to the board to criticize that staff member, or recommends that person be fired, the staffer has a built-in advocate. When there's a problem between the pastor and a staff member, if the board backs their lead pastor, the staffer has to change his or her behavior or resign. But if a board backs a staffer instead, their leader may choose to leave. While I can't prove this, I believe that 90 percent of all pastors are tender people while 10 percent are tough guys – and it's the tough guys that pastor the large churches. They have the power to fire staff unilaterally – or delegate that authority to an executive pastor – and know instinctively what to do when attacked from within. For this reason, I needed *more* authority to deal with staff, not *less*.

My fifth mistake is that *I was unsure at times how to deal with my opponents*. When I came to the church initially, I was determined to get along with everybody. My go-to verse for pastoral relationships was Romans 12:18: "If it is possible, as far as it depends on you, live at peace with everyone." I tried to greet everyone with a smile, listen to people's problems or concerns, and treat everyone with respect. But I also had to follow the Lord's leadership, which meant that on occasion, after I made a firm decision, some people would leave the church and blame me on their way out the door.

Every Christian leader gains enemies. Jesus had them both inside and outside his inner circle. Paul had many as well, some of whom he identified by name (like Alexander and Hymenaeus). While pastors don't wish to hate anyone, there are always individuals who allow a disagreement with their pastor to turn into hatred. As most pastors know, we are criticized more for what we *don't* do than what we do *wrong*. (Of course, this is highly unfair because there are thousands of things we *could* be doing at any one time.) The more impactful the pastor, the more adversaries he collects, which is why many high-visibility pastors now employ bodyguards.

One of a pastor's most important jobs is to keep church systems operating in a healthy manner. In many churches, the pastor ultimately oversees the worship system, educational system, outreach system, and financial system, among others. For systems to work at their optimal level, a pastor needs to ensure that only spiritually and emotionally healthy individuals assume leadership roles, and those leaders need to be fully committed to the pastor's agenda. Even one resistant or dysfunctional leader can harm a system. The pastor of a healthy church may also need to prevent unhealthy people from assuming leadership as well as gradually removing any unhealthy individuals who are already in leadership. In so doing, he exercises his role as guardian of God's flock (Acts 20:29-31). Yet when certain individuals sense the pastor doesn't want them in leadership, he gains enemies, even if he isn't directly involved in keeping them out.

Over the course of my career in various churches, I have also made enemies for enforcing biblical and ecclesiastical standards. Like most pastors, I've had to speak to leaders about issues like not attending church services, sabotaging the church's mission, engaging in inappropriate relationships, and failing to tell the truth. While I've tried to handle these matters sensitively but firmly – and sometimes I was the only person who *could* do it – many people resent it when a pastor enforces standards, and the pastor becomes their enemy.

In the end, all my enemies found each other.

I've heard of pastors who continually sense that they *might* have offended specific attendees. They're always setting up meetings to try and resolve matters. This approach may work fine with small group relationships, but it's counterproductive to implement in a larger church setting. It's challenging to lead a church, run a staff, prepare biblical messages, counsel wounded people, and constantly chase down people you *might* have offended. One such meeting can render you useless for an entire week. If I *knew* that someone was upset with me, I'd try and work things out, but much of the time, churchgoers won't tell you how they're really feeling anyway. But if too many complain all at once, it can have disastrous consequences.

When I was a young pastor, I secretly envied a megachurch pastor whose church was nearby. One day, I enjoyed an extended lunch with him. He told me that a staff member who was single had engaged in sexual immorality and that the board decided to put him through a restoration program, so they employed him as a church janitor. The cabinet behind the pastor's desk was filled with letters of complaint from churchgoers about this decision. Scores of attendees criticized the pastor for being too lenient while a comparable number believed he was too strict. The pastor was in torment about the situation and had no idea that extending grace to a brother would result in such vehement opposition. Eighteen months later, that pastor was dead. When pastors enter ministry, they can't envision that they'll have *any* enemies. When they leave ministry – or leave this life prematurely – it may be because they had too *many*.

My final mistake is that *I started to feel powerless*. On paper, the church bylaws stated that the senior pastor was to be the leader of the church in all its activities. But as the board began chipping away at my positional and spiritual authority, I started becoming confused about my role. For example, the day before our team left for Moldova, Kim asked me if she could buy some large suitcases to transport items overseas that our church normally supplied. Ordinarily, I would have approved that expense myself, but I wasn't sure whether it was included in the proposal that Kim had made to the board several months earlier. If it wasn't, should one of us have called the chairman for approval? What if he had to poll the entire board first? Because systems were changing, I began to feel awkward and uncertain as a leader.

The board used to average one tough meeting a year, but now we were having difficult meetings more often. The agenda for board meetings was increasingly focused on facility and finance issues, and while I needed to have input on those topics, I was more interested in reaching people for Christ. Over the course of my ministry, I worked *with* the board, but now it felt like I was working *for* them. A few months before resigning, I came home late from a meeting and told Kim that I didn't know how much longer I could endure working with them. (She immediately went online and started looking for pastoral jobs for me.) That meeting went four hours before we got to my report, which was the first time we discussed spiritual matters all night. Since this was the first time that I ever had major problems with a board, I was hoping matters would miraculously change, but I was too drained to bring it about. Wickman observes:

> When a pastor begins to feel that he has little effect on how things go, he begins to detach from the decision-making process, feelings of increasing helplessness and hopelessness develop and feelings of benign resignation set in . . . Powerlessness is a precursor to weariness, anger and despair.[2]

In a recent study of pastors who have left church ministry, the number one reason cited was conflict. Pastors felt blocked or frustrated as they tried to bring new life to their congregations.[3] Hoge and Wenger explain:

> They were not doctrinal differences or inflammatory issues such as the ordination of gay and lesbian ministers, but rather the day-to-day functioning of the congregation: the style of the pastor and of worship, the relationships among staff, and the handling of finances and building space. Congregations clash over small things. Pastors and lay leaders clash when there is a difference in styles of leadership. They clash when worship traditions are challenged or modified. They quarrel over money and how it is spent. We reflected on this and came to believe that the conflicts most often experienced by our par-

ticipants are ones that could probably be resolved and in the process offer growth experiences for both pastor and congregation. Instead, they became catapults out of parish ministry.[4]

If I knew that I had one or two supporters on the board, I could have collaborated with them to work through my differences with the entire group, but I no longer felt that I had any allies. When I sensed the board starting to turn on me, I had two extended conversations with the chairman – even suggesting that we hire a noted consultant who *wanted* to come to our church – but nothing changed. During my final board two meetings, I sensed that the board felt they no longer needed to work with me on anything. Instead of negotiation, they seemed to favor imposition.

While the board and I weren't in sync on certain matters, maybe I was in denial about the gap between us. Too often, pastors assume that the conflicts they're having with their boards are minor while the board members view the conflicts as major – and the first time the pastor hears that something is amiss is when the board asks him to resign. In fact, most pastors who experience a forced exit claim that "I never saw it coming." Pinion cites a study conducted by Wayne Kiser of 250 churches that underwent serious conflict and concludes, "'It is typically people perpetrated. Someone disagrees with the pastor, begins a quiet crusade among others in the congregation and forces the pastor to resign.' Unfortunately, most pastors do not learn about a member's disagreement until it is too late."[5]

While the former board never asked me to resign, I did not learn that our relationship was intractable until I returned from Moldova. As a seasoned pastor, I had experienced scores of conflicts throughout my ministry and had built up a high level of toleration toward them, but newer board members can easily overreact when faced with normal conflict. Truth be told, it felt like the board was trying to strip me of authority that I had earned since becoming pastor so they could claim it for themselves. The coup was happening right before my eyes but I could not stop it because I was outnumbered, causing me to feel increasingly frustrated – and at times, helpless.

When I left home for my next-to-the-last board meeting in September, I paused and asked God to give me strength just once more. I felt like Samson pleading with the Lord to grant him enough power to complete one final task. (But I didn't ask the Lord to collapse the roof on top of anybody.) I even asked the Lord to take me away from the church for good because of my deteriorating relationship with the board.

The Lord answered my prayer in a way I didn't expect.

TAKEAWAYS FROM CHAPTER 10

For pastors:

- Assess how much responsibility you need to assume for any major conflict. When a conflict initially breaks out, we assume that we're right and our opponents are wrong. But over time, our mistakes become clearer. When it's appropriate, do your best to make things right.
- Consider putting together a small team of trusted confidants from within the church who can provide periodic feedback as to how you're really performing as pastor. This is a good way to test a board's objectivity. If the "feedback team" believes you're doing a great job, but the board doesn't, they may have their own secret agenda.
- If a conflict centers around you as the pastor, try to resolve matters but realize that you won't be able to handle matters perfectly and that you'll need counsel from qualified experts.

For board members:

- If your pastor is acting abnormally, the chairman and another member (preferably one with compassion) should sit down with him and encourage him to share how he's really feeling. While he may withhold information from you (pastors feel like they're surrendering ministerial authority when they're too vulnerable), the pastor may *want* to share some issues with you. It's better that his feelings emerge in private than from the pulpit.
- If you sense that your pastor isn't being forthcoming with the board, encourage him to find a party with whom he can be more candid.

For the congregation:

- Your sincere appreciation of your pastor's ministry can provide the emotional and spiritual fuel that he needs to keep going. It usually means more to a pastor if you thank him for his ministry during the week than on a Sunday. And while pastors appreciate sincere verbal compliments, written commendations may mean even more to them.
- Pray for your pastor continually and *let him know* that you're praying for him.

CHAPTER 11

MISTAKES THEY MADE

*L*et me switch gears and share how the board contributed to this conflict. It is the tendency of decision-making groups to assume they are infallible when conflict arises because they've deliberated carefully and believe they've examined issues from every angle. They assume that any fault must lie with others and that group decisions are 100 percent correct – and many people buy into this thinking. For example, I was recently considered to serve on a jury involving employee termination. When the judge asked prospective jurors if they believe a company is always right when it terminates an employee, most people raised their hands. For obvious reasons, I did not raise mine – and was not selected to serve.

Speed Leas cites a project where the research tried to determine who was at fault when a pastor is forced to leave a church:

> While we could find some situations that were primarily the congregation's 'fault' . . . and we could find some that were primarily the pastor's 'fault' . . . these occurrences were rare. Most of the time we found a mixture of congregational and pastoral causes that defied unraveling as to who 'started it.' Asking the question 'Whose fault is it?' in the church seemed to tangle people up . . . more than it helped . . . in our research into 127 'involuntary terminations' or firings, we found the need to find fault to be one of the most characteristic and least

helpful dimensions of the conflict . . . it is almost never the case that one party is exclusively in the wrong.[1]

While I have shared some mistakes that I made that contributed to the conflict, I do not believe it is healthy for me to blame myself for *everything* that happened as some pastors have been taught in the past. If I had handled some situations better, maybe others would have responded more favorably in return. In fact, I freely confess my lack of omnicompetence. But I can only take responsibility for my own decisions and reactions, not those of others. Since I cannot read people's hearts or motives, I will leave it up to the reader to discern whether any of the parties involved simply made mistakes or engaged in sinful conduct. With those thoughts in mind, let me share six mistakes that I believe the board made as well.

Their first mistake was *to make some decisions outside board meetings*. In the summer of 2008, Charlie, the previous chairman, brought a five-page expense policy proposal to a meeting. The policy dealt with the way that staff spent funds, and while I supported controlling expenses, the policy was complicated, used jargon I didn't understand, and felt oppressive. Whenever a staff member wanted to plan an event – or go on a mission trip – they had to submit a detailed plan to the board (including a list of all their volunteers, vendors, and expenditures) and receive *their* approval before making any plans. This additional bureaucratic step would, in my view, discourage staff members from taking risks and transfer ministry authority to the board. It was a way of micromanaging the staff and, by extension, the entire ministry. I had five objections to the policy, and it was tabled temporarily. No board member ever addressed those objections.

But Charlie kept resubmitting the policy, and nearly a year later, worn down by his efforts, I agreed to its implementation if two conditions were met. First, I asked that two board members explain the policy to the staff, and second, I asked that the policy be tried for ninety days, after which it would be reviewed by both parties. Both my conditions were accepted, and the policy was scheduled to go into effect after two board members met with the entire staff.

I wanted the board to hear from the staff because they both lived in different worlds. The board had theories on how money *should* be spent; the staff had firsthand experience on how funds *were* spent. The board had an ivory tower view of the church; the staff was on the ground daily. While a board needs to set policy, it can't be involved in daily operations because its members usually aren't on campus during the week. Micromanaging ministry from the board level demonstrates little confidence in the staff and defers decision-making from office halls (where decisions are made daily) to boardrooms (where decisions are made monthly). Growing, impactful churches are capable of making decisions on a dime. Stagnant, inward-focused churches create bureaucracies that slow decision-making to a crawl. Any governing board that tries to run a church without pastoral leadership is doomed to failure.

The meeting was held that June and did not go well. It took two board members two hours to say what could have been said in ten minutes. Most staff members were resistant, not because of the policy itself, but because they hadn't been consulted in its creation. They viewed the policy as a "top down" imposition.

The temporary policy took effect that June, and at the board meeting the following September, I told the board that the ninety days had expired and that it was time to review the expense policy. Charlie held up his hand and stated: "The policy is permanent." Dumbfounded, I looked around at the other board members for assistance but everyone just stared at me. I should have protested, but I was afraid I'd get angry again, so I stuffed my feelings. It was obvious that the board had agreed to this decision before the meeting. They had agreed to review the policy when it was implemented but now declined to do so.

I *expect* that board members will talk among themselves between meetings about issues. Ideally, I would meet with the chairman before the next meeting and we'd review the agenda together. But if several or all members were going underground to make decisions – either via email, phone, or in secret meetings – then our working relationship was irretrievably broken. (One pastor told me about a board where several members met before the official meeting at a restaurant. That was the *real* meeting. Then they came and imposed their wills on everyone else.) Increasingly, it felt like I was becoming irrelevant.

Their second mistake was *to talk about me behind my back but not to my face*. As a pastor for nearly four decades, I long ago realized that people would talk about me out of earshot. Every pastor must accept this reality in order to survive ministry. As Spurgeon was fond of saying, a pastor must learn to turn "one blind eye and one deaf ear" to all that is said about him.[2] But I work best with open, assertive leaders who share exactly how they feel *inside* a meeting rather than share their true feelings in the parking lot *after* the meeting.

When the board resigned, they brought up issues in their letter they had never discussed with me directly. And when the informational meetings occurred on November 8, I had never heard most of the accusations made against me before. If various board members had issues with me, why did they wait until they left the church to throw bombs at me? If they had concerns, but didn't discuss them with me directly, doesn't that demonstrate either a lack of confidence in their views or a lack of courage in expressing them? Leas believes that:

> A person being charged or condemned by others should have the right to know what those charges are and [have] an opportunity to respond to them. Denying this opportunity plays into the hands of real or potential manipulators, allows untrue or distorted information to be circulated and establishes a precedent that the way to deal with differences is to talk about rather than to talk with others. I have also found it true that individuals who talk about others out of their presence tend to exaggerate their charges, believing they will not be quoted.[3]

A few years before, I was asked to lead a workshop for a Christian leadership convention on the topic "Giving Your Pastor Feedback." It's scary for many people to talk to their pastor until they get to know him personally, but most believers don't feel comfortable confronting him if they believe that he's done or said something wrong. The pastor is perceived to be closer to God than most Christians and has the power of the pulpit to retaliate against critics (although that's highly unethical behavior). Many pastors also have forceful personalities and overreact to the slightest criticism. Some do not listen well, either, and begin responding to feedback before the person speaking with them has finished sharing. Most people figure that the pastor's wife or the board will address a pastor's shortcomings, but board members can feel intimidated by the *office* of pastor, just like anyone else. Because confronting a pastor is daunting and can become complicated, some board members prefer to fire him outright rather than use any kind of process, biblical or otherwise. Saves time.

In our case, it felt like the board arrested us, judged us, and sentenced us without using any kind of standard process and without hearing our side of any issue before they made irrevocable decisions. When Paul was mistreated by the Roman authorities, he appealed to Caesar (Acts 25:10-11). But when a pastor believes he is being mistreated by a board, where can he appeal? In a congregationally-governed assembly, he can only appeal to the church body, which usually results in division.

Because I was the lead pastor as well as a board member, the board should have consulted with me before making crucial decisions, especially concerning a staffer's status. In fact, most pastors I've consulted with after leaving the church have told me they're surprised I didn't have the authority to hire and fire staff myself. But even in our system, the board usurped their role. Leas counsels:

Healthy and fair confrontation should tell the 'offender' what is wrong, and prepare the way for negotiation (or collaboration) toward agreement and a better relationship. Confrontation which demands that things be done one way, and does not allow for others to shape the way those things are done, is oppressive and demeaning. There are times when a board or supervisor (the one with authority to direct others) must confront without negotiation or collaboration; but even in these cases the 'offender' should have ample opportunity to perform differently before being dismissed from the organization. This is often difficult and done poorly in church situations. Instead of clearly describing to an employee or volunteer what is wanted and seeking to find a way to achieve a mutually satisfactory relationship, too often church leaders avoid confrontation until all hope of improving the working relationship is lost, or they confront and expect immediate change on the part of others without looking at what else in the organization might need to be changed.[4]

When Kim and I attended the Wellness Retreat in Tennessee the month after we resigned, a nationally-known psychiatrist taught a seminar in which he presented the anatomy of a pastoral termination. He stated that an individual – sometimes a board member – feels powerless in life and senses an opportunity to exercise power in the church. While this person knows the pastor's values, the pastor doesn't know their values, which are cleverly disguised. Because this person only respects power – not reason – they use tactics that the pastor could never use, and the pastor is usually no match for such a person. The psychiatrist noted that it takes this person twelve months to break down a pastor and turn people against him. During this time, the pastor becomes so depressed that he can hardly function. The antagonist makes his plans in secret and attacks when least expected, usually when a pastor returns from a trip. This whole scenario is replicated every month in hundreds of churches. Shelley writes:

> Personal attacks . . . rarely start with a direct clash. The would-be attacker usually begins a covert warfare, going to others in the congregation, seeking those of like mind, those who deal in dissent . . . . the strategy is one of planting questions in people's minds . . . with the result of raising doubts about the pastor's competence, credibility, ministry, or motives.[5]

Greenfield expands:

> In many cases, the initial accuser enlists a few key leaders to plan some meetings to be held at his or a sympathizer's home. These meetings are secret, that is, 'invitation only,' meetings of people who the accuser believes will agree with his accusations. The primary purpose is to gather support for an eventual attack on their minister. At these meetings, the discussions assist in gathering additional evidence that the minister is to blame for the church's problems. Meticulous notes are usually taken by the accuser or one he designates to do this.

> The clergy killer knows he must work through recognized authority, this behind-the-scenes oligarchy, to accomplish his goal of getting rid of the minister. When he knows he has their backing, he will move swiftly, with careful calculation. The attack has actually been going on for some time, but the

clergy killer, when the time is right, gets his plan of attack on the agenda of the official board of the church. He arranges for the minister not to be present. The board will be called to 'an executive session,' meaning no outsiders are invited and that includes the minister.

At this crucial meeting, the clergy killer lays his charges before the assembled body of lay leaders. He will use 'statistics' to bolster his accusations. A common target is church finances, since most churches never have enough money. The shortage of money can easily be blamed on the minister's leadership . . . . The bottom line of the charges is simple: If we get rid of our minister, all of our problems will be solved, because we will bring in a new and different minister who will lead us to new heights of statistical glory.[6]

Looking back, I believe the decision to "take me out" as pastor can be traced back to the middle of the summer. While I do not believe the board as a whole agreed to push me out at that time, I suspect that was the intent of one or two members who "greased the skids" with the others. My wife intuitively sensed that board members were developing greater camaraderie outside official meetings and that the relational distance between us was increasing. (One board member even stopped attending worship services.) While I hoped that these signs of potential trouble were temporary, I wish the chairman would have clued me in to the mood of the board. He never did.

Their third mistake was *to try and run the church like a business*. The board was composed of people from the business world who kept trying to modify systems so that *they* were comfortable with the way the church was managed. They believed there was only *one* way to run things, and I wasn't running things the *right* way. But while a church can learn from business, the purpose of a church isn't to make money or reward investors but to make disciples (Matthew 28:19). If we're meeting the budget but not making disciples, we're a failure. If we're making disciples but not meeting the budget (like in many third world churches), we're a qualified success. Rediger observes:

Because the church as a whole has succumbed to the business model of operation . . . the pastor has become an employee, and parishioners the stockholders/customers. The pastor is hired to manage the small business we used to call a congregation. This means his primary task is to keep the stockholders happy; the secondary task is to produce and market an attractive product. When this mindset infects the church, the church is no longer a mission but has become a business . . . the introduction of a business mindset is producing dissonance in the church continually. For though businesses advocate mission and discipline, the budget is necessarily the bottom line. This is the reverse of how a healthy congregation functions.[7]

Like many pastors my age, I was trained to be a theologian, a preacher, a counselor, and a pastor, not a CEO. I didn't have any courses in seminary on business management or hiring employees or supervising staff. I learned about those issues on the job or through mentors or seminars. When pastors are evaluated by purely business criteria, they become confused and ineffective because they're trying to be someone they're not. And when it comes to conflict, those who are spiritually-minded will use Scripture as their authority while those who are business-oriented may lean toward corporate practices. Both sides are using a different set of rules. The pastor assumes that if he's done something wrong, the board will use Matthew 18:15 and speak with him privately about any issue needing correction, while the board uses a business model that is unfamiliar to the pastor. Addressing board members, Anthony offers the following warning about conflict management:

If you have business experience, you might be tempted to use methods that you were taught in the corporate headquarters of your company – but don't go that route. The church is not an organization; it is an organism. The body of Christ has a different set of procedures it must follow when it comes to conflict resolution.[8]

For example, years before, a staff member refused to do something that I asked him to do. Since I could not fire staffers unilaterally, I brought the incident to the board to receive their counsel. During the ensuing discussion, several members told me how such an incident would be handled in a business setting, but no one mentioned biblical principles for handling insubordination. It has been my experience that many board members believe that spiritual problems can be handled with managerial solutions. While I value the insights that business can offer the church in supervising employees, I wish biblical authority would be given the same respect.

I believe that the board tried to *impose* changes on me rather than *collaborate* with me. They stopped *asking* me about policies and started *telling* me how things were to be done. Over a period of eight years, previous boards – which included several top-level financial executives – had collaborated with me to develop a number of systems and written policies to ensure that our church was managed with integrity. I had input on every system and policy and wholeheartedly supported them both privately and publicly. But now the board wanted to impose rigid controls on the ministry without working *with* me on those changes. They used unilateral imposition to freeze the church budget, railroad through an expense policy, dismiss a staff member, and insist I use their mediator, among other things. No board I had ever served with had acted this way. But while I had precedent on my side, they had the numbers. In my opinion, they made decisions outside meetings, announced their decisions inside meetings, stood united against my objections, and then criticized me for not cooperating with them. If they were going to operate that way, why did they even need me? In the end, they decided they didn't. I was blocking their agenda and had to go. For the first time in my pastoral career, it felt like I was working for a board that demanded control of the church.

Their fourth mistake was *to put the welfare of their group ahead of the church's welfare*. This is a common problem with church groups, especially when they're in stress mode. Once they begin to deliberate in secret, group interests begin to outweigh congregational interests, and they convince themselves that many others in the church agree with them. Leas makes the following observation about Level IV of his Five Levels of Conflict:

Examples of Level IV conflict include attempts to get the pastor fired, trying to get those with whom one doesn't agree to leave the church and/or attempting to get people to join oneself in leaving. Here the objectives have shifted significantly. Rather than the good of the organization, the good of a subgroup (which can either be a minority or a majority group) becomes the critical concern. Being right and punishing become predominant themes . . . . It is at this level that factions solidify. Clear lines mark who is in and who is out of each of the camps. Strong leaders emerge, and members of factions conform to the wishes of the leaders and the will of the group. Subgroup cohesiveness is more important than the health of the total organization.[9]

If a board member was upset with me over something I had done or said, he needed to discuss that with me *directly* rather than with other board members *covertly*. One board member's *personal* issue with a pastor can become an entire board's *official* issue months later. For instance, I have a pastor friend who was abruptly terminated by his governing board, and he later concluded that he was dismissed because of his neglect to visit a prominent board member's child in the hospital after a minor procedure. That's putting the feelings of a single individual or group members ahead of the welfare of the entire church.

Whether it's because of a common cause or friendship, for some churchgoers "loyalty to long-term friends and associates is even more influential with them than their own thinking and opinions. They will take a position in a conflict more out of interpersonal allegiance than out of personal conviction."[10] This kind of thinking can happen with board members, too. Writing on groupthink, Bolt and Myers add:

The more difficult and ambiguous the situation, the more each individual relies on the judgment of other group members to define reality and the appropriate course of action. And when a group of persons who respect each other's judgment arrives at a unanimous view, each member is likely to feel the belief must be true. Victims of groupthink keep quiet about their doubts.[11]

Years before, a staff member in that church proposed that a different board buy a church vehicle for his ministry. After some discussion, the board agreed to purchase it. But upon further reflection, I called the chairman the next day to express concern that we had made the wrong decision, and after polling the other board members, the board chose not to purchase the vehicle. Looking back, it's amazing that we approved the acquisition in the first place, but I submerged my doubts when a few prominent leaders initially went along with the proposal. This kind of thinking occurs all too often inside many church boards.

I don't believe the board really knew how the vast majority of the congregation felt about their pastor or outreach director. The board seemed to be in touch with our few critics but not our many supporters. For example, a few dissidents wanted me removed as pastor because I wasn't more openly supportive of the denomination, but nobody on the staff or board cared about that issue. One non-leader wanted continual access to me but that wasn't a privilege I could grant. One woman was angry with me for a decision made by another staffer but I took the blows instead. Separately, these discontented attendees did not have a following, but if they shared their feelings with various board members, the board may have thought their feelings represented the entire church when they were really just anomalies. I wonder how often board members misjudge the mood of their congregation when they try and forcibly remove a pastor.

Their fifth mistake was *to engage in judgment rather than redemption.* The genius of Jesus' words in Matthew 18:15-20 is that when a believer sins, the aim of those who have been sinned against is to restore their believing friend rather than punish him or her. Nowhere does Jesus exclude pastors (and by extension, staff members) from his commands. (In fact, Paul applies our Savior's admonitions in Matthew 18 directly to pastors and elders in 1 Timothy 5:19-21.) Jesus' words in Matthew 18 are not first *event*-oriented but *process*-oriented. The one who experienced an offense is responsible for confronting the offender with his or her wrongdoing. If the offender repents, the estranged parties have been reconciled. But if the offender refuses to repent, the offended party takes along one or two others to witness a second encounter. Their goal is to demonstrate the seriousness of the situation or mediate between parties. If the offender repents at this point, reconciliation has been attained and the process has been completed. Believers are to make every effort to reconcile privately with those who have fallen into sin before any kind of prospective discipline is instituted.

But whenever a believer sins, church leaders aren't to rush into telling the congregation about their misbehavior. Jesus does not say, "If your brother sins against you . . . tell it to the church." Instead, Jesus states that the offended party must patiently work through the steps, which can take time if done correctly. But these steps were not followed in our case.

British evangelist Michael Green relates a story about a Christian business he was associated with that was losing money. The losses were traced to a staff member, and when he was confronted by one individual, he denied wrongdoing. But in the presence of multiple witnesses, the staff member admitted that he *had* stolen money. Green notes that "although it was painful and the offender had to leave our employment, the love and integrity with which he was confronted did in fact win our brother over . . . . He got another job, and was restored to love and full acceptance in the church he had wronged."[12] But that kind of love was never exercised in our situation. There was no pathway for restoration presented to me or my wife for any offenses we may have committed. Because of the way things were handled, it's taken us a long time to heal.

Country singer Lee Ann Womack has a song called "I'll Think of a Reason Later" where the singer recounts how much she despises another woman. The song is done with humor, but one telling line is repeated several times: "I really hate her, I'll think of a reason later." This line perfectly encapsulates how some believers – even church leaders – feel about their pastor. They can't articulate *why* they don't like him and want him to leave. They just want him *gone*.

Before we went to Moldova, any mistakes we made seemed to be interpreted by the board as a citation (like jaywalking). After we returned, any mistake was viewed as a felony. Kim didn't contact the board right away? Felony. I didn't immediately accept their mediator? Felony. I protested their lack of process in making decisions? Felony. However, in their eyes, *everything* they did was justifiable while no one – least of all me – was allowed to question their judgment.

215

Board members terminated my wife without due process (according to Scripture or church bylaws); exaggerated the charges against her; told me to tell her that she was terminated, which was humiliating for both of us; told the staff that she was fired before ever meeting with her; threatened to leave the church four times in six days; failed to show us any written evidence of her offenses; finally agreed to resign, then requested mediation; claimed I had rejected mediation; wrote an extremely critical resignation letter; went on a calling spree to announce their resignations; and then provided information to someone who tried to destroy my reputation before the congregation, resulting in people leaving the church for good.

How redemptive do *you* think those actions were?

Their final mistake was *to take shortcuts on the investigative process*. This is the area in which we felt most violated. If the board was unhappy with me for some reason, then they needed to talk with me about it. If they felt I wasn't supporting their decisions, then we needed to discuss it openly. If the board was upset with Kim at the September 22 budget meeting, then they should have discussed it with her at the time rather than waiting more than a month. This approach is like witnessing your teenager commit an action you believe is wrong, saying nothing for weeks, and then throwing him out of the house six weeks later without any discussion or warning. Who is most responsible: the teenager who did the deed or the parent who kept quiet?

Seems like retroactive justice to me.

When we returned from Moldova, the board should have sat down with us and asked us about the expenditures on the trip. They would have learned that we felt terrible about the charges for transporting the suitcases but felt we had to get them to their destination. They would have learned that *I* approved that expense, not my wife. They would have learned that I didn't think we had to call home constantly and ask the board for permission to make necessary expenditures because a board member *was* on that trip: me. If you've ever gone on a mission trip, you know that sometimes unexpected expenses arise, but no board member had ever gone on such a trip to my knowledge.

If they had interviewed us and heard our side of things, the board wouldn't have had much of a case against us. How long would such an investigation have taken? As little as two hours. Kim would have submitted a report listing and explaining all the trip expenditures as she always did. But I don't think the board wanted to hear another side. They had already made up their minds that they wanted us to leave. (A top leader told me later, "They just wanted you guys gone.") Maybe in some businesses, a supervisor just looks at the numbers and says, "I did not authorize these expenses. The employee is terminated immediately." *But this was a church*, and there was no understanding between the board and staff that if you spent *any* funds without authorization, you would be terminated. If we knew up-front that was a possibility, maybe we could have put expenses on our own credit card and sought reimbursement at a later date – but we were on a *church*-sponsored trip to Eastern Europe, and no one gave us any guidelines beforehand about paying for emergency costs.

I believe the board was extremely anxious about money and that they overreacted to what they perceived as resistance to their leadership. Rather than dialoguing about how we could better work together, they made decisions that ended up wounding many people. There have been recent stories in the press about former National Football League players who have suffered brain damage after retirement because of repeated blows to the head inflicted during their playing days. Sometimes I think that in church ministry, you have to brace yourself for repeated blows to the heart – only to find they're administered by your own team.

After hearing my story, some people have asked me, "How could the board members be Christians?" I knew them all personally, and they took their faith seriously. They were all professing believers who cared about their church. However, while they relied upon God's Word for salvation and spiritual growth, I wonder how much Scripture factored into their thinking on issues like finances and conflict.

When the board resigned, their departures triggered a backlash from their friends and matters imploded after that. While I wish that nothing had been said about potential legal action, I am still doubtful that was the real reason for their exodus. They had telegraphed their intentions during the first week of the crisis by threatening to resign four times. Since the board asked that Kim and I not visit the campus for a solid week, they hoped to operate without any interference from me. They just wanted Kim's resignation after which they hoped they would have mine. When Kim failed to resign at the October 29 meeting, they scrambled because they didn't have an adequate Plan B, which is why they promised to resign the next day, requested mediation the following morning, but resigned anyway the next evening. This makes me wonder who would have replaced me as pastor on a temporary basis had I suddenly resigned. The board might have considered Roger, and apparently my predecessor was considered as well. Since the board felt they knew how to lead a church better than their pastor, would one of *them* have volunteered?

If a board determines that its working relationship with their pastor is nearing an end, they have various options. They can allow the pastor to stay temporarily (maybe six months to a year) provided he searches seriously for another job. They can grant him a leave of absence and recommend that he seek counseling to uncover possible personality or behavioral issues. They can fire him outright without a separation package, an option that damages the church as well as the pastor and his family. (Some board members will suggest the pastor behaved so badly that he doesn't *deserve* a package, but even if that's true, his family still needs assistance.) Or they can offer the pastor a generous separation package if he'll quietly resign. However, if a board wants their pastor to leave but is unwilling to give him that package, they may pressure him to resign – and use some unholy methods in the process. Truth be told, most boards have little training or expertise in conflict resolution skills.

So many pastors are clashing with their boards these days that some new models have arisen. Some founding pastors, like Rick Warren from Saddleback Church, lead their ministries without a formal board structure. In other churches, the pastor automatically becomes the chairman and board members serve at *his* pleasure. One pastor told me recently that he is familiar with churches where each board member serves for one year and then rotates off the board, which does not allow anyone to build a power base. A trend among evangelical mega-churches is for some board members to be selected from their home church while Christian leaders outside the church also serve on the board. (These leaders communicate through technology.) But in effective churches, the board's job isn't to sabotage the pastor's vision or impose their *own* agenda on him, but to ask the pastor how they can support *his* agenda. Borden discusses the optimal roles for boards in growing churches that he oversaw in his district:

> Their responsibility was to govern, not manage or lead. They were to focus on the ends of ministry, goals set by the pastor and the pastor's staff members, not the means of ministry . . . . Board members were taught that their job in relation to the pastor and the pastor's staff members were to be their protectors and cheerleaders . . . . However, the board was not to become involved in the management of the ministry.[13]

I once had lunch with a pastor friend who leads a megachurch. He asked me, "What good is a board, anyway?" He told me in frustration that his board members were never on campus during the daytime and had no idea what was really happening, and yet they would come to a monthly meeting and block his ideas for growing the ministry. While I understood his feelings, for most of my pastoral career, I have been grateful for those lay people who have served alongside me on a governing board. Many remain good friends to this day. To be honest, I was grateful for the group that served with me until they made decisions that nearly caused the church to implode. For the sake of everyone involved, I sincerely wish we had been able to work through any differences in a more biblical, open and compassionate manner.

TAKEAWAYS FOR CHAPTER 11

For pastors:

- Teach the staff, the board, and the congregation what the New Testament says about conflict, focusing especially on Matthew 18:15-20 and 1 Timothy 5:19-21. Do it at least annually. If *you* don't teach them, they may never learn.
- Insist that if a staff or board member has something against you personally that they come to you and discuss the issue privately. If you have something against a specific staff member or board member, do the same. Modeling is a great teacher.

For church boards:

- Find a way to communicate the board's thinking and decisions to the congregation on a regular basis. While the pastor may be accountable to the board, the board is accountable to the congregation if they elect or ratify you for office.
- Do not scapegoat your pastor for all the problems in your church. How is the staff performing? How about the board? How can your board ease the pastor's burden?
- When your pastor does a great job at something – teaching, leading, or resolving a sticky issue – affirm him and let him know that you're glad he's your pastor.
- And when he messes up – and he will from time-to-time – encourage him to resolve matters with the appropriate parties at the first opportunity. And if he makes mistakes with the board, encourage him to discuss those issues as soon as possible. It is normal for Christians to confess their sins to one another and to forgive each other (James 5:16). It is abnormal for Christians to act like they never sin or to refuse to forgive those who request forgiveness.
- Never let a board member's personal anger against a pastor fester. Encourage that board member to speak with the pastor privately and work matters out. If this is not done, that board member's personal issue may later end up expanding into an official charge.

For the congregation:

- If feasible, consider spending at least an hour with your pastor on a social basis within the next three months. Ask him and his family out for dinner after Sunday services or over for dessert one evening. Get to know him as a human being, not just as a spiritual leader.
- Stand up for biblical principles even if your church friends feel differently. Those who stand up for biblical principles may end up saving both their pastor and their church. Those who surrender biblical principles for friendship may end up losing both their pastor and their church family. Think about it.

CHAPTER 12

JESUS AND THE TERMINATION TEMPLATE

*T*he greatest injustice in my lifetime happened to my father. While in his early thirties, he planted a church in Garden Grove, California by going door-to-door and inviting people to attend services. A gentle and sensitive man, he got along well with everyone and recruited a deacon board to assist him in ministry. During its first few years, the church grew numerically and became my second home. I loved hanging out on that small property.

One Sunday when I was nine, my family came home from the evening service, and my parents put my brother and sister and me to bed. But after the phone rang, my parents rousted us out of bed, placed us in the family station wagon, and drove to the home of the head deacon. When we arrived there, I noticed that a group of chairs had been arranged for an impromptu meeting. We three kids were placed in a bedroom adjacent to the living room, and while my siblings quickly fell asleep, I remained awake. Through the wall, I heard church leaders who had taught me in Sunday school verbally crucify my father. (How could they have been so thoughtless?) I was frightened because I wasn't sure what it meant – but I knew it wasn't good.

The pastor of a large church in that district later moderated a special meeting involving church members that focused on my dad. There were two primary complaints against him. First, he parted his hair on the right side of his head (which really bothered someone). Second, he left a church party thirty minutes early one Saturday night to finish his Sunday school lesson. An older woman also claimed there was a salacious incident involving my dad that occurred under the mulberry tree outside, but when questioned by the moderator, she couldn't recall anything about it. My father overwhelmingly won a vote of confidence from the congregation and stayed at the church, but in retrospect, he should have left earlier. His tenderness worked against him when he became the focus of discontent because he found confrontation difficult and tended to internalize his pain.

Two years later, two antagonists (both brothers) stopped attending the church for six months, but when new deacons were chosen, the brothers both won election, and one was named chairman. When that occurred, my father resigned immediately. At the meeting where his resignation was read, a woman cried out, "I never meant for it to come to this. I crucified the man!" My father became a milkman and eventually contracted pancreatic cancer, which also decimated his liver. He suffered in great pain for six months before dying at the age of thirty-eight. His gravestone simply reads: "Beloved Husband and Father – Present with the Lord."

I believe that the stress of the conflict compromised my father's immune system and that the cancer in the church accelerated the cancer in his body. Part of me believes that if the conflict had been handled better – and my dad had received more support from his district – he wouldn't have died so soon. In fact, I suppose that my passion for resolving pastor-church conflicts is my way of saving my father from his antagonists. Several years after his death, the instigators in my dad's situation bragged that they had gotten rid of the next two pastors. One day, my mother received a phone call from the wife of a detracting deacon, telling her that the church had voted to disband. I'm glad my father wasn't around to hear the news. It might have killed him.

While a handful of pastors *should* leave their churches because they are guilty of heresy or immorality or criminal conduct, most pastors are forced to leave a church for flimsy reasons. In my dad's case, the woman who cried out in the meeting once listed some complaints she had about my father and showed her list to a friend, who added her own complaints before sharing the list with others. Before long, the original list had grown much larger. The issues were all trivial. While my father had his flaws, he hadn't committed any major offenses.

But soon afterward, the church he planted vanished. When church-goers attack their pastor, they may be unaware that they're ultimately attacking their church at the same time.

As unjustly as my father was treated, the crucifixion of Jesus Christ remains the greatest injustice in human history. Yes, there is a redemptive thread running throughout the story, and yes, Jesus was a volunteer rather than a martyr, and yes, the Trinity planned the events of that Passover weekend from the foundation of the world – but that does not excuse the guilt of those who deliberately terminated the Messiah. My purpose in going over familiar ground is not to cast exclusive blame for Jesus' death on a single group of people. I agree with John Stott:

> This blaming of the Jewish people for the crucifixion of Jesus is extremely unfashionable today. Indeed, if it is used as a justification for slandering and persecuting the Jews (as it has been in the past), or for anti-semitism, it is absolutely indefensible. The way to avoid anti-semitic prejudice, however, is not to pretend that the Jews were innocent, but, having admitted their guilt, to add that others shared in it. This was how the apostles saw it. Herod and Pilate, Gentiles and Jews, they said, had together 'conspired' against Jesus (Acts 4:27). More important still, we ourselves are also guilty. If we were in their place, we would have done what they did.[1]

I believe there are many similarities between the way that Jesus was cruelly terminated and the way that thousands of pastors are unjustly treated in our day. In fact, a case can be made that the steps leading to Jesus' crucifixion are replicated regularly in all too many churches. While some parallels are inexact – pastors lack Jesus' perfect character and miracle-working power – the unoriginal devil uses the same template to destroy spiritual leaders as he did in our Savior's time. Why change your methodology when it's been working so well? Charles Chandler writes:

> I have worked with hundreds of ministers who have experienced forced termination . . . . I have decided a rulebook is floating around out there somewhere and it does suggest that

a few disgruntled church members can follow the above listed rules and 'kick the preacher out.' I've never seen it in writing, but its effectiveness can be seen in case after case.[2]

In re-reading the Gospels recently, I believe that the single verse that best describes Satan's strategy in attacking a leader is Mark 14:27. In this verse, Jesus quoted Zechariah 13:7 the night before his death and told his disciples, "You will all fall away, for it is written, 'I will strike the shepherd, and the sheep will be scattered.'" While the devil sometimes picks off a stray sheep or two – and even provokes some sheep to fight each other – he knows that the best way to slaughter an entire flock is to eliminate their leader. Without their shepherd, the sheep wander toward cliffs, fail to find nourishing pastures, and become easy prey for wolves.

Let me share ten parallels between the way that Jesus was mistreated twenty centuries ago and the way that many pastors are unfairly treated today.

First, *the enemies of Jesus were threatened by him.* Before Jesus arrived, the Pharisees, chief priests and elders were *the* unquestioned spiritual authorities in Israel as well as *the* undisputed arbiters of Jewish law. But in a clash with Israel's leaders, Jesus publicly challenged their authority inside a synagogue in Capernaum on the Sabbath (Mark 3:1-6; Luke 6:6-11).

Jesus met a man there with a shriveled hand. Although healing on the Sabbath was viewed as work and a violation of the popular interpretation of the Law, Jesus turned toward the Pharisees in Luke 6:9, asking them, "Which is lawful on the Sabbath: to do good or to do evil, to save life or to destroy it?" The Pharisees remained silent rather than engage Jesus in dialogue. After looking them directly in the eyes, Jesus instantly restored the man's hand to health.

While the Pharisees lived by their extra-biblical codes, Jesus always behaved within the true confines of God's written law. Although Jesus committed only good deeds, the Pharisees were convinced he was doing evil. Because Jesus could have healed the man on any other day, his behavior landed him in trouble with the religious authorities, who began to worry that he might displace them as Israel's leaders. Stott says about them:

They were proud of their nation's long history of a special relationship with God, proud of their own leadership role in this nation, and above all proud of their authority. Their contest with Jesus was essentially an authority struggle. For he challenged their authority, while at the same time possessing himself an authority which they manifestly lacked . . . He claimed authority to teach about God, to drive out demons, to forgive sins, to judge the world. In all this he was utterly unlike them, for the only authority they knew was an appeal to other authorities.[3]

Jesus not only threatened the *authority* of the Jewish leaders by spurning their man-made laws, he also threatened their *influence* with a scathing public indictment (Matthew 23), castigating them for hypocrisy, narcissism, vanity, majoring on minors, and obsessing about their spiritual images. After Jesus healed a woman with spinal issues on the Sabbath, the synagogue ruler angrily told attendees, "There are six days for work. So come and be healed on those days, not on the Sabbath." But Jesus did not relent, accusing his opponents of being "hypocrites" who lead their animals to water on the Sabbath while prohibiting supernatural deliverance for hurting people. Luke concludes, "When he said this, all his opponents were humiliated, but the people were delighted with all the wonderful things he was doing" (Luke 13:17).

Most of all, Jesus threatened their very *survival*. After Jesus raised Lazarus, the Sanhedrin concluded, "If we let him go on like this, everyone will believe in him, and then the Romans will come and take away both our place and our nation (John 11:48)," the term "place" referring either to Jerusalem itself or the temple. If Jesus kept attracting a large following, he might put the Jewish leaders out of business, rendering them irrelevant. Due to their scarcity mentality, they couldn't let that happen. While John the Baptist nobly proclaimed, "He must become greater; I must become less" (John 3:30), their sentiment was, "We must become greater; he must become less." After explaining the differences between the various parties in Israel in Jesus' day, Yancey concludes, "For all their differences, though, Essenes, Zealots, Pharisees, and Sadducees shared one goal: to preserve what was distinctively Jewish, no matter what. To that goal, Jesus represented a threat, and I'm sure I would have perceived that threat."[4]

While Jesus and the Jewish leaders contended for the soul of their nation, many pastors and church leaders fight for the soul of a congregation. There are powerbrokers in every church that sense that their influence is being displaced as the pastor's influence increases. When that happens, it's common for them to form a coalition and strike back.

During my junior year at the Christian college I attended, I took a class from a new instructor who proved to be a master teacher. He later served several churches as pastor, finally landing at a church of great prominence. After nearly fifteen years of brilliant service, a small group of old-timers felt threatened by the pastor's vision and attacked his character until he finally resigned. Like the Jewish leaders, these people were concerned that their influence on their religious institution was waning. Regardless of church size, the majority of pastors who are forced to leave a church are targeted by a faction of ten people or less.[5] Embedded in that group may be some who hate the pastor, and he may have no idea of their hatred until it's too late.

Second, *the enemies of Jesus became enraged by some of his decisions.* Luke concludes his account of Jesus healing the man with the shriveled hand in Luke 6:11: "But they were furious and began to discuss with one another what they might do to Jesus." Mark omits the comment about their anger but adds that "the Pharisees went out and began to plot with the Herodians how they might kill Jesus" (Mark 3:6). Jesus performed good deeds that infuriated his opponents. They performed evil deeds but were so spiritually sightless that they could not engage in meaningful self-reflection, so early in Jesus' ministry, they began to deliberate in secret about eliminating him.

As Mark 3:5 indicates, Jesus was also angry with the Pharisees due to their hard hearts. But Jesus' anger was *controlled* while theirs spun *out of control*. Jesus' anger was directed at *evil deeds* while theirs was directed at him *personally*. Jesus' anger resulted in a *constructive* outcome (healing) while the Pharisees' anger resulted in a *destructive* outcome (death). The Pharisees wanted everyone in Israel – even Jesus – to consult with them before operating outside of their rigid laws. Jesus ignored them and healed the man anyway.

When our mission team visited Moldova, we stayed with Mark, a pastor friend originally from Northern Ireland, his Romanian wife Mari, and their two young daughters. Mark and his wife planted a church in an extremely poor village in southern Moldova. As our team witnessed firsthand, a young married couple in the church was doing a fabulous job leading the youth ministry, which was attended by several dozen teenagers, many of them unbelievers. Those young people lacked Bibles, but they couldn't afford them, so I sensed God's Spirit prompting me to ask Mark how our church could supply Bibles for the youth. (Due to the historical Communist mindset in Moldova, sending Bibles from America is risky because the authorities often open and confiscate such packages.) Mark told me they could only purchase Bibles at a bookstore in the capital city of Chisinau, a drive of two-and-a-half hours. Fortunately, the church's driver was taking our team to the airport in Chisinau several days later, so I arranged for him to buy Bibles for the students. Their cost? About two hundred dollars. While my idea was not included in the written proposal for the trip that was approved by the board (there was no way to anticipate every need in advance), I was certain that the board would understand when I returned home and explained the situation. After all, those kids needed Bibles and they could best be purchased in their own country. Can you imagine their sense of joy and liberation when they received God's Word in their own language?

Maybe the board would have rejoiced over those Bibles had I been able to share that story with them. But when we returned home, no board member ever asked us about the *purpose* of that expense, but the *amount* was undoubtedly counted against the budget for missions. Just as Jesus enraged the religious leaders when he healed the man in the synagogue without authorization, I may have angered the board by my unauthorized decision to buy Bibles as well. It grieves me that the board never heard that those teenagers finally had their first Bibles, but they never took the time to inquire about the purpose of any other expense from that trip, either.

Third, *the enemies of Jesus plotted to destroy him*. The Gospels give us amazing insight into the real motives of the Jewish leaders toward Jesus. While their decisions were initially made in the dark, they later fully came into the light. For example, after Jesus healed the lame man at the Bethesda pool on the Sabbath, John tells us that "the Jews tried all the harder to kill him; not only was he breaking the Sabbath, but he was even calling God his own father, making himself equal with God" (John 5:18). John 7:1 tells us that Jesus purposely stayed away from Judea "because the Jews there were waiting to take his life." The attitude of the leaders became so well known that some people in Jerusalem began asking in John 7:25, "Isn't this the man they are trying to kill?" Jesus himself told the Jewish leaders that he knew about their hostility toward him in John 8:40 when he said, "As it is, you are determined to kill me, a man who has told you the truth that I heard from God." After Jesus declared that "before Abraham was born, I am!" the Jewish leaders "picked up stones to stone him" but Jesus slipped away from the temple area (John 8:58-59). After Jesus raised Lazarus from the dead, we're told about the Sanhedrin that "from that day on they plotted to take his life" (John 11:53). They were so enraged about Jesus' resuscitation of Lazarus that "the chief priests made plans to kill Lazarus as well, for on account of him many of the Jews were going over to Jesus and putting their faith in him" (John 12:10-11). And during the last week of Jesus' life, Luke tells us, "Every day he was teaching at the temple. But the chief priests, the teachers of the law and the leaders among the people were trying to kill him" (Luke 19:47).

The New Testament writers never tell us that anyone was trying to kill disciples like Peter, or James, or Thomas – just Jesus. In the same way, few people in a local church band together to eliminate the small group director, or the children's fourth grade teacher, or the office manager. No, if they go after anyone, a group almost *always* attacks the church's primary leader.

I am not suggesting that a pastor's adversaries wish to *kill* him as Jesus' enemies did. While that sort of thing *has* happened – and I have some stories in my files as evidence – it's more common for antagonists to try and remove him from office, harm his reputation, or damage his career. According to Speed Leas' Five Levels of Conflict, the fourth level involves breaking the relationship between two parties either by withdrawing yourself or convincing the other person to withdraw. The conflict is elevated from issues and emotions to eternal values and principles.[6] But the fifth level is worst of all. Leas observes:

At Level V, people believe the opposition is so evil and so virulent that simply getting rid of them will not do. The opposition must be punished or destroyed. Those at Level V conflict believe, for the safety of the church, that the bad people must be disciplined so they can do no further damage. For example, people at Level V are not satisfied with having the congregation fire a pastor. These people continue their battle at the denominational level, looking for ways to get the pastor defrocked.[7]

In my mind, it is simple to determine which side in a "religious war" represents the devil and which side represents the Lord. In a word, Satan majors in *destruction* (I Peter 5:8) while Jesus majors in *redemption* (Titus 2:13-14). Rediger tells the story of a pastor who was once a shining star in his denomination. A couple of university professors resented his charisma and success and began sabotaging his leadership. When the pastor's confidence began to wane, they accused him of mental disorders, causing his wife to divorce him in panic. The pastor left the ministry and was only able to hold menial jobs.[8] Who was doing the Lord's work? Who was doing Satan's work?

Fourth, *the enemies of Jesus began to scrutinize his life and ministry*. Mark 3:2 states that before Jesus healed the man with the shriveled hand, some Pharisees "were looking for a reason to accuse Jesus, so they watched him closely to see if he would heal on the Sabbath." After Jesus uttered "six woes" against them, Luke tells us that "the Pharisees and the teachers of the law began to oppose him fiercely and to besiege him with questions, waiting to catch him in something he might say" (Luke 11:37-52). During the last week of Jesus' life, Matthew tells us that "the Pharisees went out and laid plans to trap him in his words" (Matthew 22:15-16). Luke 20:20 adds, "Keeping a close watch on him, they sent spies, who pretended to be honest. They hoped to catch Jesus in something he said so that they might hand him over to the power and authority of the governor." Fortunately, Jesus was aware of their "evil intent" (Matthew 22:18). As a pastor, I was aware that people were constantly watching me, sometimes with a hypercritical eye. That's the price pastors pay for telling people how God wants them to live.

Many years ago, in my second pastorate, one board member became my all-time greatest antagonist. (I'll call him Phil.) While I always felt we got along personally, our visions for ministry continually clashed. Phil grew up in Wisconsin where he attended a red brick church building among proud Swedes, and he wanted to replicate that experience at our church. When I arranged for a contemporary band to lead Sunday worship, Phil's wife stayed home from church in protest, and after a while, he quit coming, too. But he returned one Sunday morning a year later. I was teaching in Mark 6 where King Herod Antipas arrested and executed John the Baptist. Phil sat twenty feet away and stared me down with his arms folded. Evidently he noticed too many parallels between Herod and himself because when the service ended, Phil cornered the board chairman to complain that I had deliberately aimed my message at *him*. To his credit, the chairman told Phil, "Look at the bulletin. We were in Mark 5 last week, and we're in Mark 6 this week."

But Phil remained unconvinced and wanted to "take the church back." He gathered together a group of seventeen people who began holding secret meetings. They began researching attendance trends, giving patterns, and church membership, trying to show that my leadership was hurting the church. Phil's group called former attendees and tried to goad them into blaming me for their exodus. (A woman called and clued me in to their tactics.) Then this coalition sat in a room and listed every complaint they could think of about each member of my family – and, of course, they found *some* things. Two group members then brought their charges to two board members who knew they were coming and thwarted their plan by answering every charge. That's the kind of support I *once* enjoyed.

It's unnerving to have people watch your life that closely. While I was used to "living in a fishbowl" as a pastor's kid, I could not lead a perfect life, and knowing people were watching me in hopes that I might stumble caused me to be overly cautious at times. It's not a recipe for being your best self and living – or leading – with abandon. But amazingly, Jesus was always himself in every situation, being far more conscious of his Father's scrutiny than that of his enemies. But no matter how hard they tried, Jesus' enemies couldn't find anything he had done or said wrong, so they advanced to the next step.

Fifth, *the enemies of Jesus accused him of trumped-up charges.* In John 8:46, Jesus asked his adversaries, "Can any of you prove me guilty of sin?" They tried but couldn't, so they continually provoked him into doing or saying something wrong. They had already determined his fate – they just hadn't decided on the most plausible accusations. Whenever Jesus spoke, they tried to twist something he said into a violation of Jewish law so they could charge him with a capital offense. In Matthew 22:15-46, the Pharisees (in league with the Herodians and Sadducees) came to Jesus on four separate occasions to trip him up, but in each case, Jesus turned the tables on them and sent them home whimpering. Because Jesus' enemies couldn't defeat him in a debate, and because of his popularity with the masses, the only way his adversaries could eliminate him was to distort his record with exaggerated charges.

When Jesus was finally arrested away from the gaze of the Passover crowds, we're told that "the chief priests and the whole Sanhedrin were looking for false evidence against Jesus so that they could put him to death. But they did not find any, though many false witnesses came forward" (Matthew 26:59). Nowadays, I suppose, Jesus' enemies would engage in opposition research on Mary and his family and every member of his disciples, trying to find something in their backgrounds, schooling, careers, or family lives that they could use to smear Jesus. Then they would leak that information to the press and let *them* ruin his reputation. But in the end, the charges against Jesus boiled down to two: the Jewish leaders accused him of *blasphemy* (Luke 22:65-71) while the Romans accused him of *sedition* (Luke 23:2), which included opposing the payment of taxes to Caesar and claiming to be a rival king. Neither accusation was true, but both *sounded* plausible, so Jesus was stigmatized by fraudulent charges. Steinke comments:

> Deceit is the hallmark of evil . . . . Deceit is cover up, falsity and darkness. The evil avoid anything that sheds light, anything that involves exposure . . . . Where there is evil, there is a lie present. The evil are not truthful . . . . The manifestation of evil I encounter most frequently in the church is the cunning, sly kind – subtle manipulation, winsome seductiveness,

shrewd innocence. In fact, I dare to say that the cunning side of evil is even assisted, enabled, and welcomed in the church.[9]

I once served on the staff of a church where the pastor's giftedness was in shepherding. (He's the only man I refer to as "pastor" to this day.) While he was a good preacher, preparing messages was hard work for him, and he had to plan teaching for the Sunday morning, Sunday evening, and Wednesday night services. On Sunday nights, he invited different people to preach, including me. But a faction in the church didn't understand his gifting and began accusing him of being too lazy to speak on Sunday nights – and threatened to leave the church if he didn't. While this group *may* have had some legitimate concerns, the charge of laziness was exaggerated, and wounded the pastor so much that he felt demoralized and could barely function. When people start *searching* for wrongdoing in a leader's life, they've become Pharisees – and their graceless attitudes usually trump *anything* a leader may have done wrong.

Sixth, *the enemies of Jesus collaborated with a close confidant to betray him.* Jesus wasn't intentionally betrayed by all twelve of his disciples, or even by two or three, although they all fled when he was arrested. No, it only takes *one* traitor to take out a spiritual leader, and Judas played that role to perfection. Whether he wanted Jesus to be a political Messiah, or he was greedy for cash, Judas was disappointed by his Master and left the upper room to arrange for his arrest. But Jesus knew that Judas wasn't loyal to him as far back as John 6:70-71 when Jesus called Judas "a devil" in front of the other eleven disciples. When he was in their company, Judas acted one way, but away from them, he acted differently. A tough business executive might have expelled Judas months before, but a shepherd keeps hoping that unconditional love will prompt the traitor to change.

In speaking with other pastors, I have discovered that it's not uncommon for an associate pastor to form an alliance with board members, sometimes because the associate wants the pastor's job. While there are many fine associates everywhere, it's essential that an associate demonstrate complete loyalty to his or her pastor. When any staff member can no longer support the senior pastor fully, he or she needs to resign rather than angle for the pastor's removal. I had lunch once with a prominent pastor who told his staff members, "If any of you try and form an alliance with a board member, you're gone. I will fire you on the spot." Since the pastor hired those staff members for his ministry team, he expected their absolute loyalty. I served as a staff member under the leadership of five senior pastors, three times as a youth pastor and twice as an associate pastor. In each situation, churchgoers complained to me about the pastor, but I always supported him publicly. In my opinion, plotting behind a pastor's back is spiritual treason.

In John 13:18, Jesus predicted his impending betrayal by quoting Psalm 41:9, which reads: "Even my close friend, whom I trusted, he who shared my bread, has lifted up his heel against me." Paul writes in 1 Corinthians 11:23, "The Lord Jesus, on the night he was betrayed, took bread, and when he had given thanks, he broke it and said, 'This is my body, which is for you. Do this in remembrance of me.'" Paul didn't refer to "the night Jesus was arrested" or "the night of his agony in Gethsemane" but "the night he was betrayed." Even though Judas had already left the Eleven when Jesus uttered his famous words, Paul contrasts Jesus' self-sacrificial giving with Judas' conniving ways. Today, we'd call Judas a "frenemy" – an enemy disguised as a friend. How much I want to imitate Jesus and treat traitors as friends! Sadly, I'm not there yet. Right now, it's enough for me not to view them as enemies. Maybe, just maybe, that's a start.

Seventh, *the enemies of Jesus formed unholy alliances against him.* By himself, Judas couldn't have succeeded in getting rid of Jesus. He needed allies. By itself, the Sanhedrin couldn't have put Jesus to death. They needed an "inside man" among The Twelve along with assistance from Rome. As one reads the Gospels, it's surprising to note all the unnatural alliances that formed against Jesus: the Pharisees and the Herodians (Mark 3:6; 12:13-17); Judas and the Sanhedrin (Matt. 26:4-5); the Sanhedrin and Pilate (Matt. 27:1-2); and Pilate and Herod Antipas (Luke 23:12). The only way that Jesus could be eliminated was for all his adversaries to collaborate toward the same goal: his crucifixion. Stott remarks:

The doctrines he taught were felt to be dangerous, even sub-
versive. The Jewish leaders were incensed by his disrespectful

attitude to the law and by his provocative claims, while the Romans heard that he was proclaiming himself King of the Jews, and so challenging the authority of Caesar. To both groups Jesus appeared to be a revolutionary thinker and preacher, and some considered him a revolutionary activist as well. So profoundly did he disturb the status quo that they determined to do away with him. In fact, they entered into an unholy alliance with one another in order to do so.[10]

Jesus predicted his death on three occasions in each of the Synoptic Gospels (Matt. 16:21-23; 17:22-23; 20:18-19; Mark 8:31-33; 9:31-32; 10:33-34; Luke 9:21-22, 44-45; 18:31-33). In each passage in Matthew, Jesus mentions *where* he will be killed (Jerusalem), *how* he will be killed (crucifixion), and what will happen *after* he's killed (resurrection). He doesn't deal with *when* or *why*. But in two of those passages (Matt. 16:21-23; 20:18-19), Jesus specifically mentions *who* will kill him. In the first passage, Jesus attributes his coming death to "the hands of the elders, chief priests and teachers of the law" – the spiritual leaders of their nation. In the second passage, Jesus predicts he will be "betrayed to the chief priests and the teachers of the law" without mentioning the elders. And in Matthew 20:19, Jesus also warns that the Jewish leaders "will turn him over to the Gentiles to be mocked and flogged and crucified."

Many of us assume that Jesus was trying to prepare his disciples for his eventual departure and ultimate return, but why did he mention *by name* the three Jewish groups that conspired against him? Is it possible that Jesus wanted his disciples to know *who* "did him in" so they would know the identity of the conspirators in case they later pursued Jesus' disciples? As conscientious Jews, I'm sure that Jesus' men didn't want to believe that their national leaders were responsible for the Messiah's execution. But Jesus predicted that the official leaders *would* conspire to take him down. He recognized and named his antagonists ahead of time. Although he shielded his disciples from the full identity of the *individuals* involved (Judas, Caiaphas, Pilate, and Herod), Jesus openly fingered the particular *groups* (the elders, chief priests, teachers of the law, and Gentiles) that plotted together to take his life.

Like Jesus, I wish I had known in advance every party that would conspire together to harm my wife and me. While I suspected *some* parties, my inability to detect them *all* ended up in devastation. In fact, it's easy to feel foolish because I was largely responsible for choosing the leaders – until I realized that Jesus chose Judas. How difficult it must have been for Jesus, knowing that a handpicked intimate would eventually sell him out!

As a pastor increasingly acquires spiritual authority, some power-brokers choose to undermine the pastor from within. But why don't *they* leave? Because they believe it's *their* church and not *his*. In one of our neighborhoods, Kim and I couldn't let our two little dogs play outside unless we were nearby because coyotes roamed the area. When we mentioned this to others, people invariably said, "Well, they were here first." That's exactly how veteran churchgoers feel toward their pastor: *they* were here *first*! And when people contemplate leaving a church, they're forced to consider leaving friends behind, so some lock arms with their friends and push out the pastor instead. They claim that "this is *our* church," like the pastor is a foreigner who invaded it and should be deported back to his homeland. But when a pastor is called to a church, it becomes *his* church as well. He uses *his* gifts to enrich it. He gives of *his* income to support it. He prays for the church and loves the church and promotes the church, so it isn't the exclusive possession of the pioneers. It's *his* church, too. But ultimately, every local church that worships and preaches Jesus Christ is subservient to *his* leadership (Colossians 1:18). It's not really *our* church or the *pastor's* church but *Jesus'* church, as he reminds us in Matthew 16:18 when he asserts, "I will build my church." How I wish that every churchgoer would remember that. We manage *his* church.

Eighth, *the enemies of Jesus encouraged a mob mentality against him.* I recently saw a sign that stated, "Never underestimate the power of stupid people in large groups." How true! Rational people can completely shut down their brains when they're in a large company of their peers. Exhibit A is the way the crowds praised Jesus when he entered Jerusalem on a young donkey but called for his crucifixion five days later. How could some of the same people call out, "Blessed is the king who comes in the name of the Lord!" on Sunday (Luke 19:38) and cry "Away with this man!" the following Friday morning (Luke 23:18)?

235

Of course, the Jewish leaders did not want to arrest Jesus publicly because they knew that the common people adored him. Mark 12:12 says, "Then they looked for a way to arrest him because they knew he had spoken the parable against them. But they were afraid of the crowd, so they left him and went away." The crowd stood with Jesus and against the Jewish leaders at this juncture. (Leaders are only afraid of "the people" when "the people" aren't afraid of the leaders and speak out against injustice.) But by the time we reach Mark 15:15, the crowd was now provoking Pilate to batter Jesus: "Wanting to satisfy the crowd, Pilate released Barabbas to them. He had Jesus flogged, and handed him over to be crucified." Stott indicts Pilate:

> Sure, Jesus was innocent. Sure, justice demanded his release. But how could he champion innocence and justice if thereby he denied the will of the people, flouted the nation's leaders, and above all provoked an uprising, thereby forfeiting the imperial favour? His conscience was drowned by the loud voices of rationalization. He compromised because he was a coward.[11]

While Pilate must bear responsibility for permitting Jesus' execution, the Gentile ruler was the only person that day that defended Jesus when the Jews turned against him. As Peter later told the Jews, "You handed him over to be killed, and you disowned him before Pilate, though he had decided to let him go. You disowned the Holy and Righteous One and asked that a murderer be released to you" (Acts 3:13-14). What a striking illustration of the power of a mob!

At the November meetings, I could not believe the behavior of some people who spoke against us. Kim and I had enjoyed meals with them. We had prayed with them and for them. We had helped them launch their ministries. We had helped them grow spiritually. But each person who stood to indict us seemed to embolden the others. I had never before witnessed such a mob mentality in a church. When a crowd becomes focused on one individual, people forget all the good that person has done and spotlight their flaws instead. Leas observes:

> Not only does conflict besmirch us when it reaches a certain level, most of us lose our ability to think clearly and rationally. Most of us aren't very good at dealing with conflict and we

don't want to go through the pain of developing those skills. Therefore, instead of functioning rationally, we overfocus on our own personal ends and on self-protection. We lose our ability to see complexity; we oversimplify; we become hyper-vigilant – looking for any sign of threat and reacting out of proportion to the amount of danger actually present. Instead of feeling powerful in conflict, most of us feel powerless and find ourselves using means that we know aren't kosher, but we don't feel completely in control of the situation.[11]

I wonder if Jesus felt like I did as he surveyed the crowd that Good Friday: "I remember healing your son several years ago. I recall the way you smiled when I taught in the temple last week. I still retain the memory when you walked up to our group and gave us food and coins. What did I ever do to have you treat me this way?"

Ninth, *the enemies of Jesus abused him without regret.* According to the Gospels, Jesus was subjected to violence even before he hung on the cross. After Jesus was charged with blasphemy by the high priest, the Jewish leaders "began to spit at him; they blindfolded him, struck him with their fists, and said, 'Prophesy!' And the guards took him and beat him" (Mark 14:65). After Pilate handed over Jesus to be crucified, his soldiers surrounded Jesus (Matthew 27:27-31):

They stripped him and put a scarlet robe on him, and then twisted together a crown of thorns and set it on his head. They put a staff in his right hand and knelt in front of him and mocked him. 'Hail, king of the Jews!' they said. They spit on him, and took the staff and struck him on the head again and again. After they had mocked him, they took off the robe and put his own clothes on him. Then they led him away to crucify him.

In addition, Jesus was mercilessly taunted by passersby who insultingly said in Matthew 27:39-40, "You who are going to destroy the temple and build it in three days, save yourself! Come down from the cross, if you are the Son of God!" Even members of the Sanhedrin were there to mock him, shouting, "He saved others, but he can't save himself! He's the King of Israel! Let him come down now from the cross, and we will believe in him" (Matthew 27:41-42). Judging from these statements, "trash talking" was prevalent centuries before being practiced in the National Football League.

Here's what gets me: there is no specific record in the Gospels that those who beat and insulted Jesus had any regrets about their actions. Some of them undoubtedly did later on – especially when they discovered his true identity on the Day of Pentecost – but they couldn't express those feelings directly to Jesus because he had died, and even after he rose again, Scripture never indicates that Jesus made himself available to any crowd of unbelievers.

When it comes to the harsh way in which many pastors (and staff members) are treated in our day, don't people see what they are doing? How can they abuse a person called by God? Don't they know that their anger puts them in a position to be controlled by evil forces? What was done to Jesus was *evil*. And the actions of a small minority operating against an innocent pastor may be evil as well. But unfortunately, too many Christians won't admit it, which is a big reason we can't eradicate this plague from our churches. Rediger writes:

> Mainline churches have been caught unprepared for the increase of evil practice and ill will in congregations. In recent years mainline Protestantism and Catholicism have tended to regard sin as normal mistakes, and evil as another name for mental disorders and illnesses. This has allowed evil to gain a foothold, even among good people. And it has left us without spiritual categories and resources for handling evil. Many religious leaders still deny the reality of evil and try to manage its consequences with tactics appropriate for normal or abnormal conflicts. The outcome is like trying to quench an electrical fire with water. The conflagration and collateral damage are increased, rather than diminished by the efforts to put the fire out . . . . Evil is real and powerful, and it is not expressed nor managed in purely rational ways. Conflict management methods that fail to acknowledge this will fail when applied to conflicts having evil components and agendas.[13]

So why haven't we heard regrets or apologies from even *one* person who banded together to betray us? (Kim is convinced that the board knows they did wrong, while I'm just as convinced they still believe that all their decisions were right.) The phrase "banded together" is the key. In the minds of some, if one person turns on a pastor, that's *betrayal*, but if an entire group does so, that's *justice*. But let's remember that when Jesus was crucified, the whole world stood against him – and the whole world was wrong.

Finally, *the enemies of Jesus were unknowingly working for Satan*. Jesus was constantly aware of the devil's attempts to discredit and destroy his ministry. While Satan offered Jesus shortcuts to avoid the cross during his temptation, Jesus resisted Satan's lures through the skillful use of Scripture (Matthew 4:1-11). Satan went away for a little while (Luke 4:13) but later returned through external (the Pharisees and the Sadducees) and internal attacks (Judas). Satan's specialty is using people who harbor bitterness against a leader and fanning the flames of that hostility until it becomes blind rage. The devil and his minions constantly probe the hearts of professing believers, searching for bitter individuals – especially inside a leader's inner circle – they can use to harm the leader. Paul writes in Ephesians 4:26-27, "In your anger do not sin. Do not let the sun go down while you are still angry, and do not give the devil a foothold." Some anger is sinful, while other anger is not – but sinful anger should be faced and confessed before a day concludes. And yet many believers feel powerful when they're angry, so powerful that they carry their anger from one day to the next. If you bump them, they'll tell you about the intensity and object of their wrath. Bitterness is contagious.

The anger of the Jewish leaders spread to Pilate, and to King Herod, and to the crowds in Jerusalem gathered for Passover. Their resentment toward Jesus climaxed in the mob's cry to crucify him. While the Father was guiding his Son's life in a sovereign fashion, Satan was working in an undetected manner. Jesus knew that the Pharisees were working for their father, the devil (John 8:44), but his disciples did not. Jesus knew that Satan had entered into Judas (Luke 22:3), but his disciples did not. If Jesus visited our churches today, he could instantly show us those in whose lives Satan had gained a foothold. Leaders could unite to defeat his influence while lovingly confronting the evil one's victims. But like Jesus' disciples, most believers do not sense the enemy's presence in their midst and are completely unaware that the devil might be using *them* to accomplish nefarious purposes. Unfortunately, the lack of a forgiving spirit can blind God's people to the hatred inside their souls. Murphy writes:

> Perhaps the major door of defeat for believers struggling with interpersonal conflicts is lack of forgiveness . . . . When we are angry with others and refuse to forgive them, we open the door to all kinds of interpersonal conflicts and sin . . . . Sin energy, like a mighty negative spiritual magnet, draws Satan and his demons. Where deep interpersonal conflicts exist among believers, the Evil One is there.[14]

Maybe those who have the gift of discerning of spirits could form an alliance with a church's pastor. These gifted believers could identify pockets of bitterness in a congregation so that potentially contentious individuals could be monitored and confronted if necessary. In this way, a church might be able to prevent attacks against a pastor from even beginning.

The best thing that Peter ever said is recorded in Matthew 16:16 when he told Jesus, "You are the Christ, the Son of the living God." Jesus commended Peter for his insight and attributed it to divine revelation. Yet a few verses later, after Jesus predicted his crucifixion, Peter told Jesus privately, "Never, Lord! This shall never happen to you!" Jesus attributed those words to the devil when he responded, "Get behind me, Satan! You are a stumbling block to me; you do not have in mind the things of God, but the things of men" (Matthew 16:21-23). If Peter could be greatly used by God one moment, and greatly used by Satan the next, isn't it possible for Christian leaders and believers today to be influenced by Satan as well? Shouldn't this knowledge humble each one of us? And yet when the devil *does* use us, we seem largely unaware of it. The Pharisees were so spiritually blind that they accused Jesus of operating by Satan's power when *they* were the real culprits (Matt. 12:24; Mark 3:22). Too many Christians insist that Satan is working through *others* when he might very well be working through *them*.

In the film *Murder on the Orient Express*, a group of nine individuals travel on that famed train from Istanbul to Paris. Along the way, a man is found murdered in his compartment with multiple stab wounds. Throughout this Agatha Christie story, the viewer wonders which of the many suspects knifed the victim until the surprise ending: they *all* stuck a knife in him – but all for different reasons. What a picture of the spiritual dynamics involved in too many churches!

I have a theory about the mentality of those who seek to target a pastor they don't like. Because they sense that what they're doing is wrong, they have to (a) exaggerate any charges to the level of a capital crime; (b) find others who agree with them to alleviate their guilt; (c) justify their actions by convincing themselves it's for the common good; and (d) work up their hatred so they follow through with their plan. While this progression sounds like the kind of diabolical rage one might find in politics or war (or the prelude to a murder), the last place we'd expect to find such irrationality is inside a church. The ultimate explanation? Satan.

I don't believe that Jesus could have been defeated by any human movement, political party, or organization alone. His execution was the result of a conspiracy between Jews and Gentiles, Pilate and Herod, and government and religion (Acts 4:25-27). His betrayal, arrest, trials, and crucifixion were all launched by a merger of human and supernatural forces (Luke 22:3; John 6:70-71; 13:2, 27). In the end, everything came down to a cosmic power struggle between Jesus and Satan – and yet superintended by a sovereign and loving God.

It is my fervent prayer that pastors, church leaders, and lay people will become so familiar with Satan's game plan for terminating pastors and staff members that they will recognize when they are tempted to fall into his trap and choose to act biblically rather than diabolically. May God give us a spiritual awareness of the enemy's methodology so we can expose and defeat his influence in the wisdom and power of the Holy Spirit.

CHAPTER 13

QUESTIONS ABOUT OUR CONFLICT

*I*f I shared my story one Sunday at your church, and I opened up the floor for questions afterward, what would *you* want to ask me? Here are seven possibilities:

1. What was it like to be the focal point of a major conflict?

It was confusing. On the one hand, a group of leaders selected by the church were upset with me, but on the other hand, I did not really know what I had done wrong. I could only guess. It's like watching an old Western where the town council accuses their sheriff of murder so they quickly move to hang him. While the sheriff knows he didn't shoot anybody, he tries to slow down the proceedings so he can find out what's really motivating the lynch mob.

At first, you assume the allegations made by the leaders are correct. After all, there are six of them but just one of you. You know you have your blind spots but wonder how you could be *that* blind. So you review your past doings and conclude, "Okay, I could have handled that situation better, and maybe I should have said this instead." But your conscience will not allow you to make the leap from "You made some minor mistakes" to "You are a horrible person who needs to leave this church immediately," and yet that's how you feel you're being treated.

My biggest concern was that board members were going to pool their complaints about my faults and then unload that list on me, just like they did with Kim. I've had people do that to me before, and it's devastating to think that believers would harbor that kind of resentment against you. In all but one case, those actions destroyed our relationship. When people come to you in love to discuss one shortcoming at a time, you can handle it. But when they dump all your mistakes on you at once, it's crushing. While it's arrogant for a pastor to think that *everybody* should love or follow him, no one expects professing Christians to act with such acrimony.

Few in the congregation had any idea there was friction between church leaders behind the scenes. Until the conflict surfaced, I had spoken with only a handful of people about my problems with the board, and then only to figure out how to work with them better. I didn't try to harm their reputations or have them removed from office. I sincerely tried to cooperate with them, but in the end, I wouldn't have been true to the Lord, the congregation, or my calling if I had surrendered myself to their micromanagement philosophy.

So being the focal point of a conflict feels terrible. Part of you wants to emulate Jonah and just throw yourself overboard, but in your saner moments, you realize that you haven't done anything worthy of banishment, so you pray for resolution while preparing for your departure.

I enjoy root canals more.

2. What was the whole conflict *really* about?

Church conflict is usually complex, so I'm hesitant to offer simplistic answers. People usually search for a single cause for a church's problems so they can have someone to blame, but matters aren't always that black and white. In retrospect, I believe that I had five unspoken value clashes with The Seven:

• Fear versus faith. Some board members were afraid the global economy might collapse. They ate a meal before every meeting and talked about the latest news in the financial world. Since the recession had negatively impacted their companies, they assumed it would also harm the church. They wanted to deal with matters proactively, and deserved commendation for their foresight. While I had more experience in trusting the Lord to bring a church through tough times, my faith seemed to be viewed as a liability rather than an asset. As the associate told Kim during his first weeks on the job, "Your faith scares me." (Kim should have responded, "And your lack of faith scares me," but she's too gracious to say that.) The board became so immersed in finances that they found it difficult to view the shortfall through a spiritual lens. Years before, previous board members used to ask, "What does God want us to do?" Now they were asking, "What will money permit us to do?" The board allowed money to dominate their thinking and dictate their decision-making, giving money far too much authority. Richard Foster writes:

> The Christian is given the high calling of using mammon without serving mammon. We are using mammon when we allow God to determine our economic decisions. We are serving mammon when we allow mammon to determine our economic decisions. We simply must decide who is going to make our decisions – God or mammon . . . . If money determines what we do or do not do, then money is our boss. If God determines what we do or do not do, then God is our boss.[1]

At some point along the line – I can't pinpoint exactly when – money began making decisions.

• Maintenance versus outreach. Our church had experienced its best-ever year statistically in 2008 and I wanted to keep the momentum going because when it stops, it's difficult to resurrect. We began 2009 with a solid reserve fund, and I wanted to save many of those funds for a rainy day but invest the rest in starting that third service to reach a younger demographic. But while I was thinking outreach, the board was thinking maintenance. Some board members believed that the roof on the original building needed to be replaced within five years so they wanted to lay aside money from the reserve fund to accomplish that goal. While I understood their desire to replace the roof, we could not budget the funds for all the upgrades needed to pull off that third service. Since they had me outnumbered six to one – seven to one, if you count the associate pastor – I believed the board was missing an opportunity. Greenfield writes:

> I have observed that when a church is more concerned with its internal operations, with 'maintenance' of the organization, than it is with ministry, it becomes vulnerable to attempts at internal political control of the organization. When a church is focused on taking care of itself, paying off its mortgage, paying its bills, and saving money, and shows little interest in outreach, evangelism, ministry, and missions, it is often headed for trouble . . . . Outreach, evangelism, ministry, and missions will keep a congregation on its knees in prayer (which always frightens Satan away). Satan can more easily invade a church that is consumed with secondary matters.[2]

While our mission and vision statements still touted the church's outreach direction, I began to sense that board members no longer supported that orientation. There was talk of focusing just on the needs of attendees and eliminating mission trips – a far cry from the way the church had operated for years. In fact, there was some sentiment on the board for just sending funds rather than people to Moldova and Kenya. This values shift occurred without any negotiation.

I recently saw a bell curve describing the life cycle of churches. Near the top of the curve on the left, a church is characterized by cooperation, risk, innovation, growth, sacrifice, and an outward focus. As the curve slopes downward, a church is characterized by control, guarantees, tradition, maintenance, safety, and an inward focus.[3] While I was trying to preserve the values that caused the church to grow, the board was pulling hard in the other direction, which would have led to decline. You can't conserve your way to growth.

• Secrecy versus transparency. Like many of my pastoral colleagues, I chose to be open and honest about the issues facing our church. I always maintained confidentiality about people's personal problems (and what was shared in counseling), but other than that, I didn't want us to have secrets. I treated people like adults who could handle important information rather than kids who couldn't handle truth. In all my dealings, I kept in mind John 1:17: "For the law was given through Moses; grace and truth came through Jesus Christ." Like Jesus, I tried to speak the *truth* with *grace*. But the board did not practice transparency. They increasingly made decisions in the dark and then kept those decisions from others – including me – under the guise of confidentiality. If you develop a culture of secrecy, you cannot be blamed for your decisions because nobody knows what they are, but you can easily blame others for theirs. Leas writes about the merits of church boards being up-front and open concerning their decisions:

> What do I mean by 'open?' I mean that the minutes of all board meetings are open to the inspection of people who do not attend. I mean that members of the board collectively or individually do not make pacts that what goes on at a particular meeting will be kept from others in the church. I mean that members of the congregation will be given ample access to the board and members of the board when they seek it.[4]

While the board always knew what *I* was thinking, I usually did not know what *they* were thinking. As making decisions in secret became more natural, they would come to meetings and announce a decision. When I protested the decision, *I* appeared like a troublemaker. As they became more clandestine, they came to meetings and imposed their collective will on me.

• Authority versus accountability. In the church's system of government, I was accountable to the governing board. Every month, I brought a written report of my current activities and future plans. If I wanted to make a major change, I'd run it by the staff, compose a document and make a board presentation. I did this during my entire ten-and-a-half year tenure.

But the board was supposed to be accountable to the *congregation*. The board presented the annual budget to the church in November 2008 but never reported to the church in any form after that, a period of one year. Before leaving for Moldova, I recommended that the board schedule an information meeting for October 11 to tell the church about our economic status, and they agreed to do that. At the board chairman's request, I even wrote out instructions for conducting the meeting, but the board cancelled it after I went overseas.

It seemed like the board wanted increased *authority* without increased *accountability*. If the board made a decision, I ended up reporting it to the congregation through announcements, emails, or all-church letters. (In fact, I wrote a newsletter article describing what happens inside a board meeting several months before the conflict went public.) While this may be standard procedure in many churches, shouldn't pastors and boards work harder at letting churchgoers know the identity of board members and their decisions? If governing leaders remain invisible, most people's concerns inside a church will automatically be directed to the pastor and staff.

By contrast, I know a church where a board member sits at a booth every Sunday and answers questions from attendees. Some churches place photos of board members on the church website or in a campus location with high visibility. Even if the pastor announces relevant decisions to the congregation at weekend services, the board still needs to make itself accountable to the wider body provided church members vote to elect or ratify board members. If a board is accountable to the congregation, it needs to report to them more than once per year – especially if the pastor has to account to the board every month.

- Business versus Scripture. In our culture, too many churches are drifting away from what the *Bible* says and are becoming increasingly enamored with what *business* says. The new paradigm says that a pastor is the CEO of a small business, the local church. You're not *called*; you're *hired*. You don't *love* the people as much as you *lead* the institution. You don't *teach* the Word as much as *communicate* a message – one that should continually advance the church's mission. Christians now expect pastors to be CEOs, lay leaders to morph into corporate directors, and money to be the bottom line. But where's the Bible in all this? While pastors and churches can profit from the insights and practices of the business community, believers should *always* consult Scripture first. Foster writes about this historic core value:

The evangelical witness affirms the primacy of Scripture as the only infallible rule of faith and practice. This cannot be stressed enough. Scripture has primacy over other writings; primacy over church tradition; primacy over individual religious experience; primacy over the individual conscience; primacy over individual revelations, dreams, and visions; primacy over culture. As the Protestant reformers put it, *Sola Scriptura*, the Scripture alone.[5]

Does it sound presumptuous to add that Scripture has primacy over business practices? Many Christian leaders *believe* what Scripture teaches for salvation and spiritual growth but *ignore* Scripture when business practices seem more relevant – especially as they relate to the pastor. Let's say that a church board is upset with their pastor over something he said. Joe wants to fire the pastor outright. During a secret meeting, Bill comes to agree with Joe. Several aren't yet sure, but nobody feels like defending the pastor. After talking into the night, Joe and Bill persuade the remaining holdouts that they *will* fire the pastor. They then agree to meet again and decide when they'll talk to the pastor and what they'll say to the congregation.

During this whole episode, they never crack open their Bibles. They never discuss meeting with the pastor to share their concerns or give any thought to his restoration. They never ask for his interpretation of events or let him present any defense. They never even *ask* God for his guidance, later asking him to *bless* their decision instead. In other words, they handle matters like they were in a seventh floor office at work. Once again, where's the Bible in all this?

I cannot state with certainty that the board failed to consult Scripture before or during the conflict, but they certainly did not give that impression to either my wife or me. Due to the stress of the situation, they fell back on what they knew best: corporate practices.

3. What do you think the board's goal was in the conflict?

In my judgment, their *immediate* goal was to force me to resign as pastor. Because I had not done anything worthy of removal – and because they didn't have the votes at the congregational level – I was supposed to collapse and quit when they dismissed my wife. As a church leader later told me, they looked at us as a team rather than as individuals. In my view, their *ultimate* goal was to run the church more like a business, possibly in collaboration with the ex-associate or my predecessor.

If I had to reduce the whole conflict down to one phrase, I'd say, "Power struggle over church direction and money." I believe the board tried to control the ministry by micromanaging the money. We viewed church ministry in diametrically opposite ways.

For example, about four months before the October 24 meeting, I noticed that whenever a board member introduced an issue in a meeting, I was the only one who asked tough questions or had objections. I received the sense that my remarks were tolerated but were viewed as a minority position rather than the concerns of a seasoned pastor. Board members seemed to be working methodically toward an agenda regardless of my concerns. While I felt this way for a few months, I had it confirmed during the first week in September when Kim was in the hospital.

I received an email stating that the board had *approved* a proposal via online polling without consulting me about the issue. The proposal was to raise funds by promoting an e-script program, but as soon as I read the email, I had questions. What would the funds be used for? Who would administer this program? Who would explain it to the congregation? If the board was going to use e-script monies to supplement the general fund, I could not support the proposal because I believe that a local church should be funded by the donations of believers, not through fundraising projects. E-script was fine for a project outside the budget, but not to supplant tithes and offerings. I sent the board an email protesting their failure to include my voice or vote in their decision, but I wondered if they had been handling some decisions this way for a while and only now had I become aware of it.

I was okay with the *fact* of my leaving and the *timing* of my departure but not the *manner* in which we left. Looking back, maybe I needed a fresh challenge. For that reason, if the board had offered me a reasonable separation package, I would have taken it. Had they done so, the board would have stayed intact. The staff would have retained their positions. The congregation would have accepted our departure more easily. But if the board ever considered this option, they may have rejected it because it would have cost some money – but they may have underestimated the actual costs of their decisions. Weese and Crabtree observe that "the financial cost of a pastoral transition in a large church exceeds *twice* the annual compensation package, or

10-15 percent of the annual operating budget of the church. That's money!"[6]

After we left, it took the church nearly three months to find an interim pastor. If I had been offered a peaceful exit, the associate might have stayed and helped the board govern the church. In other words, everybody would have won. Then why don't more churches choose this option? I believe it's because too many people in a conflict want to *win* and make the other party *lose*. Conflicts easily become personal. Many pastors under fire can relate to these words from Jeremiah the prophet in Jeremiah 11:18-20:

> God told me what was going on. That's how I knew.
>   You, God, opened my eyes to their evil scheming.
> I had no idea what was going on — naïve as a lamb
>   being led to slaughter!
> I didn't know they had it in for me,
>   didn't know of their behind-the-scenes plots:
> 'Let's get rid of the preacher.
>   *That* will stop the sermons!
> Let's get rid of him for good.
>   He won't be remembered for long.'
> Then I said, 'God-of-the-Angel-Armies,
>   you're a fair judge.
> You examine and cross-examine
>   human actions and motives.
> I want to see these people shown up and put down!
>   I'm an open book before you. Clear my name.'[7]

4. What would have been some alternative ways of addressing any alleged overspending?

Regardless of the staff member, the most sensible option would have been to show me as pastor written documentation of any over-spending. As staff supervisor, I would have met with that staffer – possibly with a board member present – and asked him or her to account for their expenditures. This process would have been consistent with the church's governing documents and Matthew 18:15-16. I would have discovered which expenses were legitimate, which were illegitimate, and which were questionable. If the expenses were excessive, I could have made a recommendation to the board which they could have approved or disapproved.

A second option would have been for me to call the staff member into a board meeting and ask him or her to account for their spending in that forum. The board's job would then be to engage in fact-finding. Once they had the facts, we could decide how to handle matters together.

The advantage of the above approaches is that they follow Scripture, were consistent with church bylaws, and required my input as both senior pastor and staff supervisor. If I felt that a staff member had spent money excessively, I could have relinquished discipline to the board or insisted that a staff member resign. However, such a process might also clear the staff member of major wrongdoing. Sande observes:

> It is wise to remember that many differences and offenses are the result of misunderstandings rather than actual wrongs. Therefore, when you approach another person, do so in a tentative manner. Unless you have clear, firsthand knowledge that a wrong has been done, give the other person the benefit of the doubt and be open to the possibility that you have not assessed the situation correctly.[8]

Other options might include putting a staff member on probation while the board completed their investigation, or freezing a staffer's budget for a specified period of time, or warning them with a write-up that they could not spend unauthorized funds without severe consequences. But decision makers can become so anxious that they can't think creatively. Steinke writes:

> When we are flooded with anxiety, we can neither hear what is said without distortion nor respond with clarity. Bruce McEwen, a neuroendocrinologist, comments that stress limits our repertoire of responses. Fixated on what is endangering us, we forfeit our imaginative capacities. We act with a small and sometimes unproductive repertoire of behaviors. With fewer alternatives, we act foolishly . . . . Our mind is set in imagina-

tive gridlock, we obsess about the threat, and our chances of changing our thinking are almost nonexistent.[9]

If some alleged overspending had been brought to the treasurer's attention, and Kim and I were at home rather than overseas, it's possible that either the chairman or the treasurer would have contacted us and requested an explanation. We could have responded to any concerns via email or telephone and quickly cleared up matters. But because we were overseas, the offenses seemed more severe, even permanent. Cold hard numbers on a spread sheet lend themselves more readily to a "guilty" verdict than verbal interpretations of those same numbers. Leas says:

> In a conflict situation, members of a board may not want to know very much about what is happening, and they may want to take shortcuts. Uncomfortable persons don't like doing anything that might prolong their discomfort. So, incomplete information, unfair information or information excessively loaded with feelings is allowed to stand for reason and is often acted upon so that the problem can be banished quickly.[10]

When the board instituted their expense policy, no one mentioned anything about a "zero tolerance policy." In other words, if you violate the policy, you are automatically terminated. The financial systems of the church had operated one way for years, and now they were changing. Couldn't the board allow for *any* mistakes?

In a related manner, I have struggled with the amount of overspending that the board claimed my wife did. Why didn't they let us see *their* documentation concerning any alleged overspending? As a board member, I saw spread sheets on donations, budgets, and savings every month. Assuming the treasurer had compiled a spread sheet of Kim's expenses, wasn't I as the pastor entitled to see it? On October 24, when the board made their shocking announcement, shouldn't they have prepared a copy of the "smoking gun" for me to view? Kim and I might have been able to understand her release better had we seen documentation, but we never saw *anything* coherent even though we asked for the information twice. I could never in good conscience allow a church board to terminate *any* staff member for overspending based solely on *verbal* charges. They would need to convince me using *concrete* evidence.

But if they showed Kim the numbers and let her explain, she might have ended up in "slap the hand territory" or even "exoneration territory," and dismissal wouldn't have been an option. The board and I agreed that if giving didn't improve markedly over the final quarter, we'd be forced to cut staff salaries across the board or release a full-time staffer. While Kim was our most productive staff member, her ministry budgets were also larger than anyone else's.

On several occasions, I encouraged the board to analyze congregational giving by meeting with the financial secretary. She recorded who donated funds on which date all year long, and by looking at giving patterns (without looking at names), the board could have learned a great deal. All we needed to meet the budget was five more tithing units. But the board just wanted to curtail spending without even considering how to raise revenue.

The board may also have sought someone to blame for the church's financial stresses and Kim became the scapegoat. When anxiety in a congregation increases, people unconsciously attempt to exonerate themselves by locating a problem person (or persons) or condition. In the Old Testament, the priest ceremonially placed the sins of the people on a scapegoat and killed it as a means of purifying them. In medieval times, a community in stress identified someone as the "witch" and burned that person at the stake to cleanse the community. Today "the dysfunctional congregation identifies someone as the 'patient,' the symptom bearer, and blames that person (or a group) for all the problems in the church."[11] This person is not the real problem but becomes the visible expression of the issues buried deeply within the congregation – but it's healthier for a pastor and church leaders to assume responsibility *together* for their church.

But no one person was to blame because we were falling behind our budget. The economy was tanking. One of our most generous givers had moved away. And we were going through a time when we weren't attracting as many newcomers as usual. My long-term way of dealing with the shortfall was to teach on biblical stewardship and grow more and better givers, as well as reach more people for Christ who would become givers. Short-term, I agreed with the board that we needed to reduce all the spending we could. But the board never considered how to generate more revenue through donations, and it's easy for that scarcity mindset to become your permanent way of thinking.

5. Why did you wait seven weeks to resign instead of leaving sooner?

I come from the "it's always too soon to quit" school of ministry. My biblical heroes are Jeremiah and Timothy, two sensitive men who suffered much but refused to bail on God's call. In thirty-six years of church ministry, I'd been falsely accused of wrongdoing several times, and nothing hurts more – or makes one angrier. However, if you run every time your detractors accuse you of something, you'll be useless to the kingdom – and never learn how to face down critics. There comes a time when you must stand for what's right and counter lies with truth. Some pastors might have resigned during or following the October 24 meeting, but I never sensed that God wanted me to abandon my ministry. In the end, I'm glad I persevered or we never would have learned what really happened.

So when I sensed we were having problems, why didn't I contemplate leaving? It's because God had called me to the church and I wanted to be faithful to that call. Something inside told me that my feelings were temporary, that I'd eventually feel stronger and get along better with the board. I didn't feel that our issues were insurmountable, but maybe I was in denial.

In talking to many pastors that have been forcibly removed from their churches, their biggest regret is that they walked away without telling their story. (When I tell my story to Christian leaders, they usually shrug their shoulders and ask, "What else is new?" When I tell the story to people who work in secular companies, their response is, "You've got to be kidding!") Many pastors remain silent because they have absorbed the idea that church unity is more important than truth-telling. We're told that Jesus refused to defend himself against his tormentors and that we need to follow his example (even though Jesus' crucifixion initially *fractured* his disciples while *uniting* his detractors).

But Jesus *did* defend himself verbally many times throughout his ministry even though his enemies sought to kill him. He didn't surrender himself to them at the first or even tenth opportunity (for example, see Luke 4:28-30; John 8:58-59; 10:39; 12:36). In fact, in the Book of Acts, there are many occasions where a Christian leader tells his story (sometimes to enemies, other times to friends) to avoid censure, persecution, or imprisonment. Here's a brief list of such instances:

• In Acts 5, Peter and John tell their story to the Sanhedrin in Jerusalem.
• In Acts 7, Stephen tells his story to the Sanhedrin right before his stoning.
• In Acts 10, Peter tells his story about the sheet from heaven filled with animals to Cornelius' household – a story he repeats before skeptical apostles in Jerusalem in Acts 11.
• In Acts 15, Paul and Barnabas tell the story of Gentile salvation to believers in Samaria, Phoenicia, and Jerusalem.
• In Acts 16, Paul and Silas challenge their arrest before the authorities in Philippi.
• In Acts 22, Paul defends himself before a crowd in Jerusalem.
• In Acts 23, Paul defends himself before the Sanhedrin, again in Jerusalem.
• In Acts 24, Paul tells his story to Felix; in Acts 25, to Festus; and in Acts 26, to Agrippa.
• In Acts 28, Paul defends himself before Jewish leaders in Rome.

The stakes were high for these leaders. The gospel was on the line. Some leaders might have encouraged Paul to "take one for the team" without issuing a defense. But this was not the style of the early Christians who defended their faith (and their own conduct) at every turn and *never* considered truth to be subservient to unity. Of course, there are four apologetic accounts of Jesus' words and deeds in the Gospels as well. The principle remains clear: Jesus' followers – especially leaders – have the *right* to defend themselves against public accusations.

I don't agree with the false dichotomy between truth and unity. Steinke writes, "Nowhere in the Bible is tranquility preferred to truth or harmony to justice . . . . If potent issues are avoided because they might divide the community, what type of witness is the congregation to the pursuit of truth?"[12] Christians have come to believe that the truth *won't* see us free. If a board pressed me to resign – and I believed I was innocent of any charges – I'd consider calling a meeting of the congregation and relate exactly what happened and *then* resign. (Some pastors prefer to include their story in their resignation letter.) Isn't this what Stephen did in Acts 7? He could have let the mob stone him after the Jewish leaders accused him of blasphemy against the temple, but first he defended himself – and *then* he took the rocks. Think about it.

6. What was the fallout from your conflict?

Most of the members of the transition team had experienced major conflict before and knew what could happen if matters weren't handled biblically. A major conflict sets off a chain reaction of events that no one can predict or control. My prayer is that the following information will motivate spiritual leaders to address and prevent their own conflicts before they go viral.

The conflict surfaced on a Saturday and:

- The associate pastor resigned six days later.
- The entire board resigned two days after that, creating a mess that lasted for months.
- The senior pastor and outreach director resigned five weeks after the board left.
- The youth pastor resigned about the same time, so ...
- The top ten leaders in the church all left within six weeks of each other.
- Some left the church after the November 8 meetings and never returned either because they disagreed with the way the pastor and outreach director were treated or because they were friends with ex-board members or the associate pastor.
- Some attendees left the church but eventually returned, some of whom Kim and I personally encouraged to go back.
- Some churchgoers cut back on their donations because of accusations made by the former associate pastor and board. While those accusations were intended to harm my wife and me, they hurt the church just as much.

- Some people who may not have been biblically qualified became leaders, including dissidents that the consultant advised should not become leaders for the next two years.
- All outreach ministries and mission trips came to a halt. Since the latest statistics indicate that only two percent of Christians share their faith, it takes a special person to model and motivate people for outreach. The desire to mediate the conflict from inside the church was justified. Kim's passion and giftedness for outreach and missions is rare.
- The health of some leaders suffered. The conflict cost people sleepless nights, peace of mind, and loss of energy. This was the third time in thirty-five years of ministry that I was the focus of personal attacks from a vocal church minority. In the first two cases, it took me six months to recover my drive. This time, it took more than a year. One vibrant pastor told me that it took him six months to recover his energy after he survived a concerted attack by staff members years before, so I suspect this may be a pattern. Because a pastor expends enormous adrenaline during a conflict, he is largely incapacitated afterward, and when he privately operates at minimal capacity, the ministry loses momentum until he recovers.
- Caring for people became an instant casualty. While Kim and I were overseas, we learned that a woman in the church had suffered tragic losses. Her brother, his wife, and her grandmother were all killed in a car accident. Because this woman and her husband had to travel several thousand miles to deal with the arrangements – and were gone for weeks – we never learned when they returned to our community and so did not minister to them in person. I'm unsure how many others from the church touched their lives, either. Because people retreat into survival mode during major conflict, the collective body lacks the energy to pastor the hard cases.
- Some people quietly suffered in pain for months, sensing they were not permitted to share their feelings with anyone. They hoped to hear the truth about what really happened, but were never told. These Shadow Christians hide in the darkness, and if their pain goes unaddressed, they eventually slip out the church's back door and never return.
- The church's reputation suffered. Someone asked a city official about a good church to visit and was told about the church, "You

don't want to go there. They're having problems." Kim and I always tried to spread good rumors about our church. This was the first time in our recollection that negative rumors were spread instead.

• Some friendships were destroyed . . . maybe permanently.

• According to a friend, the congregation splintered into the following "camps" after we left: pro-Jim ("Jimites"); anti-Jim; pro-board; anti-board; people who refused to join any camp; those happy with the process for choosing a new board and senior pastor; those unhappy with both processes; those upset that this could happen at their church; and those who left the church because they didn't like the interim pastor or new pastor.

• Many people in the church still do not know what really happened – nor do some *want* to know. If they've read this far, maybe they know now.

• Many that stayed in the church are willing to do *anything* to avoid going through such a conflict again. Steinke writes that "the healing process for midrange to severely anxious congregations takes two to five years."[13]

• Everyone lost, nobody won. When Sherlock Holmes plunged to his death over the Reichenbach Falls in Switzerland, his loss was felt not only by Dr. Watson and Scotland Yard, but by the world's readers as well. Yet when Holmes went over the falls, he took with him his arch nemesis, Professor Moriarty. If Holmes could rid the world of Moriarty, was his own death worthwhile? In our case, if the board left, was our own departure justified? Rediger notes that "if the pastor is destroyed, the whole congregation suffers, and the perpetrators win."[14] So were they the only victors? Leas writes:

> One of the most powerful realities about conflict in its most difficult manifestations is that it leaves us all feeling soiled – on-lookers (outside the organization or relationship), insiders who have not taken a position and don't want to, protagonists, antagonists, and even those who will join the family or group or congregation after 'it' is over. Those who raised the issues in the first place may have thought they were doing a 'good deed' (it's dirty business but someone has to do it), but they usually end up feeling besmirched and angry.[15]

You know what? He's right.

7. What did you learn about conflict from this experience?

Here are 25 lessons about church conflict I learned the *hard* way:

- Satan will sabotage any church that is serious about engaging in outreach.
- A pastor's detractors will exaggerate his smallest flaws and find sin where it doesn't exist.
- It is easier to discuss a pastor's mistakes with others than to speak with him directly.
- People's personal grievances against a pastor may eventually morph into official charges.
- Rather than speak with the pastor directly about his mistakes as they occur, some people prefer to hoard his mistakes to build a case against him in the future.
- Many believers would rather remove a pastor they're in conflict with than reconcile with him.
- Unresolved conflicts between leaders will eventually spill into the congregation.
- It's difficult not to make minor mistakes during a major conflict.
- Those who stand by their pastor while he's under attack will be vilified.
- Being in the middle of a conflict is like being stuck in a war zone. There is confusion and chaos everywhere, and it's hard to detect who your allies or enemies are.
- Given the right circumstances, some Christians – including leaders – will use unchristian methods to destroy a pastor and his family.
- When the pastor is the target of an attack, he needs both mediators and defenders inside the church to stand with him or he'll be forced to resign.
- If the board chairman fails to stand behind his pastor when he's attacked, the pastor probably won't survive.
- Even if they're wounded, pastors need to exercise their God-given authority in the midst of conflict and trust their pastoral instincts.

- During conflict, believers attribute the best motives to themselves ("we're doing this for the church") while attributing the worst motives to others ("they are being supremely selfish").
- Christians are blind to how cruel and irrational they can become during a conflict.
- During a major conflict, the pastor and his attackers play by different sets of rules – and the rules can change overnight.
- When leaders make people promise blanket confidentiality during a conflict, they are trying to control the flow of information – as well as their opponents.
- During conflict, leaders prefer not to tell the congregation the truth about issues because they're afraid people will either choose sides or leave the church.
- Those who fear conflict in their personal lives will flee when conflict erupts in their church.
- Congregations rarely confront individuals or groups who attack their pastor, thereby rewarding the perpetrators with victory.
- In the aftermath of a conflict, people refuse to reflect on their own role, preferring to scapegoat others, especially the pastor.
- While some attacks against a pastor are orchestrated, nobody can orchestrate the consequences.
- When a pastor is being undermined from inside a church, he may need to look for the fingerprints of his predecessor.
- In a congregationally-governed church, it's difficult to receive justice from a human perspective because decisions are based more on politics and friendships than Scripture.

In the aftermath of conflict, Steinke observes:

But congregation leaders need to ask themselves, did the pain become a teacher? Did it provoke new awareness? Did clarity develop to inform decision making? Were necessary changes implemented? If nothing is learned, if nothing changes, if important action is not taken, if new safeguards are not set in place, and if a sense of mission is not revived, the battle will return, maybe with different people over different issues but not with different functioning. Essentially, the suffering will have yielded no benefit.[16]

In our case, God displayed his sovereign care for us. For example, when the board told Kim and me to stay home the week after her dismissal, I used my time to contact Christian leaders who could help me plan my next moves. Had it been a regular work week, I wouldn't have had time to pursue that counsel, some of which I'm implementing in our new ministry. While that week off initially felt like a disciplinary measure, our mini-exile provided the impetus to gain perspective and to strategize. That week was an inadvertent gift from God.

Had the board stood firm during the last week in October, Kim would not have been the outreach director and my only option would have been to take the matter to the church at a public meeting, which I wouldn't have done. I would have been forced to negotiate a separation agreement with an extremely frugal group. But because *they* chose to resign instead, the new board offered us a separation agreement which has allowed us to heal and prepare for the future. God was orchestrating matters in his own providential way so the church could have fresh leadership and we could be free to pursue God's next assignment.

I gradually came to believe that God had a plan and that he was using my departure to accomplish his purposes. Joseph's words to his rascally brothers constantly came to mind: "You meant it for evil, but God meant it for good" (Genesis 50:20). Since those dark days three years ago, Kim has been able to visit Kenya two more times. In my case, I've written more than 250 articles on my blog (the great majority of them about pastor-church conflict) which can be accessed at www. restoringkingdombuilders.org. And I've completed an assignment as an interim pastor with a great church in beautiful New Hampshire.

I'll let Charles Wickman have the last word. He writes about forced termination: "No matter how ugly the exit may be, or what bogus reasons may be given to justify or excuse it or what painful memories it has created, it has been a testing and training place equipping us for the ministry that lies ahead."[17]

CHAPTER 14

QUESTIONS ABOUT PASTOR-CENTERED CONFLICT

*H*ow common is this kind of conflict in churches today? It's far *too* common. The problem is so severe that as of the mid-1990s, more than thirty thousand Protestant churches in the United States were in serious conflict at any given time.[1] Once a pastor has experienced forced termination, nearly 40 percent do not return to vocational ministry.[2] The church of Jesus Christ is losing too many trained, impactful ministers because current church systems reward the complaints of incessant antagonists rather than protecting pastors with fair, biblical procedures.

In a 1996 survey of pastors, 23 percent indicated they had been forced to resign or had been terminated at least once; 43 percent of forced-out pastors indicated that a faction had pushed them from office; 71 percent of the latter group said that faction numbered ten people or less; and 41 percent indicated that this had been done more than twice in the same church.[3] A 2012 study revises the number of pastors who have been forced to resign at least once to 28 percent.[4] In two surveys of pastors taken in 2005 and 2006, Richard Krejeir states that 1,500 pastors leave church ministry each month due to moral failure, spiritual burnout, or "contention in their churches."[5] A 2003 survey by Focus on the Family increases the number to 1,800 ministers per month across all denominations.[6] Steinke comments:

Church conflict is a growth industry. My experience tells me that about four out of ten congregations in any five-year period face a moderate to serious conflict. About one third of them take effective steps to recognize and address the situation. Not only are the number of incidences rising, but also the number of people who are stubborn, deceptive, and mean . . . . Against the background of the church as a loving, welcoming community, the nastiness is clearly out of place . . . . If conflict is intense and protracted, the battles drain the congregation's energy and resources. Meanwhile those embroiled in the bitter rifts demand super simple and immediate solutions – anything to ease their discomfort. Most people seek a quick return to normalcy. But the mere reduction of anxiety is fool's gold. The lessening of tensions is mistaken for the resolution of the conflict.[7]

Since many Christians have never experienced a challenge to a pastor's leadership, they are unsure how to behave when such a conflict breaks out. In our case, I watched as spiritually-oriented Christians were absolutely dumbfounded about what was really happening. People were disoriented as if a natural disaster was occurring – but it was really a *supernatural* disaster.

Let me ask and answer seven questions about pastor-centered conflict in our churches:

1. What can be done to prevent pastoral terminations from occurring?

Even though such conflicts may happen only once in a church's history – or in a believer's experience – it helps to know how to handle them in advance. In fact, I believe that Christian leaders can create biblical models to prevent the termination of innocent pastors *if we really want to do so*. However, some parties in a conflict prefer to scapegoat the pastor rather than solve a church's real problems – problems that would force individuals to engage in self-reflection and genuine repentance.

When I mentioned to a Christian leader recently that I am interested in *preventing* the forced termination of pastors, he wondered aloud what anyone could do to stop this behavior from happening. And that's the problem: we've become calloused, convincing ourselves that there is nothing that can be done when there are many ways we can address this tragedy.

For starters, the leadership community of a church (including the staff, governing board, and key lay leaders) need to reserve a few hours every year *to review what the New Testament says about conflict*. God has given us *enough* material on the topic, but it is not overwhelming. When I once listed all the key New Testament references to conflict, it came to three pages.

Once these Scriptures have been identified, *look for themes and patterns*. I tried this inside a staff meeting at my former church. We read through all those Scriptures in groups and tried to summarize their overall teaching in five sentences. We each had to grapple with the biblical texts, run them through our brains, and explain their meaning to others.

Then I'd ask those same leaders *to create clear, written guidelines for managing conflict based on Scripture*. When people create their own guidelines, they remember them better. Then I'd *present them in a formal way to the church's governing leaders for approval*. I'd include information about interpersonal conflict as well as pastor-centered conflict. A church can sometimes find guidelines from other churches online. A Christian labor attorney could provide a summary of what due process might look like in a church setting. And then, if I was the pastor, *I'd teach a series on biblical conflict management and present the guidelines to the church* as a way of saying, "This is how we deal with conflict around here." If the pastor doesn't take the initiative to teach his church about conflict from Scripture, it won't happen.

Then if a conflict surfaces and people's emotions are going haywire, the church has written documents created during calmer times that dictate how matters are to be handled. (Make sure you can locate them, though.) Most churches lack these guidelines either because they don't anticipate needing them or because they're painful to create. And because it usually requires pastoral leadership to create such documents, who wants to focus energy on termination? This is why lay people need to become involved in conflict prevention and resolution. Most churches have wise and gifted individuals who can tackle this project. Churches especially need to create policies that can kick in whenever a group tries to drive a pastor from office. Leas recommends:

> Therefore, long before conflict arises, a church should establish clear, deliberate and agreed upon processes for reviewing, evaluating and dealing with pastoral performance. This is not the routine, regular, annual organizational review and evaluation of all personnel and committees, but a special tool for those difficult times when conflict and tension over the pastor's leadership occur.[8]

If your church doesn't have these documents, it would be wise to contact other churches and secure their guidelines until your body can create its own. These procedures should be spelled out in a church's constitution and bylaws, official board documents, and staff policy handbook. Boers observes that when his church decided to establish these procedures, the leaders approached a number of churches and asked for a copy, but most had none.[9] If a church doesn't have such procedures, then the law of the jungle will take over.

In his book *The Toxic Congregation*, Lloyd Rediger has devised a process he calls The Grievance-Suggestion Procedure which is "a stepwise method that promotes orderly, reliable resolution of potentially divisive matters before they become contentious or abusive." He also includes processes for such practices as forgiveness, renewing membership vows, and prayer, concluding with specific instructions for thwarting clergy killers.[10]

If I could do it again, I'd prayerfully appoint a team of gifted people to receive conflict management training and ask them to implement biblical principles for resolving a variety of conflict issues. Ideally, anyone in the church could consult with that group to determine *how* they should address any conflicts they had with the pastor, staff members, board members, or others in the congregation. Every church needs such an objective third party *inside* their church.

2. Whose help is needed most to prevent these conflicts?

Concerning clergy members who are forced to leave their churches, researcher Marcus Tanner from Texas Tech University states, "Everybody knows this is happening, but nobody wants to talk about it. The vast majority of denominations across the country are doing absolutely nothing."[11] So let's talk about it. We need three groups of people to speak up more frequently and vociferously to arrest the escalating number of forced exits: pastors, lay people, and denominational officials.

First, *we need pastors to speak up because they are the primary communicators in church life*. It's essential that pastors show more overt support for their colleagues who undergo forced exits. Inside a church, when someone has been wounded physically or emotionally, we expect a pastor to move *toward* that person, not *away* from them. And when a pastor hears that a colleague has been forced to resign, he should move *toward* his brother, not *away* from him. While I realize that every pastor's time is precious, we can't lick this problem if pastors choose to look away. Pastors need to realize that *they* could be the ones to experience an involuntary exit next time – and it's arrogant to think otherwise.

Next, *we need lay people to speak up because many have lost their pastors due to antagonism*. As a woman from our former church asked me after we left, why did the 5 percent who were disgruntled prevail over the 95 percent who liked the pastor and his wife? Christian leaders need to train lay people how to detect, prevent, and thwart the actions of churchgoers who have decided to force out the pastor without just cause, which is why we need more resources for lay people on conflict. I recently met a former board chairman from another church who told me that he voluntarily protected his pastor whenever people verbally attacked him.

Finally, *we need denominational leaders to engage in the pursuit of righteousness concerning forced terminations*. Pastors are catching on that it may not be wise to ask a district official to intervene in a conflict situation because denominational personnel usually side with disgruntled churchgoers. Because churches are revenue sources, district officials don't want to alienate a church's leaders if they oppose their pastor because they might stop giving to the district. These officials believe it's easier for a church to call a new pastor than for the district to plant a new church. But I'm thankful that *some* district ministers are doing something about this issue. Paul Borden, who became an executive minister for an American Baptist region, admits that when congregations had conflicts in the past, the region often advocated the pastor's departure. However, Borden and his fellow leaders "knew that change would bring conflict, and we assured the pastor that when the conflict came, we would help the pastor deal with the dragons in the congregation who did not want health and growth because it affected their ability to hold influence in the congregation."[12]

In the same vein, a longtime friend left the following comment on my blog:

> I asked the pastor of our last church why he chose to be ordained in the Presbyterian Church. His answer was that it provided a level of protection from being ousted. If he was preaching the Word and the congregation did not like it, they could not vote him out without making a case to the presbytery. This more objective body could review the accusation and make a decision about the pastor's fitness. If they deemed him fit, then the presbytery would direct their attention to the accusers. If they were members-in-good-standing of the church, then the presbytery would discipline these members. If they were not members, they would be asked to leave.

While we can thank God that a few denominational leaders are addressing this issue, pastors who are not part of denominations cannot appeal to anyone official outside their church to assist them during such times, meaning that thousands of pastors must face antagonists on their own. But if Americans can band together to eradicate cancer of the body, then can't Christians of all stripes band together to eradicate this cancer in the church?

3. Why aren't Christians doing more to combat the forced termination of pastors?

I'm weary of the excuses that Christians use as to why we won't do more about this issue:

"We need to preserve the autonomy of the local church." Of course, but at the very least, we can tell stories, train leaders, expose the template, and teach believers how to deal with pastoral antagonists. The article "If You Must Terminate a Pastor" on my blog has

been viewed several thousand times (three times more than any other article), an indication that many board members and lay people want help with this topic.

"Pastors must expect to suffer like Jesus." We've been told we're going to suffer since seminary, but we had no idea that attacks from fellow Christians could be so vicious. Jesus was crucified by religious and political enemies, not by his disciples. While his men fled when he needed them most, they didn't drive the nails into his hands. Jesus was betrayed by only one follower, but pastors are routinely betrayed by staff members, board members, predecessors, and even denominational leaders – and sometimes they work in concert. To be betrayed by one person (like a spouse, co-worker, or friend) can severely wound a person for a long time, but a larger betrayal feels overwhelming, as if each party chose to burn their bridges with you forever.

"We need to maintain confidentiality about forced exits." This plea is nothing more than a cover-up for our incompetence in preventing and managing these tragedies – and is exactly what Satan wants. When professing Christians abuse and batter clergy, and pastors try to talk about it, we rush to hush them up in the name of unity. But isn't this the same tactic abusive husbands use with their wives? What would happen if we still couldn't talk about *that* problem?

"Shedding light on this issue is poor marketing for the Christian faith." But if we can make progress in alleviating this problem, wouldn't the image of many churches improve? US Films recently released a documentary film called *Betrayed: The Clergy Killer's DNA*. The film – which my wife and I have seen – "exposes what has been the best kept secret in the Church." The film is available at www.betrayedthemovie.com. Let's learn our lessons and brainstorm solutions so these conflicts don't become so destructive.

I'd like to find just a few Christians who are outraged at the way pastors are mistreated today. In Matthew 23:33-35, Jesus was *still* outraged at the way God's leaders had been treated by religious people throughout Jewish history:

> "You snakes! You brood of vipers! How will you escape being condemned to hell? Therefore I am sending you prophets and wise men and teachers. Some of them you will kill and crucify; others you will flog in your synagogues and pursue from town

to town. And so upon you will come all the righteous blood that has been shed on earth, from the blood of righteous Abel to the blood of Zechariah son of Berekiah, whom you murdered between the temple and the altar."

Jesus stood alone in condemning injustices committed against God's servants. Where are such champions today?

4. What can the average church attendee do about conflicts involving the pastor?

Pray for your pastor and church leaders. Regardless of which party starts a conflict, spiritual leaders have the responsibility to make sure it is addressed and resolved. They need divine wisdom. They need spiritual courage. They need special skills. Conflicts are disruptive, not only to congregational life, but also to life at home and work. Uphold your leaders before God.

Insist on a fair process. If you're a member, ask your leaders point-blank *how* they are intending to resolve any conflict. Are they using Scripture? Are they using a conflict-resolution model? Are they seeking counsel from parties outside the church, and if so, which ones? I'd ask for a written copy of the process and then hold the leaders accountable for carrying it out. When the outcome of a conflict is predetermined, the process is probably corrupt. But when a fair process is used, the outcome will most likely be best for all parties concerned.

Ask the leaders to share appropriate information at opportune times. Tell them you want to know as much as you can about what's happening. They won't be able to share *everything* with you for legal and moral reasons, but they do need to share *enough*. And when you receive that information, don't modify or exaggerate what you've heard.

Realize you may be dealing with evil. The conflict may not be just a difference of opinion between two parties but an all-out assault from Satan with the intent of destroying your pastor and church. Speaking of clergy killers, Rediger says that "we tend to deny, excuse, or pamper them in the church. And because we believe that love will conquer all (read, 'Be nice to everyone'), we pretend to forgive them and love them, while we wish they would also be nice or just go away. Such thinking and behavior do not work."[13] The challenge for the average attendee is that a conflict may be complex and the facts may be concealed – and those fanning the conflict's flames may be your friends.

While no pastor is immune from being forced out of a church, some are less likely to be challenged. I am thinking of three kinds of pastors: a *founding* pastor (because everyone who attends comes on his terms); a *megachurch* pastor (because one must fight through multiple layers to attack him); and a *long-tenured* pastor (because any ministry opponents probably left years before). However, I know of cases where all three types of pastors were innocent of major offenses but were still forced out by a vocal minority or by leaders in their inner circle.

5. What does Scripture say about dealing with perpetrators?

The New Testament tells us *exactly* what to do when churchgoers sin by causing division. Governing leaders are to identify the troublemakers, confront them lovingly but firmly, and ask them to repent. They are not to be allowed to harm the body in any way (Romans 16:17-18; Titus 3:10-11; 3 John 9-10). If the perpetrators remain unrepentant, they should be ostracized, told to leave the congregation, or even excommunicated.

First, *perpetrators must be identified.* Paul writes in Romans 16:17, "I urge you, brothers, to watch out for those who cause divisions and put obstacles in your way that are contrary to the teaching you have learned. Keep away from them." In 1 Timothy 1:20, Paul mentions two troublemakers, Hymenaeus and Alexander, by name. He does the same thing in 2 Timothy 2:17 (mentioning Hymenaeus and Philetus) while later declaring that Alexander the metalworker "did me a great deal of harm. The Lord will repay him for what he has done. You too should be on your guard against him, because he strongly opposed our message" (2 Timothy 4:14). Even John, the apostle of love, mentions the church boss Diotrephes, "who loves to be first," in 3 John 9-10, faulting him for "gossiping maliciously about us" and refusing "to welcome the brothers." Leaders usually don't have to engage in a "witch hunt" to find divisive people. Though pastoral antagonists hide in the shadows, it is biblical to expose them to appropriate parties.

Second, *perpetrators must be confronted.* Jesus told his followers in Luke 17:3-4, "If your brother sins, rebuke him, and if he repents, forgive him. If he sins against you seven times in a day, and seven times comes back to you and says, 'I repent,' forgive him." Jesus uses four action verbs in these verses: sin, rebuke, repent, and forgive. Jesus lays out the sequence for us. When someone sins, we rebuke them. When they repent, we forgive them. But how often do we follow *his* way? Instead, when antagonists attack God's leaders, we prematurely forgive them and dispense with our rebuking and their repenting. On a collective basis, the church of Jesus Christ perpetuates these situations by rarely if ever addressing the perpetrators.

If I'm a layman and I join a campaign to force out my pastor, and he eventually leaves, most people will either ignore my involvement or reflexively forgive me even though I've damaged the congregation. No one will rebuke me or insist I repent. A 1996 survey in *Leadership Journal* concluded that churches that fire or force out their ministers will likely do it again.[14]

Most dissidents in a conflict never admit they've done anything wrong. Pastors who have been slandered by such people wait in vain for apologies. If one person was responsible for ousting a pastor, that person might later repent, but when people make decisions collectively – like on a board or in a secret meeting – whenever they doubt their actions, they simply defend each other and tell themselves, "My friends believed this was right, and they're good people, so I'm going to trust them." I *have* heard on occasion about a repentant perpetrator who apologizes to his or her former pastor years later, but such action is rare.

Third, *perpetrators must repent or leave the fellowship.* Paul writes in Titus 3:10-11, "Warn a divisive person once, and then warn him a second time. After that, have nothing to do with him. You may be sure that such a man is warped and sinful; he is self-condemned." The "divisive person" is someone who tries to gather adherents in an attempt to divide the church and who refuses to respond to pastoral guidance.[15] If Titus encounters a churchgoer who is sinning either by his conduct or his teaching, Titus is to warn that person in private to repent. If the person corrects their behavior, Titus' warning has been successful. If the person refuses correction, Titus is to warn that individual a second time. The perpetrator is given every opportunity to

271

acknowledge and turn from error. Should his warnings fail, Titus is to "have nothing to do with him" (Titus 3:10), which refers to some form of repudiation, possibly social ostracism or formal excommunication.[16] In this passage, as in several others in the New Testament, Jesus' instructions in Matthew 18:15-17 are applied in an abbreviated fashion to an antagonist in a local church setting. Due to serious divisiveness, unrepentant persons are to be excluded from the life of their spiritual community.

If those who organize and join factions against a pastor are permitted to undermine their church with impunity, they will continue to force out God's servants until they are stopped. Paul's warning in 1 Corinthians 3:16-17 sounds like it's from the Old Testament but is found in a New Testament epistle: "Don't you know that you yourselves are God's temple and that God's spirit lives in you? If anyone destroys God's temple, God will destroy him; for God's temple is sacred, and you are that temple." The term "you yourselves" in verse 16 is not singular (as in 1 Corinthians 6:19) but plural. The entire congregation is God's temple. Speaking to the whole church, Paul says that believers who persist in divisiveness will receive divine judgment. Haugk observes that "God does not tolerate any destructive activity in his temple . . . God threatens to destroy the destroyers of his temple."[17] The word "destroy" is not specific and cannot stretch to mean either annihilation or eternal torment but "simply makes it clear that one who commits a grave sin lays himself open to a grave penalty."[18] Being infinitely creative, God has a multitude of judgments at his disposal, any one of which he could inflict upon an antagonist. Yet Paul tries to warn likely agitators so they can repent of their sin and avoid divine wrath. How often is this passage taught in our churches anymore?

If potential perpetrators knew in advance that *they* would be asked to leave their church if they tried to force out their pastor without just cause, would they still make such plans? Some might, but such a policy would give a church's governing leaders sanction to remove self-appointed vigilantes from their midst. Then why don't more churches operate this way? Greenfield writes:

> The New Testament is clear that the apostles were not intimidated by moral and organizational threats to the welfare of their church. They knew that evil in the church had to be dealt

with quickly and thoroughly. And we must follow their lead. The church must rid itself of clergy killers and pathological antagonists. Sometimes even excommunication is necessary.[19]

To that I say a hearty "Amen!"

6. What usually happens to the perpetrators?

Realistically? Nothing. Biblically, however, perpetrators need to be corrected before they strike again. This can be done by staff members, the governing board, or deputized members. However, if a transitional/interim pastor is hired after the pastor's departure, he may have to oversee this thankless task. (Some transitional pastors are trained to deal with powerbrokers and request absolute authority before being hired.) Unrepentant individuals who target their pastor sense they are immune from correction and feel free to use the same template with the next pastor. However, in such situations:

> Peace mongering is common. With tranquility and stability reigning as premium values, congregational leaders adapt to their most recalcitrant and immature people, allowing them to use threats and tantrums as levers of influence. Malcontents' complaints never seem to cease. Unwilling to confront the constant critic, leaders set the table for the unhappy souls to have a movable feast of anxiety. By appeasing rather than opposing, leaders give control to reactive forces. Feed them once and leaders can be sure they will be back for more.[20]

As far as I know, no one took action against any non-board perpetrators in our situation. My counsel to any successor is, "Watch your back. They know the template." Trull and Carter note:

> Generally speaking, an incoming minister does not need to fear those who speak well of the predecessor. Those who loved, appreciated, respected, and supported the former minister will likely do the same with the new minister. The church member of whom the minister should be wary is the one who speaks ill of the previous minister. Those who criticize, find fault with,

and express disappointment in the former minister will probably react to the new minister in the same way over time.[21]

I have to confess, this really bothers me. For decades, pastors have been told that whenever there's a major conflict in a church they're leading, they need to resign to keep the church intact. But why should the pastor leave while those who initiated the conflict are permitted to stay? I suppose it's *easier* to remove one person than many. (But wasn't this the dastardly justification of Caiaphas for killing Jesus in John 11:49-50?) And spiritually-speaking, the shepherd lays down his life for the sheep, just as Jesus did (John 10:14-15). But why don't God's people band together and ask the perpetrators to leave as well? If the *pastor* can find another church, *they* can find another church – and it's much easier for them than for him. I recently saw the highlights of a basketball game in which opposing players involved in a fight were instantly removed from the game. Why doesn't this happen in churches? Aren't we rewarding people for their divisiveness without expecting them to change?

If I was a layman and my pastor was pushed out by antagonists, I'd approach someone with leadership authority and say, "If you confront those who perpetrated this conflict, I will stay in this church. But if you don't deal with them, I will leave and find a church where they take Scripture seriously. And if anybody asks why I left, I will feel obligated to tell them." While this may sound harsh, how can church leaders take *no* action against those who have driven out their minister? Steinke writes:

> In congregations, boundary violators too often are given a long rope because others refuse to confront the trespassers. When boundaries are inappropriately crossed and people are harmed, no one wants to name the violation. It's as if the disturbance of the group's serenity is a greater offense than the viral-like behavior. Boundary violators go unattended and suffer no consequences . . . . The lack of attention only enables the repetition of the invasive behavior.[22]

In some situations, mature Christians hang around to see if church leaders will discipline the instigators. But if nothing happens after a while, these believers may leave the church permanently, especially if they see the perpetrators serving in visible positions. During a major conflict, a church is going to lose *somebody*. Isn't it better to lose *divisive* people rather than *mature* believers? Leith Anderson comments, "The result is that the church keeps the dissenters and loses the happy, healthy people to other churches. Most healthy Christians have a time limit and a tolerance level for unchristian and unhealthy attitudes and behaviors."[23]

I had a conversation recently with a Christian man. We were discussing what should be done (if anything) to churchgoers who join forces to push out their pastor. This man believes that a church should remain passive toward perpetrators because God will eventually punish them. He told me about an associate pastor who engineered the ouster of his senior pastor. The associate later contracted cancer and his wife eventually died a horrible death. Christians don't need to address the perpetrators, he said, because "God'll get 'em."

It is true that God *may* get them. The law of sowing and reaping still applies in this life (Galatians 6:7) and God promises to repay us all according to our deeds in the next life (2 Corinthians 5:10). There are cases in the New Testament where God executed swift punishment against professing believers like Ananias and Sapphira (Acts 5:1-11) and staunch unbelievers like King Herod (Acts 12:19-23). Most pastors can tell stories about the eventual demise of attendees turned into attackers. For example, a man who had led an attack on one of my former pastors died of a heart attack the day he was moving out-of-state. While God may not "take out" *every* perpetrator, how are twenty-first century believers to interpret all the biblical admonitions to confront divisive individuals in a local church? Have God's words now become irrelevant?

When I was a rookie church staff member, I witnessed an event that I have never forgotten. A few hours before a Sunday evening service, the elders met to discuss what to do about several church leaders who were involved in inappropriate behavior. I watched as the door to the pastor's study swung open and various leaders piled into cars to drive to the homes of those leaders and confront them. The serious looks on the leaders' faces told a story – they didn't sign up for this – but to their credit, they did it.

Where is the courage today that those elders displayed?

7. Can you summarize this book in one paragraph?

While pastors are gifts of the risen Christ to his church, they are fallible. Anticipate that over time, you will question one of your pastor's decisions, disagree with his teaching, or be offended by something he said to you. If your pastor wounds you personally, deal with each offense as it arises. Contact him personally and attempt to restore your relationship. Resist sharing his offenses with your network or pooling complaints with others. If you suspect your pastor is guilty of a major offense (like heresy, immorality, or criminal conduct), relay that information to your church's governing leaders so they can launch an investigation. However, the leaders should ultimately seek to restore the pastor rather than reflexively remove him from office. Because pastors are authority figures who are subject to constant criticism, Scripture has provided safeguards for how they are to be treated. These safeguards are based in the Old Testament (Deuteronomy 19:15-21) and expanded upon in the New Testament (Matthew 18:15-17; 1 Timothy 5:19-21). Every church should create a written process for resolving disputes with their pastor based upon these safeguards before they are ever needed. Church members have the right to make sure that biblical principles are followed whenever their pastor is being disciplined. These safeguards minimize the chance that a pastor will be forced to leave a congregation prematurely or that Satan will be able to influence or control their church. If God's people will patiently and compassionately follow the biblical admonitions about pastoral correction, Christians can steadily eradicate the plague of forced termination in our churches.

My favorite church building in the world is St. Paul's Cathedral in London. (Prince Charles and Lady Diana were married there.) That building is still an active house of worship even though the church was bombed by Nazi pilots during World War II. During the Battle of Britain in 1940, a group of volunteers formed called the St. Paul's Fire Watch. Every time the Nazis dropped a bomb on the church, the Fire Watch quickly extinguished the smallest spark before it could spread further. After a public appeal, 300 volunteers joined the watch, forty of whom guarded the cathedral every night. Every church needs a volunteer group that could be known as the _____ (name of church) Fire Watch. When even the smallest spark of conflict arises, this group's job would be to address it quickly.

May God raise up more *human* fire extinguishers to protect our churches and pastors!

I PLEDGE TO PROTECT
MY PASTOR

1. I pledge to protect my pastor by consistently praying for his walk with God, his family life, his personal life, his leadership challenges, and his teaching ministry.

2. I pledge to protect my pastor by knowing and practicing what the New Testament teaches about interpersonal and ecclesiastical conflict.

3. I pledge to protect my pastor by defending his life and ministry whenever others speak negatively of him in my presence.

4. I pledge to protect my pastor by insisting that anyone who complains about him go and speak with him directly.

5. I pledge to protect my pastor by always choosing to believe the best about him.

6. I pledge to protect my pastor by contacting him directly on those occasions when he has offended me in some fashion.

7. I pledge to protect my pastor by regularly praying for those to whom he accounts and for those who account to him.

8. I pledge to protect my pastor by regularly attending worship services, serving with my spiritual gifts, and giving generously of my income.

9. I pledge to protect my pastor by insisting that any charges made against him be addressed in a manner consistent with Scripture and our church's governing documents.

10. I pledge to protect my pastor by reporting to the pastor or governing board any knowledge I may obtain concerning possible attacks against him or the church.

_____   _____
Your Name   Date

SELECT BIBLIOGRAPHY

Barfoot, D. Scott, Bruce E. Winston, Charles Wickman. "Forced Pastoral Exits: An Exploratory Study." Virginia Beach, VA: Regent University, 2005.

Dobson, Edward G., Speed B. Leas, and Marshall Shelley. *Mastering Conflict and Controversy*. Portland, OR: Multnomah Press, 1992.

Faulkner, Brooks R. *Forced Termination: Redemptive Options for Ministers and Churches*. Nashville: Broadman Press, 1986.

Greenfield, Guy. *The Wounded Minister: Healing from and Preventing Personal Attacks*. Grand Rapids, MI: Baker Books, 2002.

Haugk, Kenneth C. *Antagonists in the Church: How to Identify and Deal with Destructive Conflict*. Minneapolis: Augsburg Publishing House, 1988.

Leas, Speed B. *Leadership and Conflict*. Creative Leadership Series. Ed. Lyle E. Schaller. Nashville: Abingdon, 1982.

_____. *Moving Your Church through Conflict*. Washington, DC: The Alban Institute, 1985.

Lott, David B., ed. *Conflict Management in Congregations*. Bethesda, MD: The Alban Institute, 2001.

Pinion, Gary L. *Crushed: The Perilous Side of Ministry.* Springfield, MO: 21st Century Press, 2008.

Rediger, G. Lloyd. *Clergy Killers: Guidance for Pastors and Congregations under Attack.* Louisville: Westminster John Knox Press, 1997.

Sande, Ken. *The Peacemaker: A Biblical Guide to Resolving Personal Conflict*, 3rd ed. Grand Rapids, MI: Baker Books, 2004.

Shelley, Marshall. *Well-Intentioned Dragons: Ministering to Problem People in the Church.* Vol. 1. Carol Stream, IL: Word Publishing, 1985.

Steinke, Peter L. *Congregational Leadership in Anxious Times: Being Calm and Courageous No Matter What.* Herndon, VA: The Alban Institute, 2006.

_____. *How Your Church Family Works: Understanding Congregations as Emotional Systems.* Bethesda, MD: The Alban Institute, 1993.

Wickman, Charles A. *Pastors at Risk: Protecting Your Future, Guarding Your Present.* Peoria, AZ: Intermedia Publishing Group, 2011.

NOTES

INTRODUCTION

[1] G. Lloyd Rediger, *Clergy Killers: Guidance for Pastors and Congregations under Attack* (Louisville, KY: Westminster John Knox Press, 1997), 1.

[2] Guy Greenfield, *The Wounded Minister: Healing from and Preventing Personal Attacks* (Grand Rapids, MI: Baker Books, 2001), 15.

[3] Gary L. Pinion, *Crushed: The Perilous Side of Ministry* (Springfield, MO: 21st Century Press, 2008), 97-98.

[4] Rick Warren, *The Purpose-Driven Life: What on Earth Am I Here For?* (Grand Rapids, MI: Zondervan, 2002), 247.

CHAPTER 1

[1] Speed B. Leas, *Leadership and Conflict,* Creative Leadership Series, ed. Lyle E. Schaller (Nashville: Abingdon, 1982), 116.

[2] Norman Shawchuck and Roger Heuser, *Managing the Congregation: Building Effective Systems to Serve People* (Nashville: Abingdon Press, 1996), 310.

CHAPTER 2

[1] Rediger, *Clergy Killers,* 7.

[2] Ken Sande, *The Peacemaker: A Biblical Guide to Resolving Personal Conflict,* 3rd ed. (Grand Rapids, MI: Baker Books, 2004), 171.

[3] Marlene Caroselli, *Hiring & Firing: What Every Manager Needs to Know,* rev. ed. (Mission, KS: SkillPath Publications, 1993), 72.

[4] Speed B. Leas, *Moving Your Church through Conflict* (New York: The Alban Institute, 1985), 78.

CHAPTER 3

[1] Sande, *The Peacemaker,* 146.

[2] David L. Goetz, "Forced Out," *Leadership* 17, no. 1 (1996): 46.

[3] Rediger, *Clergy Killers,* 161.

[4] Charles A. Wickman, *Pastors at Risk: Protecting Your Future, Guarding Your Present* (Peoria, AZ: Intermedia Publishing Group, 2011), 9.

[5] Paul D. Borden, *Hitting the Bullseye: How Denominations Can Aim the Congregation at the Mission Field* (Nashville: Abingdon Press, 2003), 72.

[6] Gary L. McIntosh and Robert L. Edmondson, *It Only Hurts on Monday: Why Pastors Quit and What You Can Do about It* (Carol Stream, IL: ChurchSmart Resources, 1998), 132.

[7] Ibid., 133.

[8] Brooks Faulkner, *Forced Termination: Redemptive Options for Ministers and Churches* (Nashville: Broadman Press, 1990), 78-79.

CHAPTER 4

[1] Peter L. Steinke, *Congregational Leadership in Anxious Times: Being Calm and Courageous No Matter What* (Herndon, VA: The Alban Institute, 2006), 105.

[2] Peter L. Steinke, *How Your Church Family Works: Understanding Congregations as Emotional Systems* (Washington, DC: The Alban Institute, 1993), 22.

[3] Archibald D. Hart, *Unlocking the Mystery of Your Emotions* (Dallas: Word Publishing, 1989), 76.

[4] Kenneth Haugk, *Antagonists in the Church: How to Identify and Deal with Destructive Conflict* (Minneapolis: Augsburg Publishing House, 1988), 104.

CHAPTER 5

[1] Steinke, *Congregational Leadership in Anxious Times,* 110.

[2] Speed B. Leas, "The Basics of Conflict Management in Congregations," in *Conflict Management in Congregations*, ed. David B. Lott (Bethesda, MD: The Alban Institute, 2001), 39.

[3] Leas, *Moving Your Church through Conflict*, 62.

[4] Ronald W. Richardson, *Creating a Healthier Church: Family Systems Theory, Leadership and Congregational Life,* Creative Pastoral Care and Counseling Series (Minneapolis: Fortress Press, 1996), 51.

[5] Steinke, *How Your Church Family Works,* 50.

[6] Haugk, *Antagonists in the Church,* 104.

[7] Leas, *Moving Your Church through Conflict*, 52.

[8] Martha Stout, *The Sociopath Next Door* (New York: Three Rivers Press, 2005), 98-99.

[9] Carl F. Lansing, *Legal Defense Handbook for Christians in Ministry* (Colorado Springs: NavPress, 1992), 166-167.

CHAPTER 6

[1] J. A. Thompson, *Deuteronomy: An Introduction and a Commentary,* The Tyndale Old Testament Commentaries, ed. D. J. Wiseman (Downers Grove, IL: InterVarsity Press, 1974), 217.

[2] John R. W. Stott, *Guard the Truth: The Message of 1 Timothy and Titus* (Downers Grove, IL: InterVarsity Press, 1996), 138.

[3] Peter Ackroyd, *The Life of Thomas More* [Kindle Version] (New York: Anchor Books, 1998), Chapters XXXI-XXXIII.

[4] Raymond Brown, *The Message of Deuteronomy*, The Bible Speaks Today, ed. J. A. Motyer (Downers Grove, IL: InterVarsity Press, 1993), 194.

[5] Leas, *Moving Your Church through Conflict*, 77.

[6] Steinke, *Congregational Leadership in Anxious Times*, 1.

[7] Elaine Herrin Onley, *Crying on Sunday: Surviving Forced Termination in Ministry* (Macon, GA: Smyth & Helwys, 1994), 50-51.

[8] J. Carl Laney, *A Guide to Church Disicpline* (Minneapolis: Bethany House Publishers, 1985), 120.

[9] August G. Lageman, "The Congregation: A Family System" in *Surviving in Ministry: Navigating the Pitfalls, Experiencing the Renewals*, eds. Robert R. Lutz and Bruce T. Taylor (New York: Paulist Press, 1990), 195.

[10] Edward G. Dobson, "Reconciling Battling Members," in *Mastering Conflict and Controversy*, by Edward G. Dobson, Speed B. Leas, and Marshall Shelley (Portland, OR: Multnomah Press, 1992), 160.

[11] Rachel Zoll, "More US Catholics Take Complaints to Church Court," *My Verizon*, 15 January 2012; available from http://entertainment.verizon.com; Internet.

[12] Jim Meyer, "Who Will Stop Me?", *Restoring Kingdom Builders*, 21 March 2011; available from http://blog.restoringkingdombuilders.org; Internet.

CHAPTER 7

[1] Shawchuck and Heuser, *Managing the Congregation*, 291.

[2] Steinke, *How Your Church Family Works,* 38.

[3] Roy W. Pneuman, "Nine Common Sources of Conflict in Congregations," in *Conflict Management in Congregations*, ed. David B. Lott (Bethesda, MD: The Alban Institute, 2001), 48.

[4] Cabinet and Board of Ordained Ministry, Rocky Mt. Conference, United Methodist Church, "Guidelines for Appropriate Conduct by Current and Former Pastors," 1.

[5] The Presbytery of Los Ranchos, Committee on Ministry, "Separation Ethics/ Former Pastor Policy," 17 March, 2007, 2.

[6] Goetz, "Forced Out," 46.

CHAPTER 8

[1] Bill Hybels, "Standing in the Crossfire," in *Leading Your Church through Conflict and Reconciliation: 30 Strategies to Transform Your Ministry*, ed. Marshall Shelley (Minneapolis: Bethany House Publishers, 1997), 33.

[2] John C. LaRue, Jr., "Forced Exits: Preparation and Survival," *Christianity Today Online*, 14 April 2009; available from http://christianitytoday.com; Internet.

[3] Ibid.

[4] Ibid.

[5] Leas, *Moving Your Church through Conflict*, 79.

⁶ LaRue, Jr., "Forced Exits: Preparation and Survival."

⁷ Goetz, "Forced Out," 47.

⁸ Jim Meyer, "If You Must Terminate a Pastor," *Restoring Kingdom Builders*, 14 March 2011; available from http://blog.restoringkingdombuilders.org; Internet.

⁹ Dean R. Hoge and Jacqueline E. Wenger, *Pastors in Transition: Why Clergy Leave Local Church Ministry* (Grand Rapids, MI: Wm. B. Eerdmans Publishing Co., 2005), 43-44.

¹⁰ John C. LaRue, Jr. "Forced Exits: High-Risk Churches," *Christianity Today Online*, 14 April 2009; available from http://christianitytoday.com; Internet.

¹¹ Faulkner, *Forced Termination*, 110.

¹² Loren B. Mead, *A Change of Pastors ... And How it Affects the Congregation* (Herndon, VA: The Alban Institute, 2005), 49.

CHAPTER 9

¹ C. H. Spurgeon, *Beside Still Waters: Words of Comfort for the Soul*, ed. by Roy H. Clarke (Nashville: Thomas Nelson, 1999), 46.

² Greenfield, *The Wounded Minister*, 226.

³ Neil T. Anderson, *The Bondage Breaker* (Eugene, OR: Harvest House, 1993), 198.

⁴ Marshall Shelley, *Well-Intentioned Dragons: Ministering to Problem People in the Church*, The Leadership Library, vol. 1 (Carol Stream, IL: Word Publishing, 1985), 13.

⁵ Leas, *Moving Your Church through Conflict*, 83.

⁶ Wickman, *Pastors at Risk*, VII.

⁷ Anderson, *The Bondage Breaker*, 196.

⁸ David W. Augsburger, *Helping People Forgive* (Louisville: Westminster John Knox Press, 1996), 14.

⁹ Ibid.

¹⁰ Sande, *The Peacemaker*, 210-11.

¹¹ Lewis B. Smedes, *Forgive and Forget: Healing the Hurts We Don't Deserve* (New York: Simon & Schuster, 1984), 18.

¹² Shawchuck and Heuser, *Managing the Congregation*, 267.

¹³ Greenfield, *The Wounded Minister*, 60.

¹⁴ Ibid., 64.

¹⁵ Joe E. Trull and James E. Carter, *Ministerial Ethics: Moral Formation for Church Leaders*, 2ᵈ ed. (Grand Rapids, MI: Baker Academic, 2004), 121.

¹⁶ Arthur Paul Boers, *Never Call Them Jerks: Healthy Responses to Difficult Behavior* (Washington, DC: The Alban Institute, 1999), 49-50.

¹⁷ Wickman, *Pastors at Risk*, XII.

CHAPTER 10

¹ Wickman, *Pastors at Risk*, 39.

² Ibid., 15

³ Hoge and Wenger, *Pastors in Transition*, 29.

[4] Ibid., 84.

[5] Pinion, *Crushed*, 77.

CHAPTER 11

[1] Leas, "Who's at Fault When the Pastor Gets Fired?" in *Conflict Management in Congregations*, ed. by David B. Lott (Bethesda, MD: The Alban Institute, 2001), 113-114.

[2] Charles H. Spurgeon, *Lectures to My Students* (Grand Rapids, MI: Zondervan, 1973), 321.

[3] Leas, *Moving Your Church through Conflict*, 60.

[4] Ibid., 39.

[5] Shelley, *Well-Intentioned Dragons*, 51.

[6] Greenfield, *The Wounded Minister*, 24-26.

[7] Rediger, *Clergy Killers*, 53.

[8] Michael J. Anthony, *The Effective Church Board: A Handbook for Mentoring and Training Servant Leaders* (Grand Rapids, MI: Baker Books, 1993), 161.

[9] Leas, *Moving Your Church through Conflict*, 22.

[10] Hugh F. Halverstadt, *Managing Church Conflict* (Louisville: Westminster John Knox Press, 1991), 47.

[11] Martin Bolt and David G. Myers, *The Human Connection: How People Change People* (Downers Grove, IL: InterVarsity Press, 1984), 97-98.

[12] Michael Green, *The Message of Matthew*, The Bible Speaks Today, edited by John R. W. Stott (Downers Grove, IL: InterVarsity Press, 2000), 195.

[13] Borden, *Hit the Bullseye*, 95-96.

CHAPTER 12

[1] John R. W. Stott, *The Cross of Christ* (Downers Grove, IL: InterVarsity Press, 1986), 59.

[2] Charles H. Chandler, "The Servant," Ministering to Ministers Foundation, Inc., Volume 5, Issue 4, October 2000.

[3] Stott, *The Cross of Christ*, 53-54.

[4] Philip Yancey, *The Jesus I Never Knew* (Grand Rapids, MI: Zondervan, 1995), 64.

[5] D. Scott Barfoot, Bruce E. Winston, and Charles Wickman, "Forced Pastoral Exits: An Exploratory Study" (Virginia Beach, VA: Regent University, 2005), 5.

[6] Speed B. Leas, "The Varieties of Religious Strife" in *Mastering Conflict and Controversy*, by Edward G. Dobson, Speed B. Leas, and Marshall Shelley (Portland, OR: Multnomah Press, 1992), 92-93.

[7] Ibid., 93-94.

[8] Rediger, *Clergy Killers*, 6.

[9] Peter L. Steinke, *Healthy Congregations: A Systems Approach* (Washington, DC: The Alban Institute, 1996), 60.

[10] Stott, *The Cross of Christ*, 47.

[11] Ibid., 52.

[12] Speed B. Leas, "Harvesting the Learnings of Conflict Management," in *Conflict Management in Congregations*, ed. by David B. Lott (Bethesda, MD: The Alban Institute, 2001), 10.

[13] Rediger, *Clergy Killers*, 58-59.

[14] Ed Murphy, *The Handbook for Spiritual Warfare* (Nashville: Thomas Nelson, 1992), 509-510.

CHAPTER 13

[1] Richard J. Foster, *Money, Sex & Power: The Challenge of the Disciplined Life* (San Francisco: Harper & Row, 1985), 56.

[2] Greenfield, *The Wounded Minister*, 55.

[3] Lavern Brown, *Navigating Transition: Skills for the Transition Pastor* (Huntington Beach, CA: Transition Ministries Group, 2010), 34.

[4] Leas, *Moving Your Church through Conflict*, 52.

[5] Richard J. Foster, *Streams of Living Water: Celebrating the Great Traditions of the Christian Faith* (San Francisco: HarperCollins, 1998), 222.

[6] Carolyn Weese and J. Russell Crabtree, *The Elephant in the Boardroom: Seeking the Unspoken About Pastoral Transitions* (San Francisco: Jossey-Bass, 2004), 31.

[7] Eugene H. Peterson, *The Message: The Bible in Contemporary Language* (Colorado Springs: NavPress, 2002), 1376-1377.

[8] Sande, *The Peacemaker*, 157.

[9] Steinke, *Congregational Leadership in Anxious Times*, 53.

[10] Leas, *Moving Your Church through Conflict*, 27.

[11] Shawchuck and Heuser, *Managing the Congregation*, 291.

[12] Steinke, *Congregational Leadership in Anxious Times*, 108.

[13] Ibid., 115.

[14] Rediger, *Clergy Killers*, 139.

[15] Leas, "Harvesting the Learnings of Conflict Management," 9.

[16] Steinke, *Congregational Leadership in Anxious Times*, 101.

[17] Wickman, *Pastors at Risk*, 112.

CHAPTER 14

[1] Frank Martin, *War in the Pews: A Foxhole Guide to Surviving Church Conflict* (Downers Grove, IL: InterVarsity Press, 1995), 25.

[2] Wickman, *Pastors at Risk*, XII.

[3] Goetz, "Forced Out," 42.

[4] David Briggs, "Silent Clergy Killers: 'Toxic' Congregations Lead to Widespread Job Loss," 24 April, 2012; available from www.huffingtonpost.com; Internet

[5] Richard J. Krejeir, "Statistics on Pastors," Francis A. Schaeffer Institute on Christian Leadership Development, 2007; available from www.intothyword.org; Internet

[6] Pinion, *Crushed*, 93.

[7] Steinke, *Congregational Leadership in Anxious Times*, 101.

[8] Leas, *Moving Your Church through Conflict*, 78.

[9] Boers, *Never Call Them Jerks*, 75.

[10] G. Lloyd Rediger, *The Toxic Congregation: How to Heal the Soul of Your Church* (Nashville: Abingdon Press, 2007), 93-103.

[11] Quoted in Briggs, "Silent Clergy Killers"

[12] Borden, *Hit the Bullseye*, 49.

[13] Rediger, *Clergy Killers*, 13.

[14] Greenfield, *The Wounded Minister*, 58.

[15] Ronald A. Ward, *Commentary on 1 and 2 Timothy and Titus* (Waco, TX: Word Books, 1974), 278.

[16] John R. W. Stott, *Guard the Gospel: The Message of 2 Timothy* (Downers Grove, IL: InterVarsity Press, 1973), 210.

[17] Haugk, *Antagonists in the Church*, 46.

[18] Leon Morris, *The First Epistle of Paul to the Corinthians: An Introduction and Commentary*, Tyndale New Testament Commentaries (Grand Rapids, MI: William B. Eerdmans Publishing Company, 1993), 67.

[19] Greenfield, *The Wounded Minister*, 169.

[20] Steinke, *Congregational Leadership in Anxious Times*, 102.

[21] Trull and Carter, *Ministerial Ethics*, 129.

[22] Steinke, *Congregational Leadership in Anxious Times*, 85.

[23] Leith Anderson, *Leadership That Works: Hope and Direction for Church and Parachurch Leaders in Today's Complex World* (Minneapolis: Bethany House Publishers, 1999), 31.

CPSIA information can be obtained at www.ICGtesting.com
Printed in the USA
BVOW06s2143170216

437153BV00006B/56/P